DENNIS

BUSES AND OTHER VEHICLES

One of the first Enviro 400s was this one, 'Spirit of London', built to replace the Trident destroyed by a terrorist bomb in London on 7 July 2005. It is shown here at the 2005 NEC Show launch of the Enviro 400. ADL

DENNIS

BUSES AND OTHER VEHICLES

Andy Goundry

FOREWORD BY JOHN C R DENNIS

THE CROWOOD PRESS

First published in 2020 by
The Crowood Press Ltd
Ramsbury, Marlborough
Wiltshire SN8 2HR

enquiries@crowood.com

www.crowood.com

British Library Cataloguing-in-Publication Data
A catalogue record for this book is available from the British Library.

ISBN 978 1 78500 707 1

Typeset by Jean Cussons Typesetting, Diss, Norfolk

Printed and bound in India by Replika Press Pvt Ltd

CONTENTS

FOREWORD

It is interesting to reflect that of the major UK vehicle manufacturers, Henry Ford of the USA decided that Dagenham would be his UK base following a major corporate decision. Similarly, Herbert Austin chose Longbridge in Birmingham, William Morris selected Cowley in Oxfordshire, and many others also decided that the ideal place would be where manufacturing and a potential workforce were readily available.

However, the chassis manufacturer Alexander Dennis, originally Dennis Brothers, was destined to be located in the market town of Guildford after a Devon farmer's son answered a 'situation vacant' advertisement in the early 1890s. Guildford is probably the only town in the UK that has a vehicle manufacturer that has been building vehicles continuously under its own name in the nineteenth, twentieth and twenty-first centuries.

Alexander Dennis and its forebears have been fortunate in being exempt from the industrial problems that have beset many of its larger competitors and, despite a few corporate issues in the past, has been able to weather the commercial storm. Now, under the safe ownership of its Scottish parent, it is looking forward to many more years of manufacturing in Guildford.

Andy Goundry is the ideal author to celebrate the 125-year history of Dennis in Guildford, being both an acknowledged automotive historian and also having worked as a senior engineer within the company.

John C.R. Dennis
Guildford, England
June 2019

DEDICATION

This book is dedicated to the late Bob Loveland, for many years the Dennis technical publications manager. Without his foresight in collecting a vast amount of historic material, this book would not have been possible. Thanks go also to his son, Mike, for allowing me access to Bob's collection.

ACKNOWLEDGEMENTS

Particular thanks also go to Richard Norman, Dennis chief engineer for many years, both for contributing his accounts of how some of the company's most successful products came about, and for the loan of his extensive archive materials.

Many other people have contributed both technical and historical information as well as photographs, including the following:

John Dennis, without whose family the company would never have existed!

Colin Robertson and Carrie Szeremeta, respectively chief executive and marketing manager of Alexander Dennis, for their assistance in providing photos of current and recent products, and permission to reproduce Dennis Archive material;

My ex-ADL colleagues Gary Avery, Andy Boulton, Paul Bromley, Peter Cooper, Graham Harrington, John Hood, Roger Paice and Richard Winkworth for photos, technical information and recollections;

Di Stiff and Lawrence Spring of the Surrey History Centre, for their assistance during my many visits to unearth items from the Dennis Archives;

Raymond le Mesurier-Foster of the Aldershot & District Omnibuses Rescue & Restoration Society for providing the E-Type restoration information;

Danny Chan, Joe Devanny, Neil Jennings and John Turnbull for providing images to enhance the book;

The Crowood Press for their help and guidance throughout;

Last but not least, I must thank my wife, Cecilia, for the endless cups of coffee, the hours of proofreading and forebearance of the many domestic tasks left uncompleted while this book was being put together.

TIMELINE

1895	First bicycle
	Universal Athletic Stores opened
1898	First motorized tricycle
1899	First motor quadricycle
1900	Factory moved to the Old Barracks
1901	First car
	Dennis Brothers formed as private limited company
	Rodboro' Buildings factory opened
1903	First bus
1904	Worm drive axle patented
	First commercial vehicle
1905	Woodbridge Works site purchased
1908	First fire engine
1910	Annual production exceeds 1,000 vehicles
1912	2,000th vehicle produced
1913	Dennis Brothers (1913) Ltd becomes public limited company
	Last car manufactured
	All production now at Woodbridge Works
1915	Woodbridge Works Power House opened
	Company under Ministry of Munitions control
1918	Renamed Dennis Brothers Ltd
1919	Rodboro' Buildings vacated
	White & Poppe acquired
	Raymond Dennis 60,000-mile (100,000km) world sales tour
1921	First municipal vehicle (a cesspit emptier)
	First lawnmower
1923	Annual production reaches 2,000 vehicles
1925	First dedicated bus chassis introduced (the E-Type)
1933	White & Poppe production moved to Guildford
1934	Dennisville estate build commences
1937	250th Dennis fire engine for London delivered
	O4 diesel engine introduced
1939	John and Raymond Dennis both pass away
1962	Alfred Miles fire business acquired
1964	Mercury Truck & Tractor business acquired
1966	Bus production ceases
1970	Dennis Motor Holdings set up
1972	Acquired by Hestair
	Company renamed Dennis Motors Ltd, a division of Hestair Special Vehicles
	Truck production ceases
	Tow truck and tractor business sold to Marshalls
1973	Woodbridge Works site sold, 10 acres (4ha) leased back
1976	Mower business sold
1977	Re-entry into bus market
	Dennis Motors Ltd renamed Hestair Dennis Ltd
1978	Re-entry into UK truck market
1983	Duple acquired
1985	Company renamed Dennis Specialist Vehicles Ltd
	Fire bodybuilding transferred to Carmichael
	Cab production moved from Guildford to Blackpool
1987	John Dennis Coachbuilders set up
1988	Dart launched
1989	Dennis Specialist Vehicles sold to Trinity Holdings
1990	Dennis Specialist Vehicles vacate Woodbridge Works and move to Slyfield site
1992	Carmichael Fire & Bulk acquired
	Trinity Holdings flotation
1995	Douglas Equipment & Schopf acquired
1998	Dennis Specialist Vehicles bought by Mayflower Bus & Coach
1999	Dennis Eagle sold to their management
	Douglas Schopf and Carmichael International sold
2000	TransBus International formed by merger with Henlys (as a Mayflower subsidiary)
2004	Mayflower enters administration
	TransBus assets acquired by Alexander Dennis Ltd
	Plaxton's assets acquired by their management
2005	Alexander Dennis turnover £150.3 million
2007	Last fire engine built
	Plaxton acquired by Alexander Dennis Ltd
2008	First hybrid buses in service
2018	Alexander Dennis turnover £577 million, with 2,533 buses delivered worldwide
2019	Prototype self-driving bus
	Prototype hydrogen fuel cell bus
	Alexander Dennis bought by NFI Group Inc

THE EARLY YEARS: 1895–1918

Britain's Industrial Revolution saw the rapid development of the railway system, offering for the first time a comparatively fast way to transport both goods and people over relatively long distances. However, even as the nineteenth century was drawing to a close, railway supremacy was about to be challenged and beaten by a new form of transport – the internal combustion engine.

In that time of rapid technical development, inventive Victorian minds created endless new products; many flourished briefly then disappeared, themselves overtaken by newer inventions. Such was the pace of change that few of the pioneers of this second industrial revolution, such as John Cawsey Dennis, could have imagined in their wildest dreams how their new inventions would develop.

John was born in 1871, the son of a long-established farming family from Huntshaw in Devon. Despite his deep roots in farming, John's interests lay in machinery, so at the age of sixteen he began an apprenticeship with Tardrews, a Bideford ironmonger. While still an apprentice, John applied for and was successful in obtaining a position as assistant to an ironmonger in Guildford, almost 200 miles (320km) away. Moving there at the age of twenty-three, and having no friends or family locally to occupy his time, he decided to build a bicycle, using parts bought from his new employer, Filmer and Mason.

Proud of his creation, he borrowed the window of a friendly tailor at the top of Guildford High Street to display it, an act which within a couple of hours resulted in its profitable sale. That first bicycle led to others until before long his hobby was more lucrative than his day job.

Pondering his next move, John realized that his employer bought components from Brown Brothers in London,

so if he also bought directly from them, he too could increase his profits. He went a step further and joined Brown Brothers as an employee for several months to learn as much as possible about making and sourcing engineering components.

With that knowledge under his belt, together with a ready supply of parts assured from Brown Brothers, he returned to Guildford in January 1895 to set up a bicycle shop, Universal Athletic Stores on Guildford High Street. Cycle assembly was carried out with the frame suspended from a pear tree in the garden of his shop, giving the pear tree the distinction of being the first piece of Dennis assembly tooling!

Showing the marketing initiative that characterized the company, on opening day his shop window hosted a 'Spinning Wheel Competition'. When the wheel was set spinning, the assembled onlookers were asked to estimate

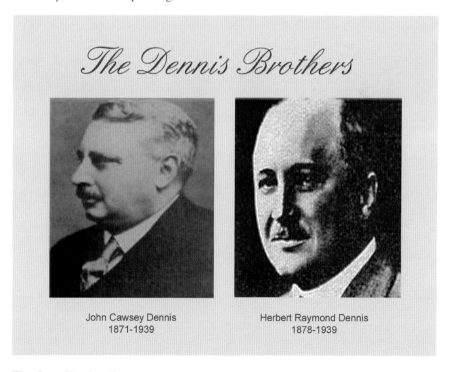

The founding brothers. AUTHOR

how long it would take to stop. It took 12 minutes and 10 seconds, during which time he had subtly indicated to his audience the engineering quality of his product, and drawn many customers into the shop.

Sales of his Speed King and Speed Queen cycles became plentiful, and soon John's younger brother, Herbert (better known by his middle name, Raymond), then still only seventeen, joined him as an equal partner in the business. Raymond provided cycling lessons to new riders, and also became an accomplished competitive cyclist, his many successes helping promote the brothers' products.

As the business developed, the brothers began to design and make many of their components, notably patenting a popular pneumatic saddle. Their component manufacturing took place in the garden of the shop, by then equipped with a small workshop containing plating vats, enamelling stoves and other equipment.

DENNIS SPEED KING QUADRICYCLE, 1899–

Configuration: Two in-line seats, convertible to single-seat tricycle by loosening four bolts
Engine: De Dion Bouton
Max. power RAC: 2.25HP
Steering: Bicycle-type handlebar
Tyres: 26in (660mm) × 2.5in (63.5mm)
Wheels: Bicycle-type, steel, spoked
Price (1899): 95 guineas (£99 15s/£99.75)
(Source: Dennis Bros. advertisement, 1900)

SPEEDING FINE

Although inevitably primitive, the tricycle must have been reasonably effective, for as John was testing his machine around the hilly streets of Guildford one summer day in 1899, a policeman saw him hurtling up Guildford High Street at a speed that he subsequently affirmed to the magistrate as at least 16mph (26km/h). Despite John's defence that the tricycle was incapable of such a speed, particularly on the High Street's 1 in 11 (9 per cent) uphill gradient, prosecution duly followed, the outcome being a not inconsiderable fine of twenty shillings. So John became one of the first, if not the first, person to fall foul of motoring law. However, that fine was repaid many times over as the Dennis brothers used this incident in their advertisements as proof of the machine's speed, measured 'on the sworn testimony of a constable'. Then – as now – speed sells!

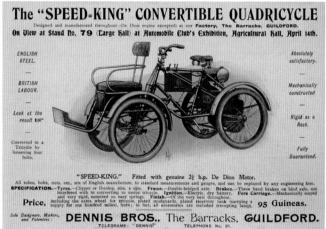

Dennis's first motorized tricycles appeared in 1898, quickly followed by quadricycles. AUTHOR

FROM TWO WHEELS TO FOUR

In a far-sighted move, in 1898 John and Raymond built a motorized tricycle fitted with a single-cylinder 3HP De Dion Bouton engine. Motorized tricycles soon became motorized quadricycles, and both tricycles and quadricycles competed with great success in several races and events, usually piloted by Raymond Dennis.

Building these new-fangled machines needed more space than the small Universal Athletic Stores garden workshop could provide and so, in 1900, the company made its first move, just around the corner into disused army barracks in Friary Street. The decision was also soon made to formalize the company, which became Dennis Brothers Limited, a private company. The first board meeting was held on 29 July 1901, with four directors, seven subscribers and capital of £7,500, subsequently increased in 1906 to a not-inconsiderable £100,000 – over £12 million at 2019 levels. Part of a document from that time discovered in the Dennis Archive notes that: 'With the extra capital, a great many new automatic labour-saving machines were installed, and by their aid the accuracy has been increased to the point of absolute interchangeability, allowing a large output of the best possible at a minimum cost.'

The same document also notes that: 'We commenced manufacturing before the passing of the Light Locomotive Act, which gives us the position of the oldest Makers in England.'

Quadricycle manufacture led to the development in 1901 of a 'proper' car, still using De Dion Bouton engines, this time an 8HP unit specially tuned for Dennis Brothers. The use of De Dion engines was typical of the brothers' understanding of their business, for this French manufacturer produced engines that were already well regarded and in relatively large-volume production. Doubtless the brothers could have developed their own engine, but this would have been both time-consuming and expensive. Initially, it was intended to market the Dennis cars under the same 'Speed King' brand as the company's previous products; however, this policy was abandoned at the 27 January 1902 board meeting in favour of adopting the simple brand 'Dennis'.

WIN TODAY, SELL TOMORROW

Quickly realizing the benefits of the publicity that could result from success in competitive motoring events, the brothers were soon entering their machines in speed and reliability trials.

One hill climb event took place in 1901 at Tilburstow,

The Dennis archives include this 1,000-mile Certificate of Performance from the 1903 Reliability Trial.
DENNIS ARCHIVES

near Caterham in Surrey. Not only was the Dennis car successful in climbing the hill, with its maximum gradient of 1 in 10 (10 per cent), faster than any other competitor, many of whom failed to climb the hill at all, but it also won the prestigious Championship of the Meeting.

Two cars were entered into the Automobile Club's 1902 reliability trial, the challenge being to complete a journey from London to Oxford without stopping, a distance of around 60 miles (100km). Both cars completed the task successfully and were awarded diplomas.

A further reliability trial in 1903, this time of 1,000 miles (1,600km) and again organized by the Automobile Club, saw the winning 16HP Dennis awarded 2,991 marks out of a possible 3,000. A 20HP car was then entered into the Club's 4,000-mile (6,400km) reliability trial in March 1906, achieving an unbroken run. That performance helped the company win the first-ever prestigious Dewar Challenge Trophy for the most outstanding motoring achievements of the previous twelve months.

Events such as these helped to develop Dennis products' reputation for excellent reliability and raised their image in the minds of the motoring public. Even at that time, though, there must have been board members unhappy at some of the innovative sales tactics employed by the brothers, for the 20 April 1906 board meeting minutes note somewhat sourly that 'profits might have been larger but for the expenses incurred in the entering of two cars in the Isle of Man Tourist Trophy Race'.

RODBORO' BUILDINGS – DENNIS'S FIRST PURPOSE-BUILT FACTORY

In 1901, motor cars were still a rarity, with probably no more than 500 in Britain. Dennis products were selling well, and the brothers continued to invest in their fledgling business, expanding further with a 27,000sq ft (2,500sq m) purpose-built office and factory on the corner of Guildford's Onslow Street and Bridge Street.

Although the plans submitted for the building described it as a facility for the manufacture of bicycles and motors, the industry's pace of change was such that bicycle production had almost ceased by the time the building came into use. Indeed, the board meeting minutes of 6 April 1905 record the decision to 'discontinue the manufacture of bicycles entirely'.

The layout of the building was novel. The ground floor housed two showrooms with space for up to twenty cars, as well as offices and the power plant for the factory. In the basement was the stores area, while the first floor contained machine shops, electroplating equipment and a polishing shop, as well as the body shop. Car assembly took place above that, along with shops for final finishing activities such as painting. Above that again were the upholstering and enamelling shops with their large drying stoves. All levels were connected by a large lift, which was used to lower the finished cars to the ground.

The building still exists today and is known locally as the Rodboro' Buildings after the Rodboro' Boot and Shoe Company who bought the premises in 1919 after the Dennis business moved again. Visually, it is largely unchanged externally, although not everyone enjoying a quiet drink in the Wetherspoons pub that now occupies part of it is aware that they are in the former factory of Britain's oldest continually functioning automotive manufacturer, and indeed one of the oldest in the world.

In 1902, an account of a visit made to these works appeared in the *Gentleman's Magazine*. The article described Dennis Brothers as 'probably the principal pioneers of the motor industry in this country' noting that 'the firm was one of the very first in England to devote its attention to automobilism'.

Rodboro' Buildings was Dennis's first purpose-built factory, opened in 1901. Demand for Dennis products was such that they moved into the new factory even before it was finished. DENNIS ARCHIVES

DENNIS 3-TON CHASSIS, 1906–c.1925

Layout and Chassis
Two-axle rigid bolted ladder frame suitable for normal-control double-deck bus, lorry or van bodywork

Engine
Type: Aster
Block material: Cast iron
Head material: Cast iron
Cylinders: 4 in-line
Cooling: Water, pumped
Bore and stroke: 120 × 130mm
Valves: Side valve
Max. power: RAC 35HP; 35hp (26kW) at 900rpm
Fuel capacity: 15gal (68ltr)

Transmission
Gearbox: Dennis 4-speed, aluminium-cased
Clutch: Cone, leather-faced
Ratios:
   1st: 3.29
   2nd: 2.01
   3rd: 1.36
   4th: 1
   Reverse: 4.33
Final drive: Dennis worm drive

Suspension and Steering
Front and rear: Steel multi-leaf springs
Steering: Worm and segment
Tyres: Front: 34in (864mm) single solid rubber
Rear: 34in (864mm) twin solid rubber
Wheels: Artillery wood pattern

Brakes
Type: Footbrake: steel drum on propellor shaft with two cast-iron contracting shoes
Handbrake: drum brakes on rear axle with cast-iron shoes, rod-operated

Dimensions
Track, rear: 66in (1,676mm)
Wheelbase: Bus 160in (4,064mm)
Lorry 150in (3,810mm)
Body length: Lorry 120in (3,048mm)
Payload: 6,720lb (3,048kg)
Capacity: 34 passengers (double-deck)

Performance
Top speed: 14.5mph (23km/h)

Price (1908)
Chassis with tyres: £650
Double-deck body: £150
Lorry body: £75
(Source: Dennis Bros. Ltd catalogue, 1908)

This superb 1902 Dennis car is owned by John Dennis, grandson of one of the founding brothers. John has participated in over sixty London–Brighton Veteran Car Runs with the car, probably an unmatched achievement by anyone. AUTHOR

All this positive publicity meant that 1903 was a year in which the company did exceptionally well. By then, the range had expanded to include a wide range of models. At the 1903 Motor Show held at Crystal Palace, they received orders for eighty-three cars at a total value of £27,900. These ranged from thirty-two 16HP tourers at 550 guineas each (£60,000 in today's money) to five motor tricycles at 95 guineas apiece. One buyer paid a £1,000 deposit to secure twenty vehicles, which was reported by *Motoring Illustrated* as 'the highest aggregate amount of business done at one stand'.

Not for nothing did Dennis describe themselves in a 1907 brochure for their cars as producing 'the pioneer car of England'!

INNOVATION AND DIVERSIFICATION

The brothers were at the forefront of technical advancement, with experiments going on continually. One of the

THE "DENNIS" TOWER WAGON

As supplied to Messrs. Dick Kerr & Co., and several Corporations

Price of 18 h.p. Chassis with guaranteed Tyres **£435**
Price of Car Wagon Body **£65**

In May 1907, this tower wagon was produced for Dick, Kerr and Co. Ltd for use in maintaining overhead cables, and was probably the first of its kind in the UK. This line drawing is from a 1908 Dennis catalogue.

BOB LOVELAND COLLECTION

THE PERILS OF NOT BUYING DENNIS

The threat from other manufacturers at this time must have been significant, causing the company to publish this stern warning to anyone tempted to buy anything other than a Dennis:

There are a large number of mushroom firms, with no backbone whatsoever, and who have been trading upon the deposits received from their clients; such firms cannot last, and if you find yourself the possessor of a Car made by such a firm, or the possessor of a Car imported by the so-called Sole Concessionaire who has to suspend business, then you have made a very inadvisable purchase. Both because of the difficulty to obtain spare parts, and the name not being kept constantly before the public, any reputation the Car may have soon goes and with it your chance of resale except at a considerable sacrifice.

most significant innovations was the development of a worm-driven rear axle, at a time when many competitors still relied on noisy and unreliable chain drives. The worm drive was patented in 1904, giving Dennis products a long-lasting and smooth transmission. This axle was so good that other manufacturers used it; the first London bus, in around 1906, had a Milnes-Daimler chassis fitted with a Dennis worm-drive axle.

As the sales of cars increased, more manufacturers jumped on the bandwagon, so the Dennis brothers looked for diversification opportunities. They quickly realized that the systems developed for moving people via motor cars could be adapted for moving goods, thereby providing significant benefits to businesses large and small who had hitherto been reliant on horse-drawn transport.

So, in 1904, Dennis built their first commercial vehicle, a 15-cwt van for Harrods department store in London, which appeared at that year's Crystal Palace Show. This appearance was so successful that the company took 160 orders, the most significant number of any manufacturer. In 1905, Dennis produced their first bus, using a 4-cylinder 28HP Aster petrol engine, with the engine and gearbox mounted on a subframe to reduce stresses. It was sold to Benjamin Richardson and plied between Kingston-upon-Thames and Richmond, carrying its passengers in a body that had previously seen service as a horse-drawn bus.

At first, the 28HP chassis was used for 3-ton (3,050kg) payload commercial vehicles as well as buses, but by 1906 a range of lower-capacity chassis was also available, with 4-cylinder engines rated from 14 to 40HP and payload capacities from 8cwt (400kg) to 5 tons (5,080kg). The 4-tonner was often used to carry a double-deck body, dedicated chassis to suit passenger applications not being introduced until 1925.

The export market was not neglected. In just two years, between 1904 and 1906, single- and double-deck buses had been shipped to Italy, Holland, South Africa, New Zealand and Australia. Raymond Dennis undertook an extended sales tour in 1908, one outcome of this visit being an order for the first buses ever seen in Russia.

Dennis built probably the UK's first tower wagon in 1907, and also one of the first breakdown trucks, for the General Cab Company of London.

By 1909, total production numbers exceeded 300 vehicles.

THE FIRST FIRE ENGINES

Typical of Dennis Brothers' continual quest for innovation and preparedness to back a hunch was the production in 1908 of their first fire engine, for the City of Bradford brigade. Traditionally, fire engines had been horse-drawn, with steam-powered piston pumps, so were not only slow to attend an incident but had limited pumping capacity when they got there. Back in 1903, Merryweather had recognized the benefits of petrol power, which would enable a motor fire engine to be on the scene of a fire quickly, rather than having to wait for steam to be raised. However, the piston pumps then in use were neither particularly quick to bring into use, nor effective. The Dennis Brothers

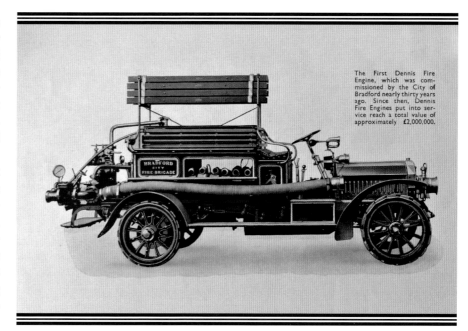

The First Dennis Fire Engine, which was commissioned by the City of Bradford nearly thirty years ago. Since then, Dennis Fire Engines put into service reach a total value of approximately £2,000,000.

This print is taken from an early **Dennis** catalogue and shows the very first fire engine, the 1908 **Bradford N-Type**. BOB LOVELAND COLLECTION

THE **DENNIS** FIRE PUMP

At the heart of every fire engine is a high-pressure water pump. This sectioned view shows the type of turbine pump that helped the early Dennis appliances quickly gain an outstanding reputation for performance and reliability.
BOB LOVELAND COLLECTION

fire engine, in contrast, used a Gwynne-Sargeant turbine pump that could begin pumping immediately. This new pump produced a much more stable water pressure than had hitherto been possible and was also much more tolerant of the dirty and sandy water supplies, which were often all that was available. This revolutionary vehicle participated in several impressive demonstrations to senior fire brigade personnel from around the country.

One of these demonstrations was held in London, where two Dennis engines, coupled together, threw a jet of water over the dome of St Paul's Cathedral, a height of 366ft (110m). Another took place nearer to home on a Guildford river bridge. The *pièce de résistance* of the day to demonstrate the capabilities of the machine was to shoot a jet of water 100ft (30m) into the air. Unfortunately, a sudden change in wind direction at the critical moment resulted in the assembled VIPs getting thoroughly soaked and the company having urgently to take over most of the available hotel accommodation to enable their guests to dry out.

In launching this machine, the N-Type, Dennis were pushing at an open door, for the government of the day had already realized the deficiencies of traditional steam-powered fire engines and were urging towns and cities to equip themselves with something better, so the launch of the Dennis appliance was incredibly timely.

The success of, and well-deserved publicity given to, the new appliance soon led to London and other fire brigades throughout Britain, and indeed throughout the world, buying Dennis fire appliances in increasing numbers. A copy of the 1908 Dennis commercial vehicle catalogue contains images of machines for various home and export customers as well as Bradford. However, it seems that the company was slightly ahead of itself in claiming these, as their sales records for 1908 indicate that payment was only received for one fire engine that year. However, 1909 saw income from sales of eight engines, to Rowley Regis, Glasgow, Kingston, Birkenhead, Christchurch, Fremantle and Birmingham. In 1910, vehicle sales numbered twenty-seven, including the first seven N-Types for London. With such widespread sales, it was not long before the name Dennis soon became synonymous with fire engines in the public's eye, where it stayed for the next century.

The chassis configuration of those first Dennis appliances generally followed the company's by then standard convention, although the usual Aster engine was replaced by either a 40/45 or 60HP 6.24-litre White & Poppe side-valve petrol engine coupled to a four-speed gearbox, with the gearing allowing an impressive 30mph (50km/h) top speed. The higher-power engine was usually fitted to vehicles with wheeled escapes. The rear axle was, of course, the patented Dennis worm-drive unit, while the wooden artillery-type wheels were either shod with 'KT' air cush-

In 1909, the New Zealand town of Christchurch took one of the first N-Type fire appliances, as shown here, becoming probably Dennis's first export fire customer. DENNIS ARCHIVES

DENNIS 60HP N-TYPE, 1908–

Layout and Chassis
Two-axle rigid bolted ladder-frame fire appliance chassis
Engine
Type: White & Poppe
Block material: Cast iron
Head material: Cast iron
Cylinders: 4 in-line
Cooling: Water, pumped
Bore and stroke: 127 × 180mm
Capacity: 9120cc
Valves: Side valve
Carburettor: White & Poppe with gravity feed
Max. power: RAC rating 60HP; 65bhp at 1,180rpm
Fuel capacity: 20gal (91ltr)
Transmission
Gearbox: Dennis 4-speed, aluminium case
Clutch: Cone clutch, leather-faced
Ratios:
    1st: 3.77
    2nd: 2.32
    3rd: 1.48
    4th: 1
    Reverse: 3.07
Final drive: Dennis worm drive, 4.85
Suspension and Steering
Front and rear: Semi-elliptic multi-leaf steel springs

Steering: Worm and segment
Tyres: 34in (864mm) solid rubber or KT air cushion, twin on rear axle
Wheels: Artillery-type wood, later cast steel hollow-spoke
Brakes
Type: Footbrake: steel drum on propellor shaft with 2 cast-iron contracting shoes
Handbrake: drum brakes on rear axle with cast-iron shoes, rod-operated
Dimensions
Overall length: 222in (5,639mm)
Overall width: 84.3in (2,140mm)
Overall height: 90in (2,286mm)
Unladen weight: 9,000lb (4,000kg) approx.
Water capacity: First aid tank: 40gal (182ltr)
Hose capacity: 1,200ft (365m) of delivery hose;
30ft (9.1m) of 5in-diameter (127mm) suction hose
Turbine pump: Three-stage Gwynne, 400gal/min (1,818 ltr/min) at 120lb/sq in (8.3 bar)
Performance
Top speed: 30mph (48km/h)
Cost
60HP: £975
(Sources: 'Instructions for Management and Control of Dennis Turbine Motor Fire Engines', c.1913/1914, and 'Dennis Motor Fire Engines' catalogue, c.1910)

THE AIRFIX N-TYPE

Several of these old appliances still exist in running order, including one that is owned by the company. This vehicle, registration number DU 179, was immortalized by Airfix in the 1960s with a delightful 1/32 scale plastic kit. It was originally used by the City of Coventry and subsequently by the industrial concern GEC before being purchased by Dennis in 1958. It can sometimes be seen in events such as the London–Brighton Commercial Vehicle Rally. The author can testify to the surprisingly impressive turn of speed of this handsome beast, which is not accompanied by an equal braking ability, making an open-air ride on it exhilarating!

Still pumping at 103 years old: this 1916 N-Type is cared for by the students at London's Royal College of Science. AUTHOR

This Black Maria prisoner transport was built in 1914 for Salford. The name 'Black Maria' apparently has its origins in a lady by the name of Maria, who in the 1840s owned Maria Lee's Lodging House in Boston, Massachusetts, USA. Maria, it seems, let the police know whenever she thought one of her lodgers was up to no good. As a result, the police attended Maria's premises so often that their horse and cart became known as the 'Black Maria'. Soon, all vehicles for moving prisoners became known as Black Marias in the UK as well as in the USA. DENNIS ARCHIVES

ion tyres or solid rubber tyres. Braking followed the typically basic standards of the day, with cast iron drum brakes on the rear axle only, augmented by a drum-type transmission brake on the rear of the gearbox, again with cast iron friction blocks.

The bodies were of the Braidwood type, named after the well-respected James Braidwood (1800–1861), who was instrumental in developing the equipment and techniques of the British fire service. A Braidwood body could carry up to ten firemen, the four on each side having to hang on for dear life in their exposed positions. The idea was that they could get on and off quickly – challenging enough on a horse-drawn appliance but far less easy on a much faster motor vehicle. Sadly, although perhaps inevitably, it was not long (1910) before the first firefighter lost his life being flung from a Dennis fire engine when it skidded on a wet road in Birmingham.

Fuel consumption was claimed to be 8–12mpg, (23–35ltr/100km), and the cost, for a typical appliance, was quoted as £850 in 1909 (around £100,000 today).

Most N-Types left the factory with a distinctive dark-blue bonnet, a finish that resulted from dipping the

Early post vans on the 30-cwt 12HP chassis of 1906 had stylish bodies to the specification of McNamara & Co., the company who for many years carried the mail on contract for the GPO. By July 1912, they had a fleet of over seventy Dennis vans. DENNIS ARCHIVES

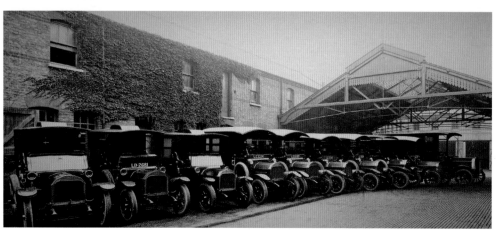

This 1912 photo shows some of the Metropolitan Asylums Board ambulances. Despite the austere name, these asylums were in fact Britain's first state hospitals, covering both physical and mental infirmity. These vehicles replaced the previous horse-drawn ambulances.

DENNIS ARCHIVES

Two of the Dennis cars owned by John Dennis. The 1909 car, nearest the camera, was repatriated from Australia by John in 1969 in a derelict condition and fastidiously rebuilt. The other car dates from 1906. AUTHOR

DENNIS 18HP MOTOR VAN CHASSIS TO CARRY 15-CWT, 1904—

Engine: Aster 4-cylinder
Max. power: RAC rating 18HP; 18hp at 900rpm
Gearbox: Dennis 3- or 4-speed plus reverse, aluminium casing
Clutch: Dennis cone clutch, leather-faced
Final drive: Dennis worm drive
Suspension: Multi-leaf springs
Brakes: Footbrake: drum at rear of gearbox
Handbrake: side expanding brakes on rear wheels, rod-operated
Wheelbase: 108in (2,743mm)
Overall length: 165in (4,190mm) approx.
Overall width: 63in (1,600mm) approx.
Overall height: 88in (2,235mm)
Top speed: 14.5mph (23km/h)
Price: Chassis £375;
Body £45
(Source: Dennis Bros. Ltd catalogue, 1908)

DENNIS 25- 30-CWT CHASSIS, 1906—

4×2 rigid ladder-frame chassis for van and ambulance bodywork (as supplied to the Metropolitan Asylums Board)
Engine: Aster 4-cylinder side valve
Max. power: RAC rating 18HP or 28HP; 18hp or 28hp at 900rpm
Gearbox: Dennis 3- or 4-speed, aluminium-cased
Clutch: Cone, leather-faced
Final drive: Dennis worm drive
Suspension: Steel multi-leaf springs
Tyres: 34in (864mm) solid rubber on artillery wood pattern wheels
Brakes: Footbrake: steel drum on propellor shaft with 2 cast-iron contracting shoes
Handbrake: drum brakes on rear axle with cast-iron shoes, rod-operated
Wheelbase: Ambulance 150in (3,810mm); van: 126in (3,200mm)
Overall length: Ambulance 200in (5,055mm) approx. including rear steps; van 181in (4,597mm) approx.
Body length: Ambulance 82in (2,083mm); van 96in (2,438mm)
Overall width: 60in (1,524mm)
Overall height: Ambulance 97.5in (2,477mm); van 101in (2,565mm) approx.
Payload: 2,800lb/3,360lb (1,270kg/1,524kg)
Capacity: Ambulance: stretcher plus four passengers
Van: approx. 220cu ft (6cu m)
Top speed: 16mph (26km/h)
Price: 18HP chassis with tyres £435;
28HP chassis with tyre £520
Ambulance body: £100
Van body: £75
(Source: Dennis Bros. Ltd catalogue, 1908)

DENNIS 18/24HP CAR, *c*.1906–1913

Layout and Chassis
Chassis suitable for 2- or 4-seat bodywork
Engine
Type: Aster
Block material: Cast iron
Head material: Cast iron
Cylinders: 4 in-line
Cooling: Water, thermo-syphon
Bore and stroke: 18HP: 90 × 110mm; 24HP: 100 × 150mm
Carburettor: Variable single-jet
Max. power: RAC rating 18HP/24HP
Fuel capacity: 9gal (41ltr)
Transmission
Gearbox: Dennis 4-speed and reverse, aluminium casing

Clutch: Hele-Shaw patent disc clutch
Final drive: Dennis worm drive
Suspension and Steering
Front and rear: Semi-elliptic multi-leaf springs
Steering: Worm and segment
Tyres: 810 × 90 pneumatic
Wheels: Artillery wood pattern
Brakes
Type: Rear only: internally expanding drums with cast iron shoes. Independent shoe pairs for footbrake and handbrake
Price (1911)
18HP chassis with tyres: £325
24HP chassis with tyres: £440
4-seat touring body, less hood and windscreen: £55
2-seat body: £50
(Source: Dennis Bros. catalogue, *c*.1911)

bonnet panels in a hot cyanide solution; this proved a better alternative to paint, which was often severely affected by engine heat.

The same chassis type was used for the ambulance bodies that were also offered by the company. One of the first customers for these was the Metropolitan Asylums Board of London, who by 1912 had a fifty-strong fleet.

Sales success in fire engines was matched by thriving orders for buses and other heavier vehicles at the expense of the original cars. Indeed, in 1909 the company issued a statement confirming that it was still building 'passenger cars'. In truth, however, the manufacture of Dennis cars was a relatively short-lived venture. Fittingly, three of the few remaining vehicles are in the care of John Dennis, grandson of one of the original Dennis brothers.

ANOTHER NEW FACTORY – WOODBRIDGE WORKS

Even though the Rodboro' Buildings factory was extended twice, in 1903 and 1905, rapid growth in sales of the broadening product range meant that the factory's capacity was again soon exceeded, and a new facility was needed.

In August 1905, the company purchased a 10-acre (4ha) site at Woodbridge Hill, then a greenfield location on the edge of Guildford. To save money, one of the first buildings on the site was the disused 29,000sq ft (2,700sq m), 5,500-seat Torrey-Alexander Mission Hall from Brixton, south

London, which after being dismantled was transported 30 miles (50km) to Guildford and re-erected to become No. 1 shop, going on to perform a useful function for a further eighty years. No. 2 shop was soon built, followed by Nos 3 and 4 shops. Nos 5, 6 and 7 shops, providing an additional 124,000sq ft (11,500sq m) of space were laid down in 1916 to support the war effort.

All production had been moved from Rodboro' Buildings to the new Woodbridge Works by 1913, with the office functions following in 1919.

Dennis seized every opportunity to promote their patented worm drive axle, including this impressive mosaic on the floor of the Woodbridge Works reception area, reportedly crafted by Italian experts. RICHARD NORMAN

The factory had its own railway system, complete with a couple of loading docks and several locomotives. In later years, although the rail link to the national network was lifted, the tracks remained in situ inside the factory, albeit with the gaps between the rails filled in. One of the first locomotives, which ran until 1942, was designed in house and based on a Dennis tractor from 1909.

Employee welfare was considered important from the outset, with the board meeting minutes of 5 March 1907 noting the plans to create football and cricket grounds for the newly formed Dennis Athletic Club. Even before that, the idea of offering efficiency bonuses to staff was under discussion by the board.

The new Woodbridge Works was intended to impress potential customers from around the world as well as being a state-of-the-art vehicle manufacturing facility. The reception area floor, for example, was of marble, with an inlaid worm and wheel motif promoting the company's innovative axle design, an icon that also featured in the firm's letterhead.

The factory was surprisingly advanced environmentally, with considerable attention having been paid to ease of operation and decent working conditions. For example, the offices were equipped with effective ventilation, which gave an air change every twenty minutes. They were located on the first floor, to allow the entire ground floor

POWER HOUSE

The power house equipment included two massive 270bhp 4-cylinder 4-stroke single-acting Sulzer air-blast injection diesel engines running at 187rpm, each coupled to a 180kW dynamo to supply 440-volt power to the factory. A third Sulzer set was added in 1917, and a fourth should have followed shortly afterwards. The ship bringing it to the UK, however, was sunk in the North Sea by a U-boat, and the fourth engine eventually only arrived in 1924.

Further expansion of the power-generating capability became necessary in the early 1930s, when engine production was moved to Guildford from Coventry. After consideration of the relative costs of taking this power from the public supply versus generating it in-house, two additional high-speed Mirrlees-Ricardo 300bhp 900rpm 6-cylinder diesel engines were installed, each coupled to a 205kW dynamo. They were shortly followed by a third set, collectively producing 615kW and nearly doubling the capacity of the powerhouse.

The Mirrlees-Ricardo engines, together with their dynamos and a huge rotary converter, were at the time the biggest high-speed diesel-engined generating plant in the UK, while the original Sulzer installations remained operational right up to 1986. It is an impressive measure of their reliability that during the World War I the Sulzer engines regularly ran non-stop for five weeks at a time.

Sadly, very little physical or documented evidence remains of the Woodbridge Power House. However, memories linger, and Richard Norman, a one-time Dennis apprentice who was to become their chief designer, recalls that 'when the wind blew from the north, exhaust fumes were drawn from the power house into the office ventilation system. Complaints to the maintenance manager, one Tom Ralph, were brushed off with the riposte that pollution levels were no worse than standing next to the adjacent A3 road!'

Inside the Woodbridge Works power house, showing the Sulzer engines. RICHARD NORMAN

Charabancs with a folding canvas roof were a popular configuration for the earliest buses. This particular vehicle, however, which was supplied to T. Copp of Ilfracombe in May 1910, was built with a fixed roof and side curtains. Unlike this example, most charabancs at least offered doors to keep the passengers from falling out! DENNIS ARCHIVES

Woodbridge Works. No. 1 shop can be seen in the bottom right-hand of this aerial photo. Alongside it is the power house, with the offices facing the main London Waterloo–Portsmouth railway line at the bottom of the picture. This image was taken in the early Hestair days, shortly before they began to sell off the site as part of the retrenchment and rationalization of the business. North Gate, the main entrance to the site, can be seen in the centre right of the picture, adjacent to what is now known locally as the Dennis roundabout under the A3 Guildford bypass. By the end of the Hestair era, all of the site had been sold off other than No. 11 shop, which was located at the top right of this picture and was where all remaining functions of the company had been crammed. Ironically, even after the move to the new Slyfield factory, No. 11 shop remained standing, although derelict, for many years. RICHARD NORMAN

to be devoted to manufacturing and avoid the need to lift heavy components between levels.

By 1911, water was being obtained from artesian wells on-site, while gas for the case-hardening furnaces was generated by burning wood shavings and sawdust from the wood-working shop. Electricity came initially from the fledgling public supply, although in 1915 the company invested in their own power house, a highly impressive building with tiled walls and floors that contained an extensive range of generating equipment.

Perhaps one of the company's greatest strengths in those pre-Great War years of rapid growth was their ability to understand the needs of their customers, however unusual, together with their willingness to produce specialized vehicles to meet those needs alongside their more standard ranges. Their 1909 'Fire Engine and Ambulance Catalogue' made this clear, proclaiming confidently that 'the makers are prepared to submit designs and estimates for any variation from their standard designs.' This flexibility was made possible by the Woodbridge Hill factory making complete vehicles rather than just bodies or chassis.

By 1910, Dennis's claimed proudly, and justifiably, that their fire engines operated all over the world, from Auckland to Zanzibar, while over 1,000 Dennis lorries and vans were at work moving goods around Britain.

By then, Woodbridge Works employed more than 400 staff and was producing 1,000 vehicles annually. The factory covered over 260,000sq ft (24,150sq m) by 1916, making it one of the largest commercial vehicle factories in Europe at that time. The product range was both broad and diverse, with chassis capacities from 15 cwt (760kg) to 5 tons (5,080kg), usually fitted with either lorry or van bodywork for haulage work or bodied as single- or double-deck buses.

FIRE FIGHTING ON THE WATER

The early days of fire-fighting on the water were, like those on land, characterized by slow responses as steam-powered craft and pumps needed lengthy preparation times before they arrived on scene of the blaze. In 1905, Bristol Fire Brigade took delivery of a steam fire float, *Salamander*, equipped with Merryweather piston pumps. *Salamander* served at Avonmouth Docks for many years, and on one occasion in 1917 demonstrated the major drawback of steam power. A fire was discovered at 7.30am in a transit shed at Avonmouth Dock, and *Salamander* was called out. By 8:30am, shore appliances had almost extinguished the fire. Meanwhile, *Salamander* had finally raised sufficient steam to lend a hand and arrived at 8:36am!

Even before that incident, Bristol's far-sighted port authority, having recognized the potential of the Dennis N-Type internal combustion fire engine, and more particularly its highly effective turbine pump, had commissioned a fire float that incorporated that same Dennis equipment into what they hoped would be a radical and efficient marine fire-fighting vessel for use in Portishead Harbour. The resulting boat entered service in 1916 and was named *Denny* (apparently after the small island in the Severn Estuary rather than being a play on the Dennis name).

The Bristol authority's faith was not misplaced, and this first experimental effort on their part soon led to such vessels being commissioned worldwide, although sadly none with the same Dennis equipment on board.

The *Denny* featured a steel hull containing a White & Poppe engine together with a turbine pump as used in the N-Type fire engine. The power unit, mounted towards the rear of the hull, provided power both to

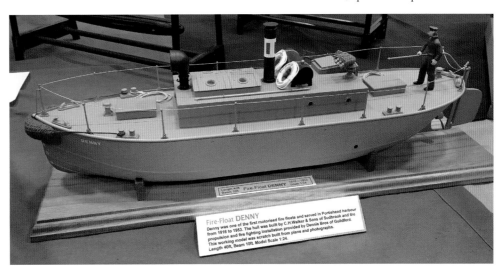

Sadly the full-size fire float no longer exists, but this magnificent 1/24 scale model built by Richard Norman, Guildford's long-serving chief designer, faithfully portrays the layout of the craft. AUTHOR

This 34-seater was built on a 30HP chassis, and was one of five supplied to West Bridgford Urban District Council in January 1914.
DENNIS ARCHIVES

the boat's propeller and to the fire pump itself. It seems that the unfortunate engineman responsible for managing the engine was incarcerated in splendid isolation in the bowels of the hull alongside the engine in what must have been a very unpleasant, fume-laden, environment. How he received his instructions to adjust speed remains a matter for conjecture, for the photographs and drawings that remain show no evidence of a speaking tube or any other form of communication device with the helmsman!

Nevertheless, the *Denny* must have been a success, for it remained in service in Portishead until 1953.

In 1916, Dennis joined forces with Mr W. A. Stevens to produce the Dennis-Stevens bus, which had a 4-cylinder Dennis petrol engine driving a generator, which in turn powered electric motors driving the rear axle, so creating one of the first of the hybrid vehicles now so much in favour a century later. However, at the time they found few customers, the most notable being Cardiff and Walsall corporations, with production ceasing by 1922.

FIRE FLOAT HULL

Between 1873 and 1886, a massive construction task took place to create the first railway tunnel under the River Severn, linking South Gloucestershire to Monmouthshire in South Wales. Its completion has been regarded as the crowning achievement of the civil engineer Sir John Hawkshaw, the chief engineer of the GWR.

Such was the scale and duration of this development that the contractor, Thomas A. Walker, developed a whole small town, Sudbrook, at the site. Sudbrook contained both housing for the workers, and a steel fabrication factory, run by his nephew C. W. Walker, to produce the tunnel lining plates.

With the completion of the tunnel in 1886, the fabrication factory looked around for other work and decided to become a constructor of steel boat hulls, a brave move at a time when the vast majority of boats were still of conventional timber construction. Walkers were approached by the Portishead authorities and duly constructed the 40ft-long (12m), 10ft-beam (3m) steel hull for the fire float.

THE DENNIS LOCO TRACTOR

One intriguing vehicle of this era was the combined tractor and irrigation machine. This machine was designed for multiple duties, from ploughing to winching to spraying water for irrigation, using a 250gal/min turbine pump driven from the vehicle's engine. It is not clear how many of these machines were produced; however, in around 1914, one, fitted with a 35HP 4-cylinder petrol-paraffin engine, was put to an unusual duty by Major Frank Dutton of the South African Railways. At that time, their railway faced considerable challenges in providing and maintaining vital yet little-used branch lines to remote rural communities.

Dutton identified that the heavy weight of the then-prevalent steam engines was a limiting factor in delivering and maintaining these lines, for the heavy loco weight dictated more substantial track and foundations and more gentle gradients. He rationalized that an internal combustion-powered locomotive would be significantly lighter than a steam engine, allowing a much lighter and cheaper infrastructure, yet still providing adequate traction if this was supplied by a rubber tyre in contact with a hard road surface rather than the relatively low grip given by a regular railway wheel on a steel rail. The resulting 'loco-tractor' had four driving wheels fitted with solid rubber tyres running on strips of roadway either side of the railway track, together with a four-wheeled bogie running on the rails to provide the guidance.

A short test track was laid near Johannesburg in 1917 to

The loco-tractor in the lower view was developed in South Africa from the 1914 tractor in the upper photo. It was intended as a locomotive for branch line goods trains. Unfortunately, the concept did not live up to its early promise, and was soon abandoned.
BOB LOVELAND COLLECTION

test the system. The four wheels of the Dennis tractor, with solid rubber tyres, were retained, but the front wheels could be lifted from the ground and an easily removable four-wheeled rail bogie placed underneath. This intriguing machine could thus run on rails where possible, and then, by removing the rail bogie, continue its journey as a regular road vehicle.

The trials, it appears, were successful, the Dennis loco-tractor towing up to six full trailers with ease. However, although some rail branch lines to Dutton's design were subsequently built in South Africa and elsewhere, no further Dennis tractors were used. Other donor units were provided, mainly by the Yorkshire Steam Patent Wagon Company – whose successors, in a twist of fate, themselves become part of the Dennis family at a later date.

Sustained experience in operating the system soon demonstrated that the benefits of the system were not as great as had been claimed, and not great enough to outweigh the added complexity, so such systems were short-lived.

WORLD WAR I PRODUCTION

Storm Clouds Gather

Dennis's 2,000th vehicle was made in 1912, meaning that by 1913 Dennis single- and double-deck buses were a common sight on Britain's roads, single-deckers usually being based on the 30-cwt (1,520kg) chassis and double-deckers on the 3- to 4-ton (3,050–4,060kg) chassis. In March

1913, Dennis Brothers (1913) Ltd was floated as a public company with £300,000 of share capital.

Even before then, war was in the air, and the newly formed public company quickly decided to cease passenger car production in favour of concentrating on the commercial vehicles for which they were by then renowned. In part, this was in response to the government's recognition that the coming war would need far more in the way of

DENNIS COMBINED TRACTOR AND IRRIGATION MACHINE, 1908–

Engine: RAC rating 30HP
Length: 171in (4,343mm)
Width: 76in (1,930mm) approx.
Wheelbase: 108in (2,743mm)
Gearbox: 3-speed: 2.5, 5, 9mph (4, 8, 14.5km/h), plus reverse
Rear axle: Dennis worm drive
Suspension: Multi-leaf steel springs
Turbine pump: 250gal/min (1,138ltr/min) at 60–70psi (4.14–4.83 bar)
Winch: 50ft (15.25m) steel rope
(Source: Dennis Bros. catalogue, 1908)

reliable mechanized transportation than was readily available.

In 1911, the War Department announced a subsidy, or subvention, scheme. The scheme invited civilians who purchased an approved model of lorry to receive an annual subsidy in return for, if necessary, making their vehicle available for War Department use in the event of war. Such a subsidy system was not a new concept; the War Depart-

ment had already used something similar to provide some 14,000 horses for the Boer War in South Africa.

The vehicle types approved for this subsidy were selected through rigorous acceptance testing by the War Department; thus owners who participated in the scheme not only received the cash subsidy but invested in the vehicle in the knowledge that the design had successfully passed an extremely tough test schedule, and should, therefore, be long-lasting.

Dennis was at the forefront of manufacturers submitting vehicles for these tests, using their standard 3-tonner introduced in 1913. The War Department testing identified only one significant change as necessary: this was to fit an improved engine and cooling system. A White & Poppe engine was duly installed, together with a more robust replaceable-tube radiator, this becoming the specification of the production vehicles.

About 700 vehicles in total were registered for the subsidy scheme, and on the day war was declared, telegrams requisitioning these vehicles were sent out to their owners. Their mobilization was complete within only five days, and some 950 lorries, including those already owned by the War Department, were dispatched to France.

Unfortunately, however, despite all this planning and preparation, the opposing forces became bogged down in the trenches, and ground conditions meant that little use could be made of the lorries for the next three years.

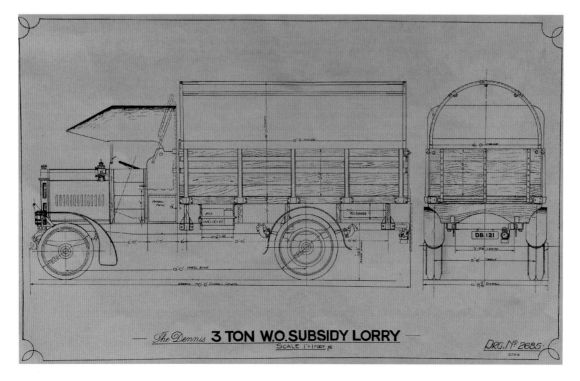

The Dennis **3 TON W.O. SUBSIDY LORRY**
SCALE 1" = 1 FOOT

DRG. N° 2685

This drawing appeared in the brochure for the A-Type 'subsidy' lorry. DENNIS ARCHIVES

THE EARLY YEARS: 1895–1918 ■ 27

DENNIS A-TYPE WAR DEPARTMENT SUBVENTION CHASSIS, 1913

Layout and chassis
4 × 2 World War I military lorry with ladder frame
suitable for various body types
Engine
Type: White & Poppe
Block material: Cast iron
Head material: Cast iron
Cylinders: 4 in-line
Cooling: Water, pump-assisted, built-up radiator with
removable tanks
Bore and stroke: 110 × 150mm
Valves: Side valve
Carburettor: Claudel-Hobson, gravity feed
Max. power: RAC rating 30HP; 40bhp at 1,000rpm
Transmission
Gearbox: Dennis
Clutch: External cone type, Ferodo-faced
Ratios:
    1st: 4.57
    2nd: 2.78
    3rd: 1.68
    4th: 1
    Reverse: 4.57

Final drive: Torque tube into Dennis worm-drive axle
Suspension and Steering
Front and rear: Semi-elliptic multi-leaf springs
Steering: Worm and sector
Tyres: Solid rubber; front 880 × 120mm, rear 1,050 ×
120mm
Wheels: Bolt-on spoked steel, twin rear wheels
Brakes
Type: Footbrake: contracting drum behind gearbox
Handbrake: cam-operated expanding type on rear wheels,
rod-operated
2 sprags at rear to War Office pattern
Dimensions
Track at rear: 66in (1,676mm)
Wheelbase: 132in (3,353mm)
Overall length: 246in (6,248mm) approx.
Overall width: 84in (2,134mm)
Overall height: 102in (2,590mm) approx. to top of cab
Ground clearance: 11.5in (292mm)
Unladen weight: 8,400lb (3,810kg) approx.
Payload: Military 7,840lb (3,556kg);
Civilian 10,080lb (4,572kg)
Top speed: 16mph (26km/h)
(Source: Dennis Bros. 'Model A Subvention Vehicle'
brochure, 1913)

THE SUBSIDY SCHEME

If an operator of an approved vehicle type signed
up to the scheme, they received £110, paid in three
instalments over three years, the first being paid when
the vehicle was enrolled into the scheme. In return,
the owner had to do no more than keep the vehicle in a
good state of repair and allow it to be inspected by the
War Department every six months.

In the event of war, if the War Department then
wished to acquire the lorry from its owner for military
use, the owner would be paid the original purchase
price of the vehicle, minus a reduction of 7.5 per cent
for depreciation for every six months of its age. The
final sum calculated in this way was then topped up by
a further 25 per cent.

The War Effort

Materials to build 1,000 of these lorries were already on
order when the war broke out, so the company was in a
good position when the government placed an order with
Dennis for twenty lorries per week. In October 1915, the
company came under the control of the Ministry of Munitions, which meant that the company then worked towards
Britain's war effort full-time.

In May 1916, the order was increased to twenty-five
'military wagons' per week, with Dennis then promising
to produce thirty-five vehicles per week from June 1917,
on condition that the Ministry of Munitions contributed
50 per cent of the cost of expanding Woodbridge Works.

Woodbridge Works toiled day and night to produce over
7,000 subvention lorries, as well as fire engines and fire
pumps over the four and a half years of the World War I.
Indeed, Dennis's vehicle manufacturing proved so crucial to
the war effort that when the company became a 'controlled
manufacturer' of the Ministry of Munitions, the young men
of its workforce were issued with special badges to ward off

The Dennis A-Type lorry played a major part in the Great War, with 7,000 being built between 1914 and 1918. This convoy is probably on its way to the Western Front. DENNIS ARCHIVES

DENNIS PORTABLE FIRE PUMP, 1916–

Configuration: No. 1 man-portable or trailer fire pump
Engine: 4-stroke single-cylinder water-cooled petrol
Max. power: 3.5bhp at 1,800rpm
Fuel capacity: 0.75gal (3.4ltr)
Pump output: 130gal/min (590ltr/min) at 40psi

Weight: 252lb (114kg), pumping set less trailer undercarriage
Price (1931): Pumping set only: £125
Trailer undercarriage: £25
(Source: Dennis Bros. booklet 'Off the Stones', 1931, and Dennis Bros. publication No. 973, 1939)

criticism for not being in uniform. This badge protected the men against approaches from 'feather girls' – women who would approach any man who had not joined up and present him with a white feather, symbolizing cowardice.

THE COLLAPSE OF THE MARKET

Ironically, the end of World War I brought sudden and dramatic change to the fortunes of the Dennis business. After working almost flat out producing lorries for the War Department, that work vanished virtually overnight as the vast fleet of trucks that Dennis had toiled so hard to build began to be returned to Britain to be sold off for civilian use, thereby reducing the opportunities for new vehicle sales dramatically. These may have been vehicles built for war, but they had plenty of life left in them; company records show orders still being placed for spares for some vehicles in Scotland in 1944, after twenty-seven years of service.

At that point, Dennis had an almost impossible problem: they had one of the biggest truck-making factories in Europe, capable of building around 2,500 trucks per year, but a minimal market. Lesser companies might have thrown in the towel there and then, but the Dennis brothers picked themselves up and set out to develop both new markets and new models.

PORTABLE PUMP

One little-known aspect of Dennis production played a small but vital part in the horrendous battles of the Great War. When the conflict moved to the Somme area, the troops regularly found themselves in truly terrible conditions, often waist-deep in water and mud, and without clean water supplies. Realizing that something had to be done, and noting Dennis's great success with their fire engines, senior officers approached Dennis management with an urgent request to develop and produce some form of portable pump that could be used to ease the dire conditions faced by the troops.

Although Dennis had not previously considered the concept of a stationary pump, they soon came up with a small pack, capable of being carried by four men and using the turbine pump technology borrowed from the fire engines. These packs, weighing only 2.75 cwt (140kg), went into service in 1916 and were capable of either moving 100gal/min (450ltr/min) of water or sending a 0.75in (19mm) jet of water 70ft (21m) into the air. After the war, similar units, retailing at £125, were sold to customers as diverse as His Majesty the King of Siam, His Highness the Sultan of Johore, and one Rudyard Kipling Esq.

The portable pump was designed and manufactured very quickly in response to an urgent War Office need for a pump to provide drinking water to the troops in Europe. It went on to become the forerunner of the trailer pumps used in their thousands in World War II.

BOB LOVELAND COLLECTION

CHAPTER TWO

BETWEEN THE WARS: 1918–1939

Civilian versions of the wartime A-Type lorry were soon on sale after World War I, with an improved payload. DENNIS ARCHIVES

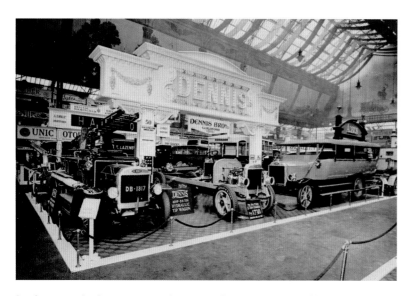

In those early days, motor show stands were ornate affairs. This photo shows the Dennis stand at Olympia in 1919. Note that prices were proudly held at pre-war levels. BOB LOVELAND COLLECTION

Urgent decisions were needed at the end of World War I. The company faced empty order books yet had one of the biggest truck-making factories in Europe and a skilled post-war workforce of 1,100. One option would have been to close the business. At the first post-war board meeting, however, the Dennis directors made two key decisions: first, to diversify their product range and, second, to intensify export activity.

Later events proved these decisions to be inspired. Fortunately, the cash to fund this activity was available thanks to the Dennis brothers' prewar foresight in retaining much of their profits as reserves in the company – a saving grace at this difficult time.

NEW PRODUCTS AND NEW MARKETS

In 1918, the company returned to its original name of Dennis Brothers Ltd with John and Raymond Dennis as joint managing directors. Sir Raymond, knighted in 1920 in recognition of the firm's wartime efforts, was an inspired sales director, selling Dennis vehicles around the world. To make further export headway, in December 1919, Raymond set out on a marathon 60,000-mile (100,000km) world tour to identify new markets, promote Dennis products and appoint agents. One of his key selling points on this mammoth mission was to highlight the sterling reliability of both the Dennis military vehicles and the fire engines, whose performance was becoming legendary. In particular, in 1917 a pair of Dennis fire engines had pumped water continuously for ten days and seventeen days respectively in a massive fire in the Greek town of Salonika.

THE FIRST MUNICIPAL VEHICLES

In seeking new sales, Dennis sought out opportunities to offer innovative products into markets where the Dennis brand was already well understood and respected. They also actively looked for new products that could use some of their existing technology, to avoid too big a leap into the unknown.

Some of the new ventures, therefore, sought to strengthen the existing Dennis relationship with local authorities. First, drawing on their experience with fire pumps, in 1921 they launched an innovative vacuum cesspool emptier following an approach from a Buckinghamshire council. Cesspool emptying was at that time a particularly unpleasant operation, involving horse-drawn vehicles and manual pumps that frequently became blocked.

The Dennis brothers duly came up with a vehicle to do the job in a much cleaner and less obnoxious way. Their machine used an engine-driven vacuum pump to suck out the contents of the cesspool. The pump incorporated a patented reversing valve to blow any obstructions out of the suction pipe as they arose. This equipment, which included a 750gal (3,400ltr) holding tank, was mounted on a unique short-wheelbase chassis. Very soon these innovative vehicles were adopted by municipal authorities across the UK, and their success led to Dennis setting up a dedicated municipal vehicle department.

The new department quickly developed gully-emptying vehicles, some of which were dual-purpose and were also used for cesspool emptying. Refuse-collection and street-washing vehicles were also added to the range, the latter making use of the turbine pump used on fire appliances.

The launch of the Dennis cesspool emptier in 1921 marked a revolution in municipal vehicles. This Stepney vehicle was typical of hundreds sold to local authorities. BOB LOVELAND COLLECTION

Dusty conditions were a major concern to early motorists, leading to the introduction of street watering vehicles to damp down the dust, like this 1930 Dennis. BOB LOVELAND COLLECTION

A typical moving-floor refuse lorry. Note the lofty seating for the unfortunate loaders! BOB LOVELAND COLLECTION

The first refuse-collection vehicles were loaded by dropping the refuse on to the floor of the vehicle. This floor was movable and was wound forward in steps as required to provide more space. When full, the load was dumped by reversing the floor movement. Later models physically compressed the rubbish, enabling much more to be carried.

Lawnmowers

Another new venture, in 1921, was the manufacture of motor mowers, mainly large machines that enabled the local authorities to keep their many hectares of parkland in trim. The first mower had a Blackburne two-stroke petrol engine but was not a great success. A fully revised machine with a Dennis-designed four-stroke engine then appeared in 1922 and was quickly acclaimed as an excellent

A mower catalogue of the 1920s. BOB LOVELAND COLLECTION

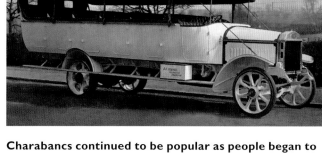

Charabancs continued to be popular as people began to travel again after World War I. This 1921 40HP example was owned by B. E. Dening of Taunton. DENNIS ARCHIVES

piece of engineering. Indeed, it was so well regarded that it remained in production for nearly twenty years.

Always quick to spot publicity potential, the company soon promoted the efficiency benefits of their mowers, proudly proclaiming that 'one man with a Dennis mower could cut in one day as much as two men and a horse could mow in two days'.

In 1928, Dennis mowers were granted a royal warrant after supplying a motor mower to the Royal Gardens at Windsor. Dennis mowers went on to be used exclusively by such varied customers as the Royal Air Force, London County Council, most if not all county cricket grounds, and innumerable owners of country estates both in the UK and overseas.

NEW MODELS GALORE

If World War I had done nothing else, it had firmly established the superiority of trucks over horses when it came to moving goods. While the market in 1918 was swamped

This 1920 view shows the Woodbridge Works body shop. The ash-framed structure of the charabancs in build is evident. DENNIS ARCHIVES

with large numbers of ex-military A-type lorries, these were limited to a 3-ton (3,050kg) payload. Dennis realized that higher-capacity models would generate sales, so quickly introduced 4- and 5-ton (4,060kg and 5,080kg) versions of the original army truck. These were successful in recovering some of the lost sales; then, as now, the concept of one person, or vehicle, being able to do more than their competitors, was attractive to customers.

Another quick fix was ideally placed to capture the needs of a population now able to travel and enjoy free time after their wartime privations. This was the introduction of a 40HP charabanc, based on an extended-wheelbase version of the military A-Type chassis. The company was able to put this model into production quickly only because, whether by accident or design, they had in 1913 secured adequate stocks of the timber necessary for body construction.

New models started to appear almost every year, but despite this proliferation of chassis types, sales of Dennis trucks and buses remained limited. In 1924, however, the company launched a successful new normal-control chassis, somewhat confusingly called the 30-cwt although its payload was in fact up to 43 cwt (2,180kg). It used robust truck components, compared to the lighter and shorter-lived car components used by others. This approach was, interestingly, mirrored by the company some sixty years later, when the Dennis Dart midibus took the bus market by storm. The 30-cwt had a straight-framed chassis, pneumatic tyres and a Dennis 4-cylinder 17.9HP petrol engine with a four-speed gearbox. In passenger form, it could accommodate 16- to 22-seat bodywork.

The 30-cwt continued in production until 1931.

DENNIS LIGHT-WEIGHT GOODS CHASSIS

1.	2.	3.	4.	5.		6.	7.	8.
Model and Capacity N.C.=Normal Control. F.C.=Forward Control.	Chassis Price	Weights				Tax	Body Dimensions	
		Weight in cwts. (approx.) Less Petrol Spare Wheel, Water and Tools.	Weight allowed for Body and Cab in cwts.	Gross Running Weight under Guarantee. Tons.	Cwts.		Recommended Length and Width of Platform (Inside).	Maximum Length of Body behind Driver's Cab to M.O.T. Regulations.
35 cwt. N.C. ...	£272	32¼	7¾	4	0	£25	10′ 0″×6′ 6″	11′ 8¾″
40 cwt. N.C. ...	£275	33½	12	4	10	£30	11′ 3″×6′ 6″	11′ 8¾″
45 cwt. N.C. ...	£283	34	12	4	16	£30	11′ 3″×6′ 6″	11′ 8¾″
45 cwt. F.C. ...	£283	34	12	4	16	£30	13′ 6″×6′ 6″	14′ 5¼″
45 cwt. N.C. Long	£300	35½	12	4	16	£30	14′ 0″×6′ 6″	14′ 6⅝″
45 cwt. F.C. Long	£300	35½	12	4	16	£30	17′ 0″×6′ 6″	17′ 3¼″
50 cwt. N.C. ...	£300	36½	13	5	5	£30	11′ 3″×6′ 6″	11′ 8¾″
50 cwt. F.C. ...	£300	36½	13	5	5	£30	13′ 6″×6′ 6″	14′ 5¼″
50 cwt. N.C. Long	£325	37½	12	5	5	£30	14′ 0″×6′ 6″	14′ 6⅝″
70 cwt. N.C. Short	£400	40	Special light 10	6	5	£30	9′ 0″×6′ 10″	—
80 cwt. N.C. ...	£400	41	14	6	15	£35	13′ 6″×6′ 10″	13′ 10⅜″
Light 4 ton. N.C.	£350	38	11¾	6	15	£30	14′ 6″×6′ 10″	—
75 cwt. N.C. ... Rigid 6-wheel.	£400	43¾	13	6	15	£35	14′ 6″×6′ 6″	15′ 3″
80 cwt. N.C. ... Articulated 6-wheel	£425	Chassis 34 Cab 3¾	Trailer with platform body 22	8	0	£35	16′ 0″×6′ 6″	—
120-cwt. N.C. ... Articulated 6-wheel	£550	—	—	10	10	£50	20′ 0″×6′ 6″	—

DENNIS HEAVY-DUTY GOODS CHASSIS

1.	2.	3.	4.	5.		6.	7.	8.
Model and Capacity N.C.=Normal Control. F.C.=Forward Control.	Chassis Price P.=Petrol. O.=Oil.	Weights				Tax With Platform body.	Body Dimensions	
		Weight in cwts. (approx.) Less Fuel, Spare Wheel, Water and Tools.	Weight allowed for Body and Cab in cwts.	Gross Running Weight under Guarantee. Tons.	Cwts.		Recommended Length and Width of Platform (Inside).	Maximum Length of Body behind Driver's Cab M.O.T. Regulations.
4 Ton. N.C. 140	P. £575	67	20	8	10	£50	14′ 6″×7′ 0″	15′ 6¼″
	†O. £750	—		8	10		14′ 6″×7′ 0″	15′ 6¼″
4 Ton. F.C. 126	P £575	68	20	8	10	£50	16′ 9″×7′ 0″	17′ 0½″
	†O. £750	—		8	10		16′ 9″×7′ 0″	17′ 0½″
4 Ton. F.C. 140	P. £575	68½	20	8	10	£50	18′ 3″×7′ 0″	19′ 2″
	†O. £750	—		8	10		18′ 3″×7′ 0″	19′ 2″
5 Ton. F.C. 126	P. £600	69	20	9	15	£70	16′ 9″×7′ 0″	17′ 0½″
	†O. £775	—		9	15		16′ 9″×7′ 0″	17′ 0½″
5 Ton. F.C. 140	P. £600	69½	20	9	15	£70	18′ 3″×7′ 0″	19′ 2″
	†O. £775	—		9	15		18′ 3″×7′ 0″	19′ 2″
7/7½ Ton. F.C. 124	P. £750	70		12	0	£70	16′ 3″×7′ 0″	16′ 10″
7/7½ Ton. F.C. 159	P £750.	71¼		12	0	£70	19′ 0″×7′ 0″	21′ 8″
7/7½ Ton. F.C. 124	†O. £925	73¼		12	0	—	16′ 3″×7′ 0″	16′ 10″
7/7½ Ton. F.C. 159	†O. £925	74½		12	0	—	19′ 0″×7′ 0″	21′ 8″
12 Ton F.C. ... 6-wheeler with single driven axle.	P. £1,050	96		19	0	£90	21′ 6″×7′ 0″	22′ 6⅛″
	P. £1,200	100		19	0	£90	21′ 6″×7′ 0″	22′ 0⅛″
	†O. £1,225			19	0	—	21′ 6″×7′ 0″	22′ 6⅛″
10/12 Ton. F.C. 6-wheel with two driven axles.	*O. £1,600			19	0	—	24′ 0″×7′ 0″	24′ 3⅝″

TOP: **Almost all of the lighter chassis in the mid-1930s were taxation class specials. These were based on the 40/45-cwt model and retained the same 4-cylinder petrol engine, gearbox and axles, but had different wheel and tyre equipment to take advantage of specific taxation classes.** BOB LOVELAND COLLECTION

BOTTOM: **The heavy-duty goods chassis list of 1934 shows the wide range of prices, from £575 for a 4-ton payload up to £1,600 for a 12-tonner.** BOB LOVELAND COLLECTION

Vehicles capable of carrying higher payloads were also developed, including in 1924 a new 4-ton (4,060kg) chassis powered by a 4-cylinder engine. It had a very competitive list price of £860 (around £52,000 at 2019 levels). A longer-wheelbase version was also offered for bus use, which proved popular with London operators for double-deck bodywork.

In 1925, Dennis introduced a 2- to 2.5-ton (2,030–2,540kg) payload chassis for both passenger and goods use. An attempt was made to sell this model via a dedicated sales outlet, Dennis-Portland, in Great Portland Street in London. This was set up to compete with the growing number of car manufacturers using their high street outlets to also sell light commercial vehicles. While the Portland sales outlet was not a success, the vehicle itself became extremely popular. Indeed, by the late 1920s, Dennis had become Britain's largest producer of commercial vehicles; by 1927, its profits were £335,000. Such profits made mergers and acquisitions an option: Guy and Leyland were both considered.

'To a very great extent Great Britain owes her pre-eminence in commercial motor cars to the foresight, energy and resource of the firm of Dennis Bros Ltd., Guildford.'
The Times

This view taken from the sales brochure shows the chassis and running gear of the highly successful 30-cwt of the later 1920s. Note *The Times* comment!
BOB LOVELAND COLLECTION

The 30-cwt chassis was the first to be offered with pneumatic tyres as an option, and was equally suited to either passenger or goods duties. The 1926 eighteen-seat passenger version shown here proved popular amongst rural customers, who appreciated its excellent economy and performance. DENNIS ARCHIVES

Built in 1924 on a 40/50HP 4-ton chassis, this Nottingham Corporation double-decker is an early example of a covered-top double-decker. It carries thirty-seat bodywork built by Short Brothers. Upper-deck headroom must have been minimal. DENNIS ARCHIVES

The 30-cwt chassis was very popular for van use, such as this immaculate demonstrator. DENNIS ARCHIVES

DENNIS 30-CWT CHASSIS, 1930

Layout and Chassis
4×2 rigid normal- or forward-control ladder chassis for van, lorry or bus bodywork
Engine
Type: Dennis petrol
Block material: Cast iron
Head material: Cast iron
Cylinders: 4 in-line
Cooling: Water, pumped
Bore and stroke: 85 × 120mm
Valves: Side valve
Max. power: RAC rating 30HP; 36bhp at 2,000rpm
Fuel capacity: 9.5gal (43ltr)
Transmission
Gearbox: Dennis 4-speed and reverse, aluminium casing
Clutch: External cone-type, fabric-faced
Ratios:
  1st: 4.6
  2nd: 2.82
  3rd: 1.63
  4th: 1
  Reverse: 3.94
Final drive: Torque tube to Dennis worm-drive rear axle
Suspension and Steering
Front and rear: Semi-elliptic multi-leaf steel springs
Steering: Worm and nut

Tyres: Air cushion: 720mm × 110mm front, 720mm × 140mm rear
or Pneumatic: 33in × 5in (838mm × 127mm) front, 34in × 7in (864mm × 178mm) rear
Wheels: Cushion tyres: hollow-spoke cast steel
  Pneumatic tyres: detachable pressed-steel disc wheels
Brakes
Type: Rear only: internally expanding drums with asbestos linings, independent shoe pairs for footbrake and handbrake
Size: 16in (406mm) diameter
Dimensions
Track: 56in (1,422mm) approx. front, 56in (1,422mm) rear
Wheelbase: 132in (3,353mm)
Overall length: 200in (5,070mm)
Overall width: 67.5in (1,711mm) over chassis;
  86in (2,184mm) over typical body
Unladen weight: 3,416lb (1,549kg) on cushion tyres;
  3,304lb (1,499kg) on pneumatic tyres
Payload: 3,472lb (1,575kg) on cushion tyres;
  3,360lb (1,524kg) on pneumatic tyres
Gross weight: 8,176lb (3,709kg)
Passenger capacity: 19 seats (typical)
Price (1930)
Normal-control chassis: From £300 (with pneumatic tyres)
Forward-control chassis: From £315 (with pneumatic tyres)
(Source: Dennis Bros. publication No. 2916, 1930)

Dennis also had the foresight to consider ways to help potential buyers to own a Dennis product. In 1929, a new subsidiary, Dennis Contracts, was created to operate a hire-purchase scheme, in many respects foreshadowing the leasing contracts that are so widespread today.

Despite the severe trading conditions in the immediate post-war period, the company continued to invest in buildings and equipment to expand the capabilities of Woodbridge Works, with shops 8, 9, 10 and 11 added between 1925 and 1936. By then, Woodbridge Works covered 31 acres (13ha), which included almost 13 acres (5ha) of workshops.

Well after the introduction of pneumatic tyres, solid tyres, which could be much smaller, were popular for duties where a low body height was needed, such as bin emptying. DENNIS ARCHIVES

The 40/45-cwt Chassis – the Ace

In 1933, Dennis produced an unusual-looking but very successful range, the 40/45-cwt (2,030–2,290kg) payload model popularly, if inaccurately, known as the Ace. Key to the normal-control version of the 40/45-cwt was that the front axle was set well back, resulting in an extremely short 9ft 6in (2.9m) wheelbase. This gave excellent manoeuvrability but resulted in the engine and radiator being positioned well forward like a snout – so it was no surprise that the 40/45-cwt soon acquired the nickname of 'Flying Pig'. The engine used in all models was the D3 24.8HP petrol unit.

A forward-control version was also offered, which was often used for 23-to 26-seat passenger bodies.

Its versatility meant that the 40/45-cwt chassis was used on a wide range of products, from buses through to lorries, tankers, and even gully-emptiers. Older readers may remember the gully-emptier being immortalized as a Meccano model for young budding engineers to build.

The chief designer responsible for the design of the 40/45-cwt Ace was none other than Erling Poppe, son of P. A. Poppe, one of the founders of White & Poppe.

Production continued until 1940.

The 40/45-cwt chassis was also sold with a third, trailing, axle giving exceptional manoeuvrability and increasing the payload to 3.5 tons (3,560kg). It was available both as normal and forward control.

LEFT: **It's easy to see from this picture why the 40/45-cwt, or Ace, was better known as the Flying Pig on account of the long snout protruding beyond the front axle. However, it was an extremely practical configuration, the set-back axle giving the Ace exceptional manoeuvrability in tight conditions. This superbly restored fuel tanker is owned by Joe Devanny, and can regularly be seen at the Goodwood Revival.** AUTHOR

The Ace lorry was more correctly known as the 40/45-cwt model. This 1933 vehicle appears regularly at rallies, mainly near its home in Lancashire. It was originally used at Woodbridge Works between 1933 and 1968 as, it is believed, a prototype 60-cwt model, before restoration in 1999. JOHN TURNBULL

DENNIS 40/45-CWT CHASSIS (ACE), 1933–1940

Layout and chassis
4×2 rigid ladder-frame chassis for normal- or forward-control van, lorry or bus bodywork

Engine
Type: Dennis petrol
Block material: Cast iron
Head material: Cast iron
Cylinders: 4 in-line
Cooling: Water, pumped
Bore and stroke: 100 × 120mm
Capacity: 3770cc
Valves: Side valve
Carburettor: Zenith down-draught
Max. power: RAC rating 24.8HP; 60bhp at 2,250rpm
Fuel capacity: 15gal (68ltr)

Transmission
Gearbox: Dennis 4-speed and reverse, aluminium casing
Clutch: Wet cone-type, fabric-faced
Final drive: Dennis spiral bevel

Suspension and Steering
Front and rear: Semi-elliptic multi-leaf springs
Steering: Worm and nut
Tyres: 40-cwt: 6.50 × 20; 45-cwt: 32 × 6
Wheels: Detachable disc wheels – single front, twin rear

Brakes
Type: Footbrake: hydraulically applied drum brakes on all four wheels
Size: 12.75in (324mm) diameter

Dimensions
Track: 62in (1,575mm) front and rear
Wheelbase: 114in (2,896mm)
　　　138in (3,505mm)
Overall length: 40-cwt 220.75in (5,607mm), chassis;
　　　45-cwt 248.75in (6,318mm), chassis
Overall width: 40-cwt: 76.25in (1,937mm), chassis;
　　　45-cwt 77in (1,956mm), chassis
Unladen weight: 40-cwt: 3,752lb (1,702kg);
　　　45-cwt 114in w/b 3,808lb (1,727kg),
138in w/b 3,976lb (1,804kg)

Performance
Top speed: 30mph (48km/h)

Prices (1937)
40-cwt normal-control chassis, 114in w/b: £290
45-cwt normal- or forward-control chassis, 114in w/b: £298
Coachbuilt steel-panelled cab: £50
Pressed steel forward-control cab: £35
Hinge-sided lorry body: £35
(Source: Dennis Bros. publication 993, 1937)

The Ace chassis were very popular for municipal work, such as gully emptying and street washing, duties which were often combined, as by this example used by **Tottenham Borough Council.** BOB LOVELAND COLLECTION

This was one of two 45-cwt vans supplied to the royal household for private transport between **Buckingham Palace** and **Windsor Castle,** earning the company a royal warrant as commercial vehicle manufacturers to **H. M. King George V.** DENNIS ARCHIVES

In the early 1930s, London County Council took a batch of these 40/45-cwt vehicles, described as 'Children's Ambulances'. DENNIS ARCHIVES

Many Aces were used for passenger transport, like this Merthyr bus, thanks to the good manoeuvrability that made them ideal for tricky rural routes. BOB LOVELAND COLLECTION

This Mace with a special body by Burlingham was used at Speke Airport, Liverpool, from 1937. BOB LOVELAND COLLECTION

This three-axle vehicle was based on the familiar 40/45-cwt chassis, the extra axle giving a higher 70-cwt (3,560kg) payload capacity. The rearmost axle steered, giving an impressively tight turning circle. DENNIS ARCHIVES

Many Dennises were used as promotional vehicles. This 40/45-cwt of around 1925 was used by CWS Paints. BOB LOVELAND COLLECTION

Special-purpose bodies seem to have been a frequent fitment on Dennis chassis, like this 1931 mobile coffee bar belonging to J. Lyons. BOB LOVELAND COLLECTION

This mid-1930s vehicle was another demonstration vehicle, this time for the tea products of the Co-operative Wholesale Society. BOB LOVELAND COLLECTION

Yet another unusual body produced in 1934 for the Sunlight Laundry by Eagle Engineering. BOB LOVELAND COLLECTION

DENNIS 80-CWT CHASSIS, 1933–

Configuration: 4×2 rigid ladder-frame chassis for normal- or forward-control van, lorry or bus bodywork
Engine: Dennis C-type 4-cylinder petrol
Capacity: 3770cc
Max. power: RAC rating 24.8HP; 75bhp at 3,000rpm
Gearbox: Dennis 4-speed and reverse, aluminium casing; optional 5-speed gearbox

Rear axle: Dennis spiral bevel
Suspension: Semi-elliptic multi-leaf springs on both axles
Wheelbase: 132in (3,353mm)
Length (chassis): 245.75in (6,242mm)
Width (chassis): 82in (2,083mm)
Weight (chassis): 4,592lb (2,083kg)
Top speed: 30mph (48km/h)
Price (1937): £400 (chassis)
(Source: Dennis Bros. publication No. 12c, 1937)

The Light 4-Ton

The 14ft 6in (4.42m) wheelbase Light 4-ton normal-control model was not based on the 40/45-cwt range but was a completely new design. The engine was the 4-cylinder petrol as used in the 45/45-cwt. The vehicle's styling was rather Americanized and was also adopted by the 1937 2- to 3-ton (3,050kg) Ajax.

The Dennis Ajax drop-sided lorry.

The Ajax normal control 2- to 3-ton (2,030–3,050kg) payload chassis was introduced in 1937 to replace the 40/45-cwt range. Unlike the 40/45-cwt, no articulated tractor versions were offered. It retained the C-type 3.77-litre petrol engine and four-speed gearbox of the earlier range. Competition meant that only 102 were built, compared to almost 7,500 of the earlier range. BOB LOVELAND COLLECTION

DENNIS AJAX, 1933–

Configuration: 4×2 rigid ladder-frame chassis for normal-control lorry bodywork of 2-, 2.5- or 3-ton payload
Engine: Dennis C-type 4-cylinder petrol
Max. power: RAC rating 24.8 HP; 75bhp at 3,000rpm
Capacity: 3770cc
Gearbox: Dennis 4-speed and reverse, aluminium casing, optional 5-speed gearbox
Clutch: Wet single plate, fabric-faced
Rear axle: Dennis spiral bevel
Suspension: Semi-elliptic multi-leaf springs on both axles

Wheelbase: 131in (3,327mm)
 150in (3,810mm)
Overall length (chassis): 192.6in (4,893mm)
 235.6in (5,985mm)
Overall width (chassis): 76.5in (1,943mm)
Unladen weight (chassis): 2-ton payload 3,808–3,892lb
 (1,727–1,765kg);
 2.5-ton payload: 3,864–3,940lb (1,753–1,787kg)
 3–ton payload 4,088–4,172lb (1,854–1,892kg)
Top speed: 30mph (48km/h)
(Source: Dennis Bros. publication No. 18, 1937)

The 7/7.5-ton

Unlike other models, this chassis designation referred to the gross weight, the actual payload being around 4 tons (4,060kg). It was a two-axle rigid forward-control vehicle powered by the usual D3 petrol engine, with options of either Dorman-Ricardo 4HW 4-cylinder or Gardner 6-cylinder oil engines. Vehicles with 6-cylinder engines had a short opening bonnet between the radiator and the front scuttle.

The 1932 brochure for this 12-ton (12,190kg) heavy-duty forward-control 6×4 shows wheelbase options of 16ft 9in (5.10m) and 18ft 6.5in (5.65m). The short-wheelbase model had a payload of 5 tons 8 cwt (5,490kg). It was powered by a Dennis 6-cylinder petrol engine driving into a four-speed gearbox and on to the twin worm-drive rear axles. In chassis/scuttle form it was priced at £1,445. Only thirty-three were sold before the model was withdrawn in 1936. BOB LOVELAND COLLECTION

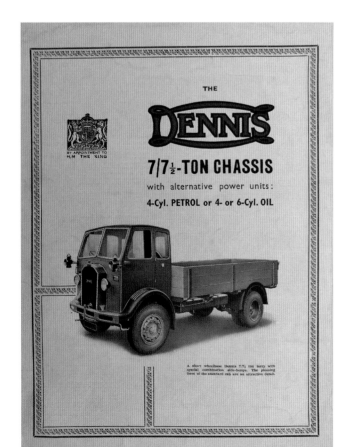

THE

DENNIS
7/7½-TON CHASSIS
with alternative power units:
4-Cyl. PETROL or 4- or 6-Cyl. OIL

BY APPOINTMENT TO
H.M THE KING

A short wheelbase Dennis 7/7½ ton lorry with special combination side-lamps. The pleasing lines of the standard cab are an attractive detail.

Publication No. 8410

The 1934 brochure for this heavy duty 7/7.5-tonner confirms that it was capable of a 12-ton (12,190kg) GVW, the same as the Max, which replaced it in 1937. BOB LOVELAND COLLECTION

DENNIS 7/7.5-TON CHASSIS, 1934–

Configuration: 2-axle rigid forward-control goods chassis
Engine: Dennis 4-cylinder petrol, RAC rating 30HP; 85bhp
or Dorman-Ricardo heavy oil engine, 72bhp
or Gardner heavy oil engine, 95bhp
Capacity: 5702cc
Gearbox: Dennis 4-speed or 5-speed, aluminium case
Rear axle: Dennis worm drive, ratio 8.25:1
Suspension: Semi-elliptic multi-leaf springs on both axles

Wheelbase: 148in (3,759mm)
  189in (4,801mm)
Overall length: 247.5in (6,287mm)
  298.5in (7,582mm)
Overall width: 89.5in (2,274mm)
Unladen weight: Dennis petrol engine: 7,728–7,896lb
  (3,505–3,582kg)
Dorman-Ricardo engine: 8,120–8,288lb (3,683–3,759kg)
  Gardner engine and 5-speed gearbox: 8,932–9,100lb
  (4,052–4,128kg)
Price (1935): £750 with petrol engine
(Source: Dennis Bros. Ltd. publication No. 8410, 1934)

DENNIS 12-TON CHASSIS, 1932–

Configuration: 3-axle rigid forward-control goods chassis
Engine: Dennis 6-cylinder petrol
Max. power: 108bhp at 2,250rpm
Capacity: 6126cc
Gearbox: Dennis 4-speed constant mesh, aluminium case
Final drive: 2 Dennis worm-drive axles, leading axle incorporating third differential
Suspension: Semi-elliptic multi-leaf springs on all axles

Wheelbase: 201in (5,105mm)
  222.5in (5,652mm)
Overall length: 331in (8,407mm)
  359.6in (9,134mm)
Overall width: 90in (2,286mm)
Unladen weight: 14,784–15,008lb (6,706–6,808kg)
Price (1932) Chassis: £1,445 less driver's cabin
All-steel 3-way tipping body and driver's cab: £470
(Source: Dennis Bros. Publication no. 5876C, 1932)

The Max

The 1937 Commercial Motor Show saw the launch of the Max, a 6- to 8-ton (6,100–8,130kg) payload forward-control truck. Its name was a reference to its ability to carry the maximum load then legally permissible on a 12-ton (12,190kg) GVW two-axle vehicle. It shared much with the Lance and Lancet passenger chassis and went on to become extremely popular.

In 1939, a twin-steer three-axle version with a 10.5-ton (10,670kg) payload called Max Major was offered; however, only two were sold before the outbreak of World War II.

The Max Major was a 10.5-ton (10,670kg) payload, 18-ton (18,290kg) gross weight twin-steer chassis, built at the request of the Yorkshire woollen trade. BOB LOVELAND COLLECTION

DENNIS MAX, 1937–

Layout and Chassis
4×2 rigid ladder-frame forward-control goods chassis
Engine
Type: Dennis Big Four petrol
Block material: Cast iron
Head material: Cast iron
Cylinders: 4 in-line
Cooling: Water, pumped
Bore and stroke: 120 × 150mm
Valves: Overhead valve
Max. power: 95bhp at 2,000rpm (est.)
Max. torque: 290lb ft at 1,000rpm (est.)
or
Type: Dennis O4-type diesel
Block material: Cast iron
Head material: Cast iron
Cylinders: 4 in-line
Cooling: Water, pumped
Bore and stroke: 117.47 × 150mm
Capacity: 6500cc
Valves: Overhead, 4 valves per cylinder
Max. power: 95bhp at 2,000rpm
Max. torque: 320lb ft at 1,200rpm (est.)
Fuel capacity: 33gal (150ltr)
Transmission
Gearbox: Dennis 4-speed plus reverse, alloy casing
Ratios:
   1st: 5.32
   2nd: 2.79
   3rd: 1.69

   4th: 1
   Reverse: 6.3
or
Gearbox: Dennis 5-speed plus reverse, alloy casing
Ratios:
   1st: 5.19
   2nd: 2.94
   3rd: 1.55
   4th: 1
   5th: 0.69
   Reverse: 6.66
Clutch: Twin dry plate
Final drive: Dennis worm drive
Suspension and Steering
Front and rear: Semi-elliptic multi-leaf springs
Steering: Worm and nut
Tyres: 36in × 8in high-pressure pneumatic
Wheels: Detachable steel disc
Brakes
Type: Drum brakes on all four wheels, hydraulically actuated with vacuum-servo assistance
Size: 17in (432mm) diameter
Dimensions
Track: 75.5in (1,918mm) front, 70in (1,778mm) rear
Wheelbase: 144in (3,658mm)
   168in (4,267mm)
Overall length (chassis): 215in (5,461mm)
   262in (6,655mm)
Overall width (chassis): 89.5in (2,273mm)
Unladen weight: Petrol: 7,280–7,336lb (3,302–3,328kg)
   Diesel: 7,672–7,728lb (3,480–3,505kg)
(Source: Dennis Bros. publication No. 47C, 1937)

The 5-Tonner/Pax

In 1939, a 5-ton (5,080kg) payload chassis with an unladen weight of only 2 tons 2 cwt (2,130kg) was introduced. This showed just how much truck technology had developed in only fifteen years: the similar payload 5- to 6-tonner of fifteen years before had an unladen weight of 3.5 tons (3,560kg). A number of these 5-tonners were built during World War II, afterwards being renamed Pax (for peace).

The first of the forward-control versions had the traditional upright front panel and windscreen. However, this soon gave way to the gently curving front that subsequently characterized Dennis models for over a decade.

THE FIRST DEDICATED BUS AND COACH CHASSIS

E- and F-Type Single-Deckers

As the post-war passenger-carrying market developed, new models specifically tailored for passenger-carrying started to appear, their lower floor levels meaning fewer steps for the passengers to climb.

One significant new model of 1925 was the single-deck E-Type. It had a low-line dropped-frame chassis with an underslung worm-drive rear axle to minimize the floor height, and was powered by the same 4-cylinder petrol engine of 5.7-litre capacity as the previous 4-ton (4,060kg) chassis. Servo-operated four-wheel brakes were fitted from 1926 once Scotland Yard had ceased their objection to front-wheel brakes.

Cushion tyres, a compromise between traditional solid tyres and the as-yet rare pneumatics, were used at this time on some passenger vehicles. It was not until May 1925 that Scotland Yard authorized the use of pneumatic tyres on single-deck buses. A Dennis thirty-seater belonging to Admiral was the first pneumatic tyre-equipped bus to operate in London.

The range was extended in 1929 by the addition of the ES-Type with a Dennis 6-cylinder 37.3HP petrol engine. A 1930 update saw the ES become the EV-Type, distinguished visually by having a much less protruding radiator. Although designed as a bus, some E-Types were built as fire engines and side-hinged tippers, where the low chassis line gave clear benefits.

The F-Type, effectively a normal-control version of the forward-control E-Type, was launched at the 1927 Commercial Vehicle Show. It was popular for coaches, generally with 20- to 28-seat bodywork. The 5.7-litre engine made it a fast and reliable performer, but for even more performance the FS-Type was offered in 1929, fitted with the 6-cylinder engine of the ES.

Around 150 F-types were built. Production of both E- and F-Types ceased in 1930 with the introduction of the Arrow.

DENNIS PASSENGER CHASSIS

1. Model and Capacity. N.C.=Normal Control. F.C.=Forward Control.	2. Chassis Price P.=Petrol O.=Oil.	3. Weights — Total Weight of Chassis, including Fuel and all Equipment.	4. Gross Running Weight under Guarantee. Tons. Cwts.		5. Tax	6. Maximum Length of Body behind Driver's Seat to M.O.T. Regulations.	7. No. of Cylinders. Side Valves unless otherwise stated.	8. Bore and Stroke. P=Petrol O=Oil	9. Cubic Capacity. c.c.
ACE. N.C. 20 Seats.	P. £300	38½	4	5	£36	14' 8½"	4	100×120 P	3,770
MACE. F.C. 23-26 Seats.	P. £350	45¼	5	5	£48	17' 3"	4	100×120 P	3,770
LANCET. N.C. 32 Seats.	P. £650	77¼	7	15	£57-12-0	19' 5"	4	110×150 P	5,702
†LANCET. N.C. 32 Seats	†O. £825	80	7	15	—	19' 5"	4	117·5×150 †O	6,515
LANCET. F.C. 36-39 Seats.	P. £650	77¼	7	15	£67-4-0	23' 0"	4	110×150 P	5,702
†LANCET. F.C. 36-39 Seats.	†O. £825	80	7	15	—	23' 0"	4	117·5×150 †O	6,515
LANCET 6. F.C. 30-39 Seats.	P. £750	82	8	10	£67-4-0	22' 11"	6 O.H.V.	100×130 P	6,126
LANCE 4. F.C. 56 Seats.	P. £900	81	10	10	£86-8-0	21' 0"	4	110×150 P	5,702
LANCE. F.C. 56 Seats.	P. £1,000	83	10	10	£86-8-0	21' 0"	6 O.H.V.	100×130 P	6,126
†LANCE. F.C. 56 Seats.	†O. £1,075	83	10	10	—	21' 0"	4	117·5×150 †O	6,515

This 1934 data sheet of passenger models shows a broad range of prices: from £300 for a twenty-seat Ace chassis to £1,075 for a 56-seat Lance. BOB LOVELAND COLLECTION

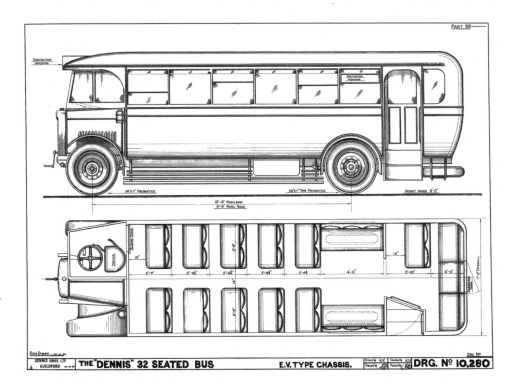

This drawing of the E-Type bus dates from 1929. BOB LOVELAND COLLECTION

The E-Type was introduced in 1925 and became an immediate success. This 1929 ES was still in regular stage carriage service as recently as 2018! It is seen here, however, at the 1995 Dennis Centenary event at Wroughton. BOB LOVELAND COLLECTION

The F-Type was introduced in 1927 as a normal-control version of the E-Type, and became a popular coach chassis. This particularly well-appointed 1928 vehicle was used on Greyline Parlour Coaches Eastbourne–London service. It had folding tables fitted to the rear of each of the twenty-four seats, curtains and interior lighting. DENNIS ARCHIVES

These F-Type buses were some of the first Dennises to see service in Hong Kong in around 1928. BOB LOVELAND COLLECTION

H-Type Double-Decker

In 1928 Dennis's first purpose-designed double-decker, the H-Type, was introduced, replacing the stalwart normal-control 4-ton (4,060kg) chassis. Double-deckers had been around for some time previously, in both horse-drawn and (later) motorized form. However, they were invariably based on goods vehicle chassis, thus were comparatively tall, making fitment of a solid roof rarely practical.

The H-Type, in contrast, had a low frame and an underslung worm axle, enabling a solid roof to be fitted if required, setting the scene for the industry-standard configuration of double-deckers for years to come. It was fitted with the D3 4-cylinder 30HP petrol engine as used in the E-type, although the separate engine subframe used in earlier models was discontinued.

A version with a larger 6-cylinder engine was marketed in 1929, designated the HS-Type, and a further 1930 update saw the model designation become the HV-Type. Pneumatic tyres were introduced on double-deckers in 1928, many older chassis being retrofitted.

The H-Type was superseded in 1930 by the Lance.

E-TYPE RESTORATION

Many old buses finished their days with their still vaguely serviceable bodies being sold on as accommodation for various purposes. Two 1928 E-Types, originally built for Aldershot & District and sold after eight years in service, were given a new lease of life as holiday homes located in a Hampshire field. They provided accommodation for many happy holidaymakers for some decades before finally falling into disuse by the 1980s.

Restoration of these vehicles was considered, but their prolonged exposure to the elements meant that at least one of the bodies was just too far gone. However, they yielded many useful spares when they were rescued in 1996 by a registered charity, the Aldershot & District Omnibuses Rescue & Restoration Society.

Another 1928 Aldershot & District E-Type ended its days as a home on the river bank at Walton-on-Thames. However, that was far from the end of the road for this particular bus, for the dwelling was later extended by building a property around it. This protected the chassis from the wind and rain that had dealt the last rites to the other pair of E-Types. Hidden from view, it lay undisturbed for seventy years, until uncovered by workers clearing the site for development. Fortunately, they contacted the nearby Cobham Bus Museum to advise of their 'find' rather than taking the easy option of using their demolition machinery to clear away the remains.

The museum recovered the remarkably sound chassis, which was then passed to the society, who began a lengthy and ongoing restoration. At the time of writing, this is progressing steadily, with the rebuilt engine now running and the chassis having driven around the society premises. The focus is now on restoration of a Strachan & Brown body, with much of the intricate wooden framing completed, thanks to the skills of a craftsman whose work also graces the restorations of both HMS *Victory* and HMS *Warrior*. When completed it is believed that it will be the only operational E-Type still in existence.

The ADORRS group are progressing well with their intensive restoration of an ex-Aldershot E-Type, as shown in these before and after photos. More details of this painstaking and unique project can be found on the Society's website (www. adorrs.co.uk). RAY LE MESURIER-FOSTER

The H-Type was Dennis's first forward-control double-decker, introduced in 1927. Unusually, this one retained an open-top deck. DENNIS ARCHIVES

'To a very great extent Great Britain owes her pre-eminence in commercial motor cars to the foresight, energy and resource of the firm of Dennis Bros Ltd., Guildford.'

The Times

This view of the HV-Type chassis taken from the model's brochure shows how the frame is swept up over the rear axle to keep the floor level as low as possible. BOB LOVELAND COLLECTION

DENNIS HV-TYPE, 1930

Configuration: 4×2 rigid ladder-frame forward-control low-load-line chassis
Engine: Dennis 4-cylinder 85bhp petrol
Capacity: 5700cc
Gearbox: 4-speed plus reverse, aluminium casing
Rear axle: Dennis underslung worm drive
Suspension: Semi-elliptic springs on both axles
Wheelbase: 198.75in (5,048mm)
Overall length: 300in (7,620mm)
Overall width: 90in (2,286mm)
Overall height (typical): 157.5in (4,001mm)
Unladen weight (chassis): 8,064lb (3,658kg)
Price (1930): £970 (chassis)
(Source: Dennis Bros. publication No. HV2, 1930)

The GL was a derivative of the G-Type and was introduced in 1929. Again normal-control, it had a chassis frame even lower than that of the G-Type, and was in many respects a 4-cylinder version of the Dart chassis. In 1931, it was offered with the new Dennis 17.9HP 4-cylinder overhead-valve petrol engine.

The GL range saw diverse applications. Many were built as fire engines, selling well overseas as well as in Great Britain. Ambulance variants were also sold, including six to Guildford's St John Ambulance brigade.

The G-Type

The normal-control G-Type made its debut at the 1927 Commercial Motor Show to replace the earlier 30-cwt chassis for passenger-carrying duties, although goods vehicles continued to make use of the 30-cwt chassis until the mid-1930s. As with the other passenger chassis, it featured a dropped frame and underslung worm-drive axle. It was almost 3ft (900mm) longer than the 30-cwt, making it suitable for twenty-seat bodies. The 2.72-litre 4-cylinder 17.9HP petrol engine was retained, with vacuum servo-operated brakes as an option.

The normal-control GL was a useful small bus for rural operators, seating twenty passengers. This 1931 example was owned by Guildford operator Yellow Bus Services. BOB LOVELAND COLLECTION

The Arrow

Both normal- and forward-control versions of the single-deck Arrow were announced at Olympia in 1929, with a hefty price tag of £1,025 putting it on a par with the AEC Reliance. Even when the Arrow was launched, most operators were specifying forward-control chassis to provide maximum passenger accommodation, so the normal-control version of Arrow found few takers. The Arrow was 6 cwt (300kg) lighter than the outgoing E-Type, had an offset driveline to reduce the floor height, and was designed to carry 32-seat bodywork. A new Dennis 6-cylinder 6.1-litre 100mm × 130mm 37.2HP overhead-valve engine was fitted, along with vacuum servo brakes.

The Arrow's low floor line also made it of interest as an ambulance; London County Council were one such buyer.

Arrow production ceased in 1934 after only fifty-eight were produced, to be replaced by the much cheaper Lancet.

The Arrow single-deck chassis was introduced alongside the Lance double-deck in 1929. Unlike earlier bus chassis, the frame was lowered fore and aft of the rear axle to give the lowest possible floor line. DENNIS ARCHIVES

The M-Type

The M-Type was intended to be a three-axle 75-seat bus, using a Kirkstall double-drive bogie. However, the project was abandoned, and the two prototype chassis were eventually fitted with tar-sprayer bodies for the Gas Light and Coke Company in 1930.

The Dart

The Dart was announced in 1930, another normal-control chassis for single-deck bus or coach bodywork and with

Dart buses, like this 1930 example, were popular with the London General Omnibus Company. They were probably the first one-man-operated buses in London. DENNIS ARCHIVES

This lovely old 1932 Dart still exists today, owned by the company. It can often be seen on rallies and at special events. In this view, taken in August 2009, it was in service as the wedding transport for the author's daughter. AUTHOR

Dart chassis were also used for ambulances, like the 1931 vehicle shown here, which was owned by the Guildford division of the St John Ambulance Brigade. BOB LOVELAND COLLECTION

a Dennis 6-cylinder overhead-valve 4.1-litre 85mm × 120mm 26.9HP petrol engine.

Notwithstanding growing preferences for forward-control chassis, the Dart became popular with small independent operators for coach applications, although it was also widely used by London General. Production continued until 1933.

The Lance

In 1930, the H-Type double-decker was replaced by the Lance, a new 56-seat forward-control model. It was initially fitted with the same Dennis 6-cylinder 37HP petrol engine as used in the Arrow, with the 34HP 6.5-litre 6-cylinder diesel engine offered later. A D3 4-cylinder 5.7-litre 30HP petrol version was also offered but was considered underpowered. It was therefore never a big seller even though the company felt it was significant enough to be given its own model designation: Lance 4. The 6-cylinder chassis weighed 4 tons 3 cwt (4,220kg) and was initially priced at £1,150.

The Lance had a profiled frame to give the lowest possible floor height, assisted by the transmission line being offset to provide an unobstructed gangway in the lower saloon. This allowed for a low-height version of only 13ft 5in (4.09m), although the standard height was 14ft 2.5in (4.33m).

The chassis saw several upgrades in 1931, most visibly a redesigned radiator, together with a revised model designation of Lance II. London General subsidiary Over-

Road testing of chassis was an exposed task in the early 1930s, as shown by this Lance chassis, which is fully laden with test weights. DENNIS ARCHIVES

In the 1930s, photographers may not have had Photoshop, but it did not stop them tweaking their images. This shot from 1931 purports to show twenty Metro-Cammell-bodied Lances for London Overground parked in Woodbridge Road, Guildford. In fact, the photographer took several images, each of four buses, then cleverly superimposed them to create an apparent line of buses. DENNIS ARCHIVES

ground were among the first customers, buying twenty-five in 1931. By 1938, the petrol engine options had been withdrawn, leaving all subsequent Lances diesel-powered.

Lance production ceased in 1940, restarting after World War II.

This early Lance operated in London. Note the lack of weather protection for the driver – a London requirement! DENNIS ARCHIVES

The Lancet

The single-deck Lancet, a low-cost successor to the Arrow, appeared at the Olympia Exhibition in 1931, with an attrac-

DENNIS LANCE, 1930–1940

Layout and Chassis
4×2 rigid ladder-frame chassis for forward-control bodywork

Engine
Type: Dennis petrol
Block material: Cast iron
Head material: Cast iron
Cylinders: 6 in-line
Cooling: Water, pump-assisted
Bore and stroke: 100 × 130mm
Capacity: 6100cc
Valves: Overhead
Max. power: RAC rating 37.2HP; 100bhp
Fuel capacity: 45gal (205ltr)
or
Type: Dennis petrol
Block material: Cast iron
Head material: Cast iron
Cylinders: 4 in-line
Cooling: Water, pump-assisted
Bore and stroke: 110 × 150mm
Capacity: 5700cc
Valves: Side valve
Max. power: RAC rating 30HP; 85bhp

Transmission
Gearbox: 4-speed plus reverse, aluminium casing
Clutch: Twin dry plate
Ratios:
    1st: 5.32
    2nd: 2.79
    3rd: 1.69
    4th: 1
    Reverse: 6.3
Final drive: Dennis offset underslung worm drive

Suspension and Steering
Front and rear: Semi-elliptic springs, optional dampers
Steering: Worm and nut
Tyres: 36in × 8in
Wheels: 10-stud steel disc; single front, twin rear

Brakes
Type: Drums all round, hydraulically actuated with vacuum-servo assistance
Size: 17in (432mm) diameter

Dimensions
Wheelbase: 198in (5,030mm)
Overall length (chassis): 310in (7,874mm)
Overall width: 89.75in (2,280mm)
Price (1931): Chassis with 6-cylinder engine £1,095
    Chassis with 4-cylinder engine: £995
(Source: Dennis Bros. publication No. 736, 1931)

The Lancet appeared in 1932 at an extremely low price of under £600. This 1933 vehicle was operated by T. S. Camplejohn. DENNIS ARCHIVES

Not all Lancets were forward-control, although normal-control sales were few in number. This 32-seat normal-control vehicle dates from around 1934. DENNIS ARCHIVES

This view shows the body framing of the Lancet II. BOB LOVELAND COLLECTION

This unusual Lancet-based vehicle was supplied to Luminastra of Bromley in 1932. It carried a light projector for sky advertising that incorporated a Sperry lamp giving a beam of 450 million candlepower. BOB LOVELAND COLLECTION

tive list price of under £600, barely half the cost of its predecessor. The D3 4-cylinder 30HP petrol engine was fitted initially, with the 34HP 6-cylinder diesel engine offered later.

Alternatively, the 37HP 6-cylinder 6.1-litre overhead-valve petrol engine as used in the Arrow could be installed in the forward-control model. Lancets of this era can be recognized by their heavy-looking pressed steel radiator grille, which protrudes from the front scuttle on forward-control vehicles, as does, unusually, the steering box.

Cheap it may have been, but the Lancet was still well-equipped and quickly gained a large following.

Lancet II, introduced at the 1935 Olympia Show, was simply an improved version of the original, able to take a longer body. Visually, the Lancet II was differentiated by sharing the cast aluminium radiator shell of the Lance rather than the chunky pressed item of the Lancet. It was also available only in forward-control configuration.

Several engine options were offered, ranging from the Dennis 6-cylinder petrol or diesel engines, a Lanova 4-cylinder diesel, or a Gardner 5LW diesel. The Gardner engine was later replaced by Dennis's own O4-type 4-cylinder diesel, an engine that quickly gained an excellent reputation for reliability and economy. Lancet II was the first single-deck chassis of the then-legal maximum 27ft 6in (8.4m) length that could accommodate forty-seat bodywork. Production continued until 1940.

The Mace

The Mace – the name deriving from Major Ace – was introduced in 1934, and shared an almost identical mechanical configuration with the Ace, including the set-back front axle. It was, however, longer, with an 11ft 6in (3.5m) wheelbase intended for passenger applications with forward-control bodywork. It attracted few sales, and production ceased in 1937.

The Arrow Minor

Of traditional layout, the Arrow Minor was introduced in 1936 but saw very few sales, and was discontinued a year later. It was based on the Light Four goods chassis and used the Dennis 24.8HP 4-cylinder petrol engine.

The Pike

The single-deck Pike replaced the Arrow Minor from 1937. It drew heavily on the components used in the Ajax goods chassis, such as the Dennis 24.8HP petrol engine. Once

THE NEW

DENNIS

Pike Chassis

(Straight-Frame Model)

For 20-Seated Passenger Bodies

DENNIS BROS., LTD., GUILDFORD, ENGLAND

Phone: Guildford 1575 (7 lines)   Grams: Dennis, Guildford

The Pike is built for the Operator who appreciates the cash value of real riding comfort, masterly performance, easy control and good visibility, coupled with the essentials of profitable and absolutely dependable service. The Pike represents Dennis passenger-transport craftsmanship in its latest and most valuable development.

The Pike was produced only between 1937 and 1940; few were sold. BOB LOVELAND COLLECTION

again it was a normal-control model, with its most striking feature being the radiator that sloped inwards to the top of the bonnet. It was intended to carry 24-seat bodywork. The Pike remained in production until 1940, although very few were sold.

The Falcon

The Falcon was Dennis's last new passenger model before the outbreak of World War II. Introduced in 1938, it was effectively a Pike, and available either in forward- or normal-control form. With a wheelbase of 16ft 6in (5.03m), it was suitable for either bus or coach bodywork. Engine options were a Dennis 4-cylinder petrol unit, a Gardner 4LK or a Perkins P6 6-cylinder diesel. Only forty-seven were manufactured before the start of the war.

DENNIS PIKE, 1937–1940

Configuration: 4×2 rigid ladder-frame chassis for normal-control bodywork
Engine: Dennis 4-cylinder petrol
Max. power: RAC rating 24.8HP; 75bhp
Capacity: 3770cc
Gearbox: 4-speed plus reverse; 5-speed optional with 0.67:1 overdrive 5th gear
Clutch: Single wet plate, fabric-faced
Final drive: Spiral bevel
Suspension: Semi-elliptic springs front and rear
Wheelbase: 150in (3,810mm)
Overall length (chassis): 250.5in (6,363mm)
Overall width (chassis): 76.5in (1,942mm)
Unladen weight (chassis): 3,920lb (1,778kg)
Capacity: 20 seats
(Source: Dennis Bros. publication No. 28C, 1937)

DHO 266 was the first Falcon to arrive at long-time Dennis customer Aldershot & District in March 1939, and was possibly one of the prototypes. BOB LOVELAND COLLECTION

FIRE APPLIANCE DEVELOPMENTS

Fire appliance sales up to 1936 had stabilized at about 100 per year, with Dennis products prominent in most brigades – London alone had 250 Dennis machines by 1937. Since the early days of the N-Type, the designs had developed considerably, and the Dennis range had expanded to include both big machines, such as the Light Six and Big Six, and

A low-cost and light fire appliance, the G-Type was developed using a long-wheelbase version of the 30-cwt chassis. This 1929 appliance saw service at Wotton-under-Edge in Gloucestershire. DENNIS ARCHIVES

Many fire brigades requested full weather protection for their crews, resulting in limousine-style bodies, such as this 1932 vehicle for Edinburgh. BOB LOVELAND COLLECTION

smaller appliances with 4-cylinder engines, such as the Ace and the Light Four, for rural areas and confined locations.

Braidwood-style bodies with their exposed and vulnerable crew positions had generally given way to configurations that minimized the risk of firefighters being ejected from the vehicle. The 'New World' body style, where the crew faced inwards, protected by the sides of the vehicle, was common. Some brigades, however, favoured enclosed or semi-enclosed limousine-style bodywork. The latter protected the crew from the elements but retained the exposed rear for easy hose and pump access.

The Ace

Ace fire appliances were popular worldwide, sales going to countries as diverse as Australia and India. Part of the

The 1936 Ace of the Dennis Works Fire Brigade giving rides to employees and their families at ADL's 2019 Guildford open day. AUTHOR

This 1936 Ace fire appliance was the pride and joy of the Dennis Works Fire Brigade, the vehicle and its crew winning many awards. It is still owned by the company today. BOB LOVELAND COLLECTION

The arrival of this 1936 canteen-bodied Ace was always a welcome sight at major incidents attended by the London Fire Brigade. BOB LOVELAND COLLECTION

Ace's success was due to that set-back front axle and relatively small size of just over 17ft (5.18m) long and 6ft 4in (1.93m) wide. This made it ideal for challenging locations such as industrial premises; indeed, the Dennis Works Fire Brigade used an Ace for many years that is still owned by the company today.

The Light Four/Big Four

The Light Four was based on the Ace but had a more conventional front axle position, while the Big Four was a heavier machine.

The Light Six

A higher-power version of the Ace called the Light Six was introduced in 1935. As the name implies, this used the Dennis 6-cylinder overhead-valve engine. Eighty-four were produced, some of which were exported, to New Zealand and elsewhere. All body styles were fitted, from Braidwood to full limousine.

The Big Six

Originally named the 80HP when it was introduced in 1930, the Big Six used a 6-cylinder side-valve engine and was typically fitted with a mid-mounted 850gal/min centrifugal pump. Rescue equipment installed on these vehicles was usually either a 30ft (9.1m) Ajax ladder made of laminated wood, or a 50ft (15.2m) wheeled escape ladder. The benefit of the mid-mounted pump over the traditional

London Fire Brigade were loyal users of the Big Four model, pictured here around 1934. The Big Four had a higher load capacity than the Ace-based Light Four. The initial D3 version had a 4-cylinder side-valve engine, while later vehicles had an all-new 6.8-litre overhead-valve engine.
DENNIS ARCHIVES

rear-mounted unit was speed, in that it avoided the delay of removing the wheeled escape before pumping operations could start. A turntable ladder could also be fitted, such as the Magirus unit fitted to a vehicle for the Belfast Fire Brigade in 1931.

The Big Six was a premium product with a premium price – £3,184 in 1939 (more than £200,000 in today's money).

Trailer Pumps

The period from 1937 leading up to World War II saw substantial purchases of trailer pumps by industrial and commercial companies as well as government departments preparing themselves for the coming war. In 1937 some 150 pumps were sold, while in 1938 sales increased to around 800, including 550 to the Home Office.

From the mid-1930s, as the probability of war increased, local councils, industrial concerns and country estates alike bought these trailer pumps in increasing quantity, with over 7,000 being built before and during World War II. This one was purchased by the Grantown-on-Spey authorities. DENNIS ARCHIVES

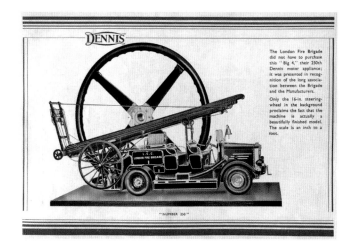

The 250th fire engine to enter into the London Fire Brigade fleet was this 1/12th scale model, presented to the brigade by Dennis in 1937. BOB LOVELAND COLLECTION

ENGINE PRODUCTION AT GUILDFORD

Although Dennis, like many other manufacturers of the time, was heavily 'vertically integrated', making almost every part of the vehicle and its running gear themselves, this did not extend to engine supply. Initially, Aster engines were used in the commercial vehicles, but by 1908 engine supply was from White & Poppe, a Coventry manufacturer of technically advanced engines. In 1919, a 'fusion of interests' amalgamated Dennis with White & Poppe, funded by an increase in the Dennis capital to £600,000: under the deal, A. J. White and P. A. Poppe joined the Dennis board.

The petrol engine range subsequently produced was impressive. A new overhead-valve petrol engine family made its appearance in 1930. It was available in both 4- and 6-cylinder versions, the 6-cylinder having a capacity of 6.1 litres. This new engine family was used widely in products such as the Dart and the 30-cwt truck chassis.

THE DENNIS TURBINE PUMP

The success of Dennis fire engines in the period leading up to World War I had been much assisted by the innovative performance of the Gwynne Turbine centrifugal pump. At some time in the 1920s, the Gwynne pump was replaced by the Tamini multi-stage centrifugal pump designed initially by Mario Tamini, of Milan, but developed further and manufactured by Dennis.

The Tamini-Dennis pump was available in three sizes. The No. 1 was generally used for trailer and portable pumps due to its light weight of only 86lb (40kg) and output of up to 200gal/min (900ltr/min). Fire engines commonly used either a No. 2 pump of 500gal/min (2,250ltr/min) or No. 3 pump, rated at 1,000gal/min (4,500ltr/min).

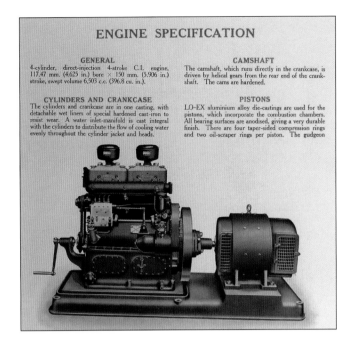

The O4 4-cylinder 6.5-litre 117mm × 150mm diesel engine was also used to power Dennis-branded stationary and mobile AC and DC 27kW and 40kW generating sets, using Crompton Parkinson generators. The success, or otherwise, of this venture is not known.

BOB LOVELAND COLLECTION

DENNIS GENERATOR SET, 1938

Configuration: Self-contained generating set
Engine: Dennis O4 4-stroke diesel
Capacity: 6503cc
Generator: Crompton Parkinson
Output options:
　　AC 27kW 400v 3-phase
　　AC 40kW 400v 3-phase
　　DC 27kW 50v or 110v
　　DC 27kW 230v
　　DC 40kW 110v or 230v
Overall length:
　　AC sets: 123in (3,124mm)
　　DC sets: 103in (2,616mm) max.
Overall height: 60in (1,524mm)
Overall width: 32in (814mm)
(Source: Dennis Bros. publication No. 73C, 1939)

However, the truck and bus market had by then moved towards diesel power, and Dennis were rather slow at entering this field, only producing their first, and not particularly impressive, diesel engine in 1931. As a stopgap, Dennis used Dorman-Ricardo and Gardner diesels in some models from 1932 followed by Perkins from 1935. The later O4 Dennis diesel engine of 1937 was, however, much better received.

THE WHITE & POPPE DEAL

In 1933, White & Poppe engine manufacturing was moved from Coventry to Guildford. This brought to an end engine production on the Coventry site that had, at its peak after World War I, employed some 33,000 people. Employment there continued, however, for the site was sold to the Triumph Motor Company for the sum of £40,000.

The conveyance for this transaction, held in the Dennis archives, records that it covered 'a piece of land situated in Holbrook Lane, with a frontage of 540ft [165m] containing 10.75 acres [4.35ha] with all factories, workshops, and other buildings and appurtenances as agreed in the deed of 7 May 1935'. Other archive documents tell us that £30,000 of the purchase price was covered by a mortgage provided to Triumph by Dennis themselves.

DENNIS AS AN EMPLOYER

Dennis was always a caring employer and recognized the problems experienced by their workforce in finding homes within a reasonable distance of the factory. Acquiring 21 acres (8.5ha) of land around the Woodbridge factory in 1934, they built 298 homes there for their increasing number of workers, including those who had moved from Coventry with the relocation of engine production. The resulting estate, Dennisville, had many of the roads named after senior Dennis people, notably Raymond Crescent and St John's Road, and still exists today. Most of today's residents, of course, are probably entirely unaware of the history of their dwellings.

Unusually, Woodbridge Works even had an on-site barber's shop, in the 1960s at least, with employees being allowed a regular fifteen-minute break for a quick 'short back and sides'!

Employees and their families were also encouraged to enjoy an active company-supported social life, with the Dennis Athletic Club providing facilities ranging from sports teams to horticulture. The Christmas parties for the children are fondly remembered by the older members of the workforce to this day.

THE GREAT DEPRESSION

The Dennis board's 1918 strategy in seeking new markets and new products had proved a great success. By 1923, production had increased to an all-time annual high of 2,000 vehicles and stayed at that level until the Great Depression of the early 1930s.

The 1920s and early 1930s had seen a relentless introduction of new and enhanced models, all promoting the traditional Dennis virtues of innovation, quality, performance and reliability: benefits that came, of course, at a price, making Dennis products amongst the more expensive in the market.

For those premium prices, though, Dennis was renowned for producing special versions of their products for specific customer orders, perhaps with non-standard wheelbases, different engines or bespoke bodies. This proliferation meant that each chassis type often underpinned a range of body types, spanning pantechnicons to fire engines to buses. As an aside, this proliferation makes the job of any historian seeking to document the Dennis model range quite a challenge.

Overall, Dennis had coped well since World War I, rising to the challenges of the lack of new vehicle orders, the years of recession and fending off the growing number of competitors such as Leyland and Bedford. By the early 1930s, however, the world was sliding headlong into a dire slump, and in those times of austerity, the expensive Dennis products, however good, were finding fewer customers. The company was forced to rethink its product strategy. As a result, it rapidly introduced the Lancet in 1931, which cost £595, compared to the earlier Arrow single-decker's massively more costly price of £1,095.

Unsurprisingly, the Lancet became a great success, doing much to keep the Dennis business profitable through the gloomy days of the depression. This was particularly important because the truck side of the company was struggling due to both the economy and a lack of diesel engines for heavier vehicles. Indeed, throughout the history of Dennis, the bus and fire engine businesses proved to be surprisingly resistant to economic depression, and this was not the only occasion where one or the other kept the company afloat.

Sadly, in May 1939 Sir Raymond Dennis passed away at the early age of fifty-nine, followed only three months later by his brother John. This precipitated the company into significant changes at the top, even as the gathering storm clouds of World War II were about to force Dennis into yet more major upheaval.

In 1933, thirty-two different Dennis models were offered, as shown by the variety of chassis in this view of the Woodbridge Works erecting shop.
DENNIS ARCHIVES

CHAPTER THREE

WORLD WAR II AND
AFTERWARDS: 1939–1972

THE WAR YEARS

As Britain entered World War II, the government quickly realized the importance of controlling vehicle construction to support the war effort. They decided that bus production would only be carried out by Daimler and Guy, depriving Dennis of one of its primary product lines. Mower and fire

ABOVE: **Some 3,000 of these Max 5-ton (5,080kg) payload trucks, most with a utility cab, were made during World War II at Woodbridge Works.** BOB LOVELAND COLLECTION

TOP RIGHT: **This wartime view shows one of the many thousands of Max trucks being fitted with its utility cab.** BOB LOVELAND COLLECTION

RIGHT: **Around 1,500 of these 3-ton (3,050kg) trucks were produced at Guildford during World War II.** DENNIS ARCHIVES

engine production was prohibited, as was producing trucks for civilian use. The company were, however, ordered to build around 3,000 Max 5-ton trucks and about 1,500 3-ton (3,060kg) normal-control trucks for the War Office, together with approximately 1,000 30-cwt (1,520kg) vehicles for the Royal Air Force. A few trucks were also allowed to be produced to support essential agricultural and municipal needs.

Orders for some 7,000 trailer fire pumps were also received. These were fitted with the Dennis 24.8HP 4-cylinder petrol engine and a No. 1 pump and became a very familiar sight around the country. Indeed, many of these ubiquitous pumps saw second lives after the war helping with the fire protection needs of both industrial sites and country estates.

A small batch of forty-three Light Six turntable ladder appliances was also built for the National Fire Service, fitted with Merryweather 100ft (30m) ladders. These were taken over by various local brigades after the war.

Dennis also assembled around 700 35-ton (35,560kg) Churchill tanks, as well as some 3,000 Carden-Loyd tracked vehicles. Subcontracted from Vickers-Armstrong, the Carden-Loyds were used by the British and Commonwealth forces in a variety of roles from troop carriers to equipment transport. One particular duty was in towing the 6-pounder anti-tank gun, and in this role, Carden-Loyd carriers were particularly active in the 1944 Normandy landings and subsequent operations.

Over 3,000 Carden-Loyd light armoured tracked vehicles were manufactured during World War II.
BOB LOVELAND COLLECTION

A further wartime venture was the 6×6 'Octolat', the name being derived from 'Light Artillery Tractor Eight-Wheel'. The Octolat had only six wheels, the fourth axle having been deleted during development to reduce both length and weight as well as improve the handling. The design was produced in response to the army needing a simple, quickly assembled and easily maintained alternative to the costly and complicated Quad 4×4 gun tractor. The Dennis design was indeed simple, steering only one of the three axles, and devoid of suspension, relying purely on the compliance of its six large tyres. It had a central driving position with a lightly armoured body. The prototypes

This shows one of the 700 Churchill tanks having its engine fitted by female as well as male workers.
DENNIS ARCHIVES

Prototypes of the Octolat, a light artillery tractor, were produced during World War II but none were sold. DENNIS ARCHIVES

were powered by Bedford engines, although a 9.8-litre Leyland engine was proposed for production units.

No production orders were received for the Octolat, although testing by both Dennis and the military was successful.

Woodbridge Works was also active in producing much additional military materiel such as tank gearboxes, Wellington bomber gun-turrets and bomb assemblies. During World War II, the site was a hive of activity, with a workforce doubled to around 3,000 and working 24 hours a day. As a 'Protected Place' under the 1939 Emergency Powers Act, security was tight. Measures included camouflaging the entire 13 acres (5ha) of factory roofing, some signs of which were still visible in aerial photos taken many years later. A Volunteer Defence Force of employees also undertook regular armed patrols of the site as well as performing fire-watching duties.

During World War II, the Dennis team were tasked with analysing a captured German 8×8 armoured vehicle on behalf of the government. DENNIS ARCHIVES

Senior politicians as well as famous stars were on hand during World War II to exhort the workforce to greater things. This view, with one of the Churchill tanks produced by the factory as the centrepiece, shows the visit of, it is believed, Minister of Labour Ernest Bevin. DENNIS ARCHIVES

World War II saw a number of high-profile visits to Woodbridge Works to encourage the workforce. This 1942 image shows the much-loved singer Gracie Fields meeting the staff on one of her visits to perform in the Dennis canteen, from which the BBC sometimes produced the midday programme 'Music While You Work'. DENNIS ARCHIVES

The factory railway connection to the main line was kept busy during World War II. Here a Southern Railway locomotive is collecting a Churchill tank. The camouflage paintwork is visible on the roof of the factory. DENNIS ARCHIVES

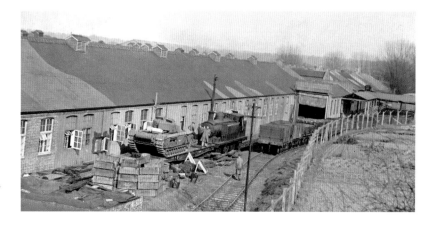

Many of the positions in the factory during World War II were filled by the women, as this photo reminds us. This iconic image was, we believe, recorded at a parade through Guildford on 26 September 1943 to mark both Civil Defence Day and the RAF Battle of Britain Commemoration. DENNIS ARCHIVES

war travel was only possible by public transport, and Dennis was perfectly placed to take advantage of this, producing a proliferation of models.

BUS AND COACH MARKET GROWTH

Early post-war days saw a massive surge in bus and coach orders, for the hard-won freedom from movement restrictions soon unleashed a pent-up demand from the population for travel. Private car ownership was still very low. Waiting lists for new cars were lengthy, as the car factories were focused on export business to generate much-needed income for Britain. For most people, therefore, early post-

The Lancet

After the war, Lancet production restarted. Little changed visually, but it was rebadged as the Lancet III/J3 and offered with the Dennis O6 6-cylinder 7.58-litre diesel engine. Around 800 were made.

In 1949, an export version, the forward-control Lancet IV, was launched, retaining the same mechanical units as the Lancet III but with a longer wheelbase. During 1950, the Lancet III chassis was also updated slightly to allow more modern full-fronted bodywork, becoming the Lancet J3A.

Little had changed visually when Lancet production restarted after World War II, as this 1947 vehicle shows. AUTHOR

ABOVE: This view of a Lancet chassis from around 1946 shows the upswept frame over the rear axle. DENNIS ARCHIVES

The 1948 Lancet IV was basically a normal control Lancet III adapted for full-fronted bodywork, and was aimed at the export market. BOB LOVELAND COLLECTION

Lancashire United Transport were Gardner engine fans, and in 1949 they specified the 5LW diesel engine for their Lancets, which were designated the J4 model. Only twenty were bought, however.

Lancet J5, J7 and J11 were export-only versions. The J5 was a left-hand-drive model of 27ft 6in (8.4m) overall length, the J7 was right-hand-drive with a 33ft (10m) length, and the J11 was also 33ft long but left-hand drive.

The Lancet J10 made its appearance in 1950, sales continuing until 1953. It was a 30ft-long (9.1m) version of the venerable J3, built to make the most of the recently relaxed Construction and Use length limits, suitable for half-cab bodywork of 7ft 6in (2.23m) width. A full-fronted body version was offered as the J10A, still at 7ft 6in wide. The J10B was an 8ft-wide (2.44m) half-cab version, while the J10C was also 8ft wide but with full-fronted bodywork. All four variants shared a body length of 30ft (9.1m) and used the Dennis O6 7.58-litre 6-cylinder diesel engine.

Eighty-four J10s were built in total.

The Pax/Triton/Teal

A small number of goods chassis, including the Pax, were fitted with passenger-carrying bodies, typically seating twenty or twenty-one people. The passenger version of the Pax was eventually rebranded as the Triton, seventy-five sales being achieved, all except one going to London County Council (LCC). The remaining vehicle went to Jersey Motor Transport. Most of these were sold in 1952/3, and the Triton was finally discontinued in 1958.

DENNIS LANCET III, 1946–

Layout and Chassis
4×2 rigid ladder-frame chassis for forward-control bodywork
Engine
Type: Dennis O6 diesel
Block material: Cast iron
Head material: Cast iron
Cylinders: 6 in-line
Cooling: Water, pump-assisted
Bore and stroke: 105 × 146mm
Capacity: 7580cc
Valves: Overhead, 4 valves per cylinder
Fuel system: CAV or Simms
Max. power: 100bhp at 1,800rpm
Max. torque: 328lb ft at 1,250rpm
Fuel capacity: 40gal (182ltr)
Transmission
Gearbox: 5-speed plus reverse
Clutch: Twin dry plate
Ratios:
  1st: 4.54
  2nd: 2.74
  3rd: 1.66
  4th: 1
  5th: 0.69
  Reverse: 5.84
Final drive: Dennis underslung worm-drive axle
Suspension and Steering
Front: Semi-elliptic springs 46.5in (1,181mm) long
Rear: Semi-elliptic springs 60in (1,524mm) long
Steering: Worm and nut
Tyres: 9.00 × 20
Wheels: Steel disc, 20 × 5; single front, twin rear
Brakes
Type: Drum, hydraulically actuated with vacuum-servo assistance
Size: 17in (432mm) diameter
Dimensions
Track: 75.5in (1,918mm) front, 70in (1,778mm) rear
Wheelbase: 209in (5,309mm)
Overall length (chassis): 322.5in (8,192mm)
Overall width: 90in (2,286mm)
Unladen weight (chassis): 8,736lb (3,963kg)
Gross weight: 18,816lb (8,535kg)
Capacity: 32 passengers approx.
(Sources: Dennis Bros. publication No. 158C, 1946 and publication No. 200C, 1948)

This Pax was new to Jersey in 1950. DENNIS ARCHIVES

The frontal appearance of this 1950 Lance K3 contrasts strongly with the more modern 'tin-front' of the 1954 K4 on the right. This photo was taken at a Dennis open day in May 2019. GARY AVERY

Introduced in the 1950s, the Teal was also based on the Pax truck chassis, but with a Perkins P6 engine. It was suitable for a forty-seat 29ft 10in (9.1m) long body. Most Teal PSVs were exported, many to Kuala Lumpur in Malaysia.

The Pax name was reintroduced for passenger variants in the 1960s, Walthamstow taking one solitary Pax BVD6 in 1962, while in 1965 one Pax IIA chassis received a 37-seat passenger body. Equipped with a Perkins 6.305 engine, this became a demonstrator before being sold to Liverpool Fire Brigade.

In 1967, a pair of Pax V goods chassis received 33-seat passenger bodies. Equipped with Perkins 6.254 engines, these went to Llandudno Urban District Council. Their unique feature was a sprag ratchet fitted to the rear axle as a safety device when operated on the hilly Great Orme service. Registered in September 1968, the two Paxes were probably the last Dennis passenger chassis for more than a decade.

The Lance III

The Lance was reintroduced in 1947, rebranded as Lance III. It was available initially in two versions: the K2, which had a Gardner 6LW engine, and the K3 with the 7.58-litre Dennis O6 unit. Transmission options were four- or five-speed constant-mesh gearboxes, while visually a new cast aluminium radiator was used, similar to that featured on models from the Lancet II onwards. Unsurprising, given their Gardner preference, Lancashire United took the nineteen K2s that were built, while Aldershot & District bought all but nine of the forty-nine K3s.

In 1954, both K2 and K3 gave way to the K4 version, which had a Gardner 5LW diesel engine and was readily

Like the Arrow single-decker, the Lance chassis had a dropped frame to lower the floor height, and the drivetrain was also offset for the same reason.
DENNIS ARCHIVES

identifiable by a wide, modern-looking 'tin-front' bonnet and grille covering the radiator. The K4 was not a success, with only thirty-two built, ensuring its early demise in 1954. All went to Aldershot & District.

The Falcon

The lightweight single-deck Falcon was reintroduced in 1948 in both normal- and forward-control form. Various

This is a 1951 brochure for the Falcon, which was reintroduced in 1948. BOB LOVELAND COLLECTION

This very early Falcon P5 in the livery of Guildford operator Yellow Bus was registered in 1952, according to the operator's records, and could have been a Dennis prototype vehicle. BOB LOVELAND COLLECTION

DENNIS FALCON, 1948–1956

Configuration: 4×2 rigid ladder-frame chassis for forward- and normal-control bodywork
Engine: Dennis 6-cylinder diesel
Max. power: 75bhp at 2,000rpm; later 87bhp at 2,000rpm
Capacity: 5060cc; later 5500cc
Gearbox: 4-speed plus reverse; later 5-speed plus reverse, constant mesh
Rear axle: 2-speed spiral bevel
Suspension: semi-elliptic springs front and rear
Wheelbase: 205in (5,207mm)
Overall length (chassis): 327in (8,306mm)
Overall width: 90in (2,286mm), legal max.
Unladen weight (chassis): 7,168lb (3,251kg)
GVW: 17,200lb (7,802kg)
(Sources: Dennis Bros. publications Nos 271C and 346C, 1951/2)

engines were used, including the Dennis D3 4-cylinder petrol unit, the Perkins P6 diesel, and Gardner 4LK or 4LW diesels. In 1950, a new Dennis 6-cylinder 5.1-litre diesel engine was added, which increased to 5.5 litres in 1952.

Aldershot & District again took Falcons, this time with normal-control bodywork. Between 1948 and 1956, 258 Falcons found homes.

The Dominant

By 1950, many manufacturers were releasing chassis with horizontal diesel engines mounted amidships under the floor to enable almost the whole length of the vehicle to be used for passengers. Dennis made their first venture into this underfloor-engined market in 1950 with the Dominant. Fitted with the Dennis O6 7.58-litre engine as well as a novel Hobbs semi-automatic transmission, it was uncompetitively heavy, and only two were bodied. One went to the ever-faithful Aldershot & District after the chassis' 1950 Commercial Vehicle Show appearance. The other was the factory demonstrator, which had a 130bhp supercharged version of the engine fitted, and this eventually went to Trimdon Motor Services in County Durham. Although the Hobbs gearbox attracted much attention initially, it must have been troublesome in service, for both vehicles were later converted to manual transmissions, using the Dennis twin-plate clutch and O-type gearboxes. A third, left-hand-drive, chassis was also built and exhibited at the show, but it is believed this was never bodied.

This view taken at the 1950 Commercial Vehicle Show shows one of the only two Dominants ever bodied.
BOB LOVELAND COLLECTION

Only two Dominants saw service; this one went to Aldershot & District. BOB LOVELAND COLLECTION

This Lancet UF was new to Glenton Tours in 1958.
BOB LOVELAND COLLECTION

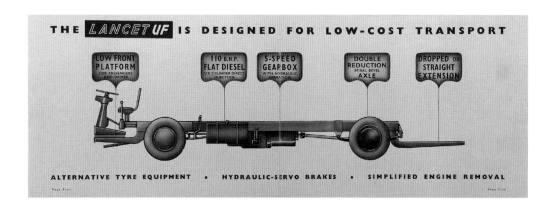

The Lancet UF was Dennis's second attempt at breaking into the burgeoning underfloor-engined bus and coach market. It found few sales, even to the ever-faithful Aldershot & District. BOB LOVELAND COLLECTION

The Lancet UF

Moving on from the overweight Dominant, the Lancet UF went on sale in 1953 and was a similarly underfloor-engined vehicle, still with a maximum width of 8ft (2.44m) and length of 30ft (9.1m), but significantly lighter by 19 cwt (970kg), with a chassis weight of 3 tons 17 cwt (3,900kg). It had a dropped chassis forward of the front axle, giving the driver a low position and offering a shallow entry step for passengers. Optionally, a dropped extension at the rear was available if rear-entrance bodywork was needed. Again, the O6 horizontal underfloor engine was used, this time with a five-speed manual gearbox driving a double-reduction rear axle. The prototype was designated LU1, while the sixty production chassis were designated LU2. Most versions looked comparatively modern, with flat-fronted bodywork unencumbered by a radiator grille. Significant orders were placed by East Kent Road Car and Newport Corporation.

An unusual Routemaster-style full-power hydraulic brake system was fitted. This was possibly to save weight, as the hydraulic valves and accumulators would have been

DENNIS LANCET UF, 1953–1961

Configuration: 4×2 rigid underfloor-engined chassis for forward-control bodywork
Engine: Horizontal Dennis O6 6-cylinder diesel
Capacity: 7585cc
Max. power: 110bhp
Max. torque: 328lb ft
Gearbox: 5-speed plus reverse
Rear axle: Double-reduction spiral bevel
Suspension: Semi-elliptic leaf springs front and rear
Wheelbase: 196in (4,978mm)
Overall length (chassis): 351in (8,915mm)
Overall width: 96in (2,438mm)
Unladen weight: 8,624lb (3,912kg)
(Source: Dennis Bros. publication No. 294C, 1952)

lighter than the traditional air valves and tanks. This type of brake system was not regarded favourably by operators, which may explain why the Lancet UF was never a big seller, losing out to competing models such as the AEC Reliance and Leyland Tiger Cub. After trying the demonstrator, even Aldershot & District opted for AECs, one of the few times they bought from anywhere other than Dennis.

The LU2 was discontinued in 1961. However, other versions of the Lancet UF followed: LU4 and LU5. Both used the same chassis as the earlier LU2 although the LU4 received a bigger engine, the 8-litre version of the O6. Neither was successful, both achieving only five sales before the models were withdrawn in 1961.

The Pelican

Pelican was the third attempt at a lightweight underfloor-engined single-decker for 30ft (9.1m) bodywork, appearing at the 1954 Commercial Motor Show in chassis form.

The Pelican of 1954 was Dennis's third and least successful attempt on the underfloor PSV market, the only chassis finding a home being the demonstrator.

BOB LOVELAND COLLECTION

DENNIS PELICAN, 1954

Configuration: 4×2 rigid ladder-frame underfloor-engined chassis for forward-control bodywork
Engine: Dennis 6-cylinder diesel
Capacity: 5500cc
Gearbox: Dennis 5-speed constant mesh
Rear axle: Single-speed spiral bevel; 2-speed optional
Suspension: Semi-elliptic springs, telescopic shock absorbers on front axle
Wheelbase: 196in (4,978mm)
Overall length (body): 360in (9,144mm)
Overall width (body): 96in (2,438mm)
Unladen weight (chassis): 7,504lb (3,404kg)
GVW (max.): 20,720lb (9,399kg)
Capacity:
    Bus: 44 passengers
    Coach: 41 passengers plus 0.5 tons (508kg) luggage
Top speed: 53mph (85km/h)
(Source: Dennis Bros. specification, 1954)

It had a chassis weight of 3 tons 7 cwt (3,400kg) and used a Dennis 6-cylinder 5.5-litre diesel engine coupled to a five-speed constant-mesh gearbox. Although soundly engineered, and with the weight reduced to an acceptable level, it was just too late to market. The post-war boom in new bus and coach sales was all but over, and the market was dominated by the well-established AEC Reliance and Leyland Tiger Cub.

Only one Pelican was ever sold, the demonstrator, PU2, which in 1956 went to local operator Yellow Bus Services of Guildford. When Yellow Bus was later sold to Aldershot & District, the Pelican went to Trimdon Motor Services of Co. Durham. They, in turn, sold it on to Daisy Bus Services of Brigg in Lincolnshire. The demonstrator was fitted with Duple 44-seat bodywork, and this bodywork was eventually removed from the Pelican and transferred to an AEC Reliance chassis. The prototype chassis, PU1, was ultimately dismantled.

The Heron

Although the Heron was a forward-control goods chassis, some were bodied as special-purpose welfare buses for carrying disabled passengers, usually having up to eleven seats plus a tail-lift for wheelchairs.

The Gladiator

The Gladiator was a passenger-carrying version of the Hefty commercial vehicle chassis; indeed, the original brochure called it the Hefty. It used the 8-litre O6 diesel engine, with the option of a Gardner 8.4-litre 6-cylinder diesel. All were exported to Greece.

DENNIS GLADIATOR, c.1955

Configuration: 4×2 rigid ladder-frame front-engined chassis for forward-control bodywork
Engine: Dennis O6 6-cylinder diesel
Capacity: 8030cc
Max. power: 120bhp
Max. torque: 368lb ft
or
Engine: Gardner 6LW 6-cylinder diesel
Capacity: 8400cc
Max. power: 112bhp
Max. torque: 358lb ft
Gearbox: Dennis 6/5 4-, 5- or 6-speed
Rear axle: Dennis double reduction, spiral bevel
Suspension: Semi-elliptic leaf springs
Brakes: Full air-actuated two-leading-shoe wedge drum brakes
(Source: Dennis Bros. publications Nos 106, 120P, 121P, 126P, 128P and 131P, undated)

The Stork

A handful of these goods vehicle chassis also received bus bodywork: Walthamstow Borough Council took all six between 1956 and 1960 for use as school buses.

The SP6

The Dennis archives contain a typed specification sheet from P. Walder Garage, Wetzikon, apparently the sole Swiss agents for the chassis. No further information is known; however, at least one must have existed, for the document offers demonstration drives. It was intended for fourteen- to twenty-seat passenger duties, with wheelbase options of 10ft 6in (3.2m) and 11ft 8in (3.55m). Gross weight was 13,117lb (5,950kg). It was probably Stork-based since it was powered by a 6-cylinder 83bhp Perkins P6 underfloor engine. This was coupled, unusually, to a ZF five-speed gearbox, with a ZF two-speed auxiliary gearbox available as an option, giving ten forward speeds.

DENNIS SP6, c.1960

Layout and Chassis
4×2 rigid ladder-frame underfloor-engined chassis for Swiss market
Engine
Type: Perkins P6 underfloor diesel
Cylinders: 6 in-line
Cooling: Water
Bore and stroke: 88.9 × 127mm
Capacity: 4730cc
Max. power: 83bhp at 2,000rpm
Fuel capacity: 29gal (130ltr)
Transmission
Gearbox: ZF 5-speed manual with overdrive top gear
Auxiliary gearbox: ZF (provides 10 speeds)
Final drive: hypoid
Suspension and Steering
Front: Semi-elliptic springs 40.5in (1,029mm) long, hydraulic dampers
Rear: semi-elliptic springs 50in (1,270mm) long, hydraulic dampers
Tyres: 7.00 × 20 or 29 × 7-15 12-ply
Wheels: Steel disc; single front, twin rear
Brakes
Type: Drum on all wheels, hydraulically actuated; Haller exhaust brake
Dimensions
Wheelbase: 126in (3,200mm) for 14- to 18-seater; 139.75in (3,550mm) for 18- to 22-seater
Unladen weight (chassis): 4,190lb (1,900kg)
Unladen weight (bodied): 8,600–8,819lb (3,900–4,000kg) for 18-seater coach
Gross weight: 13,117lb (5,950kg)
Capacity: Bus 14–18 seats;
Coach 18–20 seats
Performance
Top speed: 65mph (105km/h)
Price
Chassis: SFr 24,800 (approx. £2,000)
Extra for auxiliary gearbox: SFr 1,800 (approx. £150)
Body: SFr 35,000–40,000 (approx. £2,900–£3,300)
(Source: Bob Loveland Collection, typewritten specification sheets headed 'Garage Walder, Ober-Wetzikon')

The Loline

In the 1950s, sales of the Lance double-decker were suffering, not least because it was little different to the products of several other manufacturers, most of whom could undercut it on price due to their much higher production volumes. In an echo of the events in future decades, Dennis management then realized that to be successful, they needed to offer vehicles that offered distinct benefits over the competition.

Bizarrely, an opportunity appeared in the Lodekka, a unique new double-deck chassis developed by Bristol Commercial Vehicles. It had a roofline lowered by about 12in (300mm) compared to a conventional decker, giving it an overall height of only 13ft 5in (4.1m) and increasing the range of routes available to the bus considerably. Being nationalized, Bristol were unable to sell this model on the open market, so Dennis were licensed to build a version of it in Guildford. It was launched at the 1956 Commercial Motor Show, badged as the Loline, and sold well to many smaller operators such as Aldershot & District. The licence agreement included a two-way exchange of technical information, Dennis developing the epicyclic gearbox for this model. Thus semi-automatic Bristol Lodekkas effectively had Dennis transmissions.

Initially, the Loline was offered with a wheelbase to suit rear-entrance bodywork. It used either a 112bhp Gardner 6LW or an 8-litre 120bhp O6 engine mated to a Dennis

The 1961 Loline III chassis. BOB LOVELAND COLLECTION

five-speed constant-mesh gearbox and Dennis double-reduction rear axle with an offset differential. Air brakes were fitted. Forty-eight of these first-generation Lolines were built.

In 1960, Loline II was launched, again at the Commercial Motor Show, with a slightly extended wheelbase to suit front-entrance bodywork. The chassis differed considerably from the Loline I, with extra strength being provided by substantial frame members around the rear wheel arches at almost full body width. This style of chassis construction was to become common on later Dennis buses. When production began, rear air suspension was fitted rather than the leaf springs used on the prototype. Alternative engines included Gardner 6LX and Leyland 0.600s.

Forty-seven production Loline IIs were built, all with front-entrance bodywork.

In 1961, Loline III appeared, featuring a different style of radiator grille with a chrome surround, and several wheelbase options. Various engines were on offer, including Gardner 6LW, 6LX and Leyland 0.600 units, while transmission options included the Dennis four- or five-speed constant-mesh units, Self-Changing Gears four- or five-speed semi-automatic units, and a Bristol five-speed box. All but two of the 184 Loline III chassis had front-entrance bodywork. Production ceased in November 1966.

The front entrance identifies this Oxford decker as a 1960 Loline II.
BOB LOVELAND COLLECTION

DENNIS LOLINE, 1956–1967

Layout and Chassis
4×2 rigid ladder-frame front-engined low-floor chassis for forward-control bodywork

Engine
Type: Dennis O6 diesel
Block material: Cast iron
Head material: Cast iron
Cylinders: 6 in-line
Cooling: Water
Bore and stroke: 108 × 146mm
Capacity: 8030cc
Valves: Overhead
Fuel pump: CAV
Max. power: 120bhp at 1,800rpm
Max. torque: 368lb ft at 1,100rpm
or
Type: Gardner 6LW diesel
Block material: Cast iron
Head material: Cast iron
Cylinders: 6 in-line
Cooling: Water
Bore and stroke: 108 × 152.4mm
Capacity: 8400cc
Valves: Overhead
Fuel pump: CAV
Max. power: 112bhp at 1,700rpm
Max. torque: 358lb ft at 1,300rpm
Fuel capacity: 34gal (155ltr)

Transmission
Gearbox: Dennis inverse drive 5-speed (4-speed optional on Loline II)
Clutch: 13.75in (39mm) diameter Dennis twin dry plate
Ratios:
   1st: 4.267
   2nd: 2.526
   3rd: 1.519
   4th: 0.971
   5th: 0.659
   Reverse: 4.33
Final drive: Dennis double-reduction drop-centre offset-differential spiral bevel

Suspension and Steering
Front: Semi-elliptic multi-leaf springs, 48in (1,219mm) long with telescopic dampers
Rear: Semi-elliptic multi-leaf springs, 60in (1,524mm) long, 57in (1,448mm) on Loline II
Steering: Marles cam and double roller
Tyres: Loline I: front 11.00 × 20 14-ply, rear 9.00 × 20 12-ply
Loline II: front 10.00 × 20 14-ply, rear 9.00 × 20 14-ply
Wheels: 10-stud disc, front 7.22 × 20 Loline I (7.33 × 20 Loline II), rear 6.00 × 20

Brakes
Type: Two-leading shoe cam-operated drums, air-actuated
Size: 15.25in (387mm) dia.

Dimensions
Track: 83.25in (2,115mm) front, 72.75in (1,848mm) rear
Wheelbase: Loline I 222in (5,639mm); Loline II 228.5in (5,804mm)
Overall length: 360in (9,144mm)
Overall width: 96in (2,438mm)
Overall height: 163in (4,140mm) unladen (typical)
Unladen weight: 11,200lb (5,080kg)
GVW: 29,120lb (13,209kg)
Capacity: 70–72 seats

Performance
Top speed: 46mph (74km/h)
(Sources: Dennis Bros. Loline I brochure, 1958 and Loline II brochure 165P, 1960)

POST-WAR TRUCK MODELS

While bus and coach sales were doing well in the early post-war years, the same could not be said of trucks. Although Dennis, perhaps unwisely, produced a host of different models, most of them sold only in minimal numbers thanks to road haulage nationalization. From 1948, this enforced centralized buying for large-volume orders, none of which Dennis was successful in winning. Dennis trucks were, however, still popular with 'own-account' operators, such as breweries, whose fleets were not covered by nationalization.

Life was becoming increasingly competitive against the likes of Leyland, Foden and Bedford. This forced Dennis to become a specialist builder focusing on fire and municipal vehicle sales, where they were more successful, in part due to innovations such as better methods of compressing the refuse in dustcarts, enabling more waste to be carried.

THE MOULTON COACH

Alex Moulton was a close friend of Alec Issigonis, the designer of the Austin Mini. In the mid-1950s, he was asked by Issigonis to design a suitable suspension for the forthcoming Mini. Moulton was a fan of rubber as a suspension medium, and his company, Moulton Developments, developed the rubber cone suspension that was highly successful on the original Mini. Moulton went on to design the small-wheeled Moulton bicycle, which within twelve months became the second-largest selling cycle in the UK. In the early 1970s, Moulton's thoughts turned to coaches, and his company came up with a radically different coach prototype, having eight small wheels and twin steering axles.

Although the coach used largely British Leyland components, at one stage Dennis had an input into the design. Ultimately, the project did not proceed beyond the prototype stage, being seen as excessively complex, with potential reliability problems arising from the complicated Hydragas suspension and steering linkages.

Although the project came to nothing, it did introduce Dennis engineers to a young designer in Moulton's team, Alan Ponsford, who subsequently provided considerable support to Dennis in structural analysis. The prototype Moulton coach has for many years been stored in the Science Museum's overspill collection at Wroughton in Wiltshire.

The Pax, introduced in 1945, was very popular with breweries and other own-account customers, who were outside the scope of the nationalized road transport operation. BOB LOVELAND COLLECTION

Despite the difficult market, Dennis continued to be imaginative in finding niche markets for which they could develop products not offered by the bigger manufacturers. In typical Dennis fashion, all the major units for these were manufactured in house, even down to the steering gear, something which would be unthinkable today.

The Pax

The 5-ton (5,080kg) capacity Pax was introduced in 1945, running to 1963 by which time 5,394 had been made, including 2,920 municipal chassis. It was available in both normal- and forward-control versions, the engine being either the C-type petrol unit or a Perkins P6 diesel. The normal-control version had a three-man cab, making it particularly useful for work such as beer delivery.

DENNIS PAX, 1945–1963

Configuration: 2-axle rigid ladder-frame normal- or forward-control goods chassis
Engine: Dennis 4-cylinder petrol
Max. power: RAC rating 24.8HP; 70bhp
Capacity: 3770cc
Gearbox: Dennis 4-speed plus reverse, aluminium case
Rear axle: Spiral bevel
Suspension: Semi-elliptic multi-leaf springs
Brakes: Hydraulically operated two-leading-shoe drum brakes on all four wheels
Wheelbase:
    114in (2,896mm)
    138in (3,505mm)
    154in (3,912mm)
Overall length (chassis): Normal control 207.5–267.25in (5,271–6,788mm);
Forward control 209–268.5in (5,309–6,820mm)
Overall width (chassis): 84in (2,134mm)
Unladen weight: 4,760–4,844lb (2,159–2,197kg), plus 224lb (102kg) for tipping gear if fitted
(Source: Dennis Bros. publication No. 178C, 1947)

The Pax had a 5-ton (5,080kg) payload capacity and was available with wheelbase options of 9ft 6in, 11ft 6in or 12ft 10in (2.9m, 3.5m or 3.92m). DENNIS ARCHIVES

The Max

The heavier Max, reintroduced in 1945, was a popular machine, with 1,599 produced right up to 1958. It used 4-cylinder engines, either the Big Four petrol or new O4 diesel. As the name implies, it was intended to take full advantage of the maximum gross weight then legally permitted on two axles.

The Max 6 of 1950 was the successor to the short-lived pre-war Max Major and was available either in rigid or articulated tractor versions. The O6 engine was used, along with a five-speed gearbox.

Almost 1,600 Max chassis were produced over a production run of around fourteen years. BOB LOVELAND COLLECTION

DENNIS MAX 6, 1950–

Configuration: 4×2 rigid or articulated ladder-frame forward-control goods chassis
Engine: Dennis O6-type 6-cylinder diesel
Capacity: 7580cc
Max. power: 100bhp
Max. torque: 315lb ft
Gearbox: Dennis 5-speed overdrive plus reverse, alloy casing
Rear axle: Dennis worm drive
Suspension: Semi-elliptic multi-leaf springs
Brakes: Drum all round, hydraulically actuated with vacuum-servo assistance
Wheelbase: 114–186in (2,896–4,724mm)
Overall length: 178.75–308.75in (4,540–7,842mm)
Overall width: 90in (2,286mm)
Unladen weight: 9,632–10,192lb (4,369–4,623kg)
GVW: 26,880lb (12,193kg)
GCW: 44,800lb (20,321kg)
(Source: Dennis Bros. publication No. 235C, 1950)

Most Max 6s were two-axle rigids, this 'Chinese 6' being an exception. DENNIS ARCHIVES

The Jubilant

The three-axle Jubilant was introduced in 1945, 314 being built over its sixteen-year production run. Jubilants were particularly popular with breweries in the southeast, especially Whitbread. The O6 engine was fitted, mated to a five-speed overdrive gearbox and driving into worm-drive rear axles.

The Jubilant made its debut at a trade fair in Barcelona. It was by all accounts an excellent truck, but sales were restricted by the policies of the nationalized British Road Services. This one was operated by the Great Western Railway. BOB LOVELAND COLLECTION

Only three eight-wheel Jubilants were ever built, including this example. BOB LOVELAND COLLECTION

All the major units of the Jubilant were manufactured in house, even down to the steering gear, something that would be unthinkable today. The wheelbase was 17ft 10.5in (5.46m) and the unladen weight of the three-axle model was 5 tons 16 cwt (5,890kg) for a 12-ton (12,190kg) GVW. BOB LOVELAND COLLECTION

DENNIS JUBILANT EIGHT-WHEEL CHASSIS, c.1950–

Configuration: 8×4 rigid ladder-frame forward-control goods chassis
Engine: Dennis 6-cylinder diesel or Gardner 6LW
Capacity: Dennis: 8000cc;
    Gardner: 8400cc
Gearbox: Dennis 5-speed plus reverse, overdrive top gear; optional 2-speed auxiliary box

Rear axle: 2 Dennis worm-drive axles, third differential in leading axle
Suspension: Semi-elliptic multi-leaf, 2-spring bogie for rear axles
Length: 348.4in (8,849mm)
Width: 89.5in (2,273mm)
Wheelbase: 214.5in (5,448mm)
Chassis weight: 15,000lb (6,800kg)
GVW: 53,760lb (24,385kg)
(Source: Dennis Bros. publication No. 163P, c.1950)

DENNIS JUBILANT 12-TON CHASSIS, 1945–

Layout and Chassis
3-axle rigid ladder-frame forward-control goods chassis

Engine
Type: Dennis O6 diesel
Block material: Cast iron
Head material: Cast iron
Cylinders: 6 in-line
Cooling: Water, pumped
Bore and stroke: 105 × 146mm
Capacity: 7580cc
Valves: Overhead, 4 valves per cylinder
Fuel system: CAV
Max. power: 100bhp at 1,800rpm
Max. torque: 315lb ft at 1,000rpm (est.)
Fuel capacity: 44gal (200ltr)

Transmission
Gearbox: Dennis 5-speed overdrive plus reverse, alloy casing; optional auxiliary 2-speed unit
Clutch: Twin dry plate
Ratios:
 1st: 5.45
 2nd: 2.94
 3rd: 1.66
 4th: 1
 5th: 0.69
 Reverse: 7.01:1
Final drive: 2 Dennis worm-drive axles, with third differential in leading axle

Suspension and Steering
Front: Semi-elliptic multi-leaf springs, 47in (1,194mm) long
Rear: Two-spring bogie suspension, using semi-elliptic multi-leaf springs
Steering: Worm and nut
Tyres: 36in × 8in high-pressure pneumatic
Wheels: Detachable steel disc, dual on rear axles

Brakes
Type: Girling 2LS drum brakes on all six wheels, hydraulically actuated with vacuum-servo assistance
Size: 16.25in (413mm) diameter

Dimensions
Track: 75.5in (1,918mm) front, 69in (1,753mm) rear
Wheelbase: 214.5in (5,448mm)
Overall length (chassis): 358in (9,093mm)
Overall width (chassis): 89in (2,261mm)
Unladen weight: 12,992lb (5,893kg)
Payload: 26,880lb (12,193kg)
(Source: Dennis Bros. publication No. 235C, 1950)

THE
DENNIS
HORLA CHASSIS
for Semi-Trailers carrying
8-TON
LOADS

An eight-wheel version was also available, although only three were produced. The eight-wheeler was designed for 24-ton (24,390kg) GVW, with an unladen weight of 6 tons 14 cwt (6,800kg). It had an additional engine option, the Gardner 6LW.

The Horla

The Horla was the normal-control version of the Pax. It was an 8-ton (8,130kg) payload articulated tractor unit with a Scammell coupling. With its 8ft 8in (2.64m) wheelbase and set-back front axle like the earlier 40/45-cwt, it had excellent manoeuvrability. The Dennis 4-cylinder 24.8HP petrol engine was fitted, together with a four-speed gearbox. Unladen weight was a miserly 2 tons 2 cwt (2,130kg). Between 1946 and 1962, 415 were built.

This brochure for the normal-control Horla 8-ton (8,130kg) payload articulated tractor dates from 1948.
BOB LOVELAND COLLECTION

DENNIS HORLA, 1946–1962

Configuration: 4×2 rigid ladder-frame normal-control articulated tractor unit
Engine: Dennis 4-cylinder petrol
Capacity: 3770cc
Max. power: RAC rating 24.8HP; 67bhp at 2,550rpm
Gearbox: Dennis 4-speed and reverse
Rear axle: Spiral bevel
Suspension: Semi-elliptic multi-leaf steel springs
Trailer coupling: Scammell-type automatic coupler
Wheelbase: 99.5in (2,527mm)
Overall length: 190.5in (4,839mm)
Unladen weight: 4,704lb (2,134kg)
(Source: Dennis Bros. publication No. 159C, 1950)

This 5-ton (5,080kg) payload Pax II dates from 1958.
GARY AVERY

This bonneted Pax of 1956 is in preservation and appeared at the Dennis 2019 open day. GARY AVERY

The Pax II and IIA

The Pax II, introduced in 1946, was given a five-speed gearbox and the O6 diesel engine; 7,109 units, including 2,662 municipal vehicles, were sold before production ceased in 1966.

The 1958 DB Series had a 9 ton 12 cwt (9,750kg) GVW and a payload of around 7 tons (7,100kg). Several wheelbases were available, from the DB1 model at 9ft 6.5in (2.91m) to the DB5 at 17ft 7in (5.36m). All versions used the 5.1-litre diesel engine, coupled to a four-speed constant mesh gearbox. The DB series retained the prewar curved-front cab, updated with a new rectangular radiator grille.

The DB series Pax II was introduced in 1958. It retained the pre-war curved front cab albeit updated with a new rectangular radiator grille. BOB LOVELAND COLLECTION

DENNIS DB SERIES PAX II, 1946–1966

Configuration: 4×2 rigid ladder-frame forward-control goods chassis
Engine: Dennis 6-cylinder diesel
Capacity: 5103cc
Max. power: 105bhp
Max. torque: 232lb ft
Gearbox: Dennis 4-speed and reverse, constant mesh
Rear axle: Spiral bevel
Suspension: Semi-elliptic multi-leaf springs
Wheelbase: DB1: 114.5in (2,909mm) ranging to DB5: 211in (5,359mm)
Overall length (chassis): DB1: 215in (5,461mm) ranging to DB5: 357.75in (9,087mm)
Unladen weight: 5,824lb (2,397kg)
Gross weight: 21,504lb (9,754kg)
(Source: Dennis Bros. sales brochure, 1958)

The Tippax, Vulture and Paxit

These were Pax-based refuse collection vehicles. The Tippax was a tipping-style design, where the body was periodically tipped forwards to compact the load and tipped rearwards to discharge it.

This unusual beast is a 1960 Vulture front-loading refuse collection vehicle sold to Liverpool Corporation. The tractor unit appears to be a late-model Horla with the restyled front mudguards. BOB LOVELAND COLLECTION

This Tippax refuse truck is shown with the body tipped forwards to compress the load. BOB LOVELAND COLLECTION

The Vulture was a strange-looking 1950s machine designed for loading refuse from the front. It had a single cab, with a loading chute containing a compression plate alongside. The loading crew, presumably, had to ride on the back of the vehicle. In the late 1950s, an articulated version was built for Liverpool Corporation, coupled to a Horla tractor. Unsurprisingly, only twenty-one Vultures were made between 1950 and 1960.

The long-running Paxit was introduced after World War II and featured positive compression of the refuse load using hydraulics. The early models carried out compression of the load intermittently. Later versions added a sophisticated continuous compaction system allowing refuse to be fed in while compaction was taking place. The discharge was still by tipping; however, the 1968 Paxit 70 introduced ejection discharge.

A small number of dustcarts were built as Vulture front loaders like this 1955 example, using the Pax chassis. Loading times were slow and they were not a great success. DENNIS ARCHIVES

This Paxit IIA dates from around 1960 and was operated by Hampstead. The load was discharged by tipping, as shown here. DENNIS ARCHIVES

The Paxit was a very popular municipal vehicle, used in large numbers by councils everywhere. This photo is of a 1963 Paxit IIA operated by Southend. DENNIS ARCHIVES

A 1951 line-up of Hampstead Paxits. BOB LOVELAND COLLECTION

The Centaur

Several versions of the Centaur were offered, including a two-axle forward-control tractor unit of 15.5 tons (15,750kg) gross weight. Other wheelbases suitable for 10 ton 4 cwt (10,360kg) GVW tipper and platform bodies were also available.

the Centaur

a new oil engined goods chassis for 23,000 lb. g.c.w.

≡DENNIS≡

DENNIS BROS LTD GUILDFORD ENGLAND

This brochure covers the Centaur, a medium-weight rigid or articulated goods chassis produced between 1946 and 1956, when it was replaced by the Condor.

BOB LOVELAND COLLECTION

In 1954, an all-steel cab was offered as an alternative to the coachbuilt version.

Altogether, 401 units had been built between 1949 and 1956, when it was replaced by the Condor (*see* below).

DENNIS CENTAUR RIGID CHASSIS, 1949–1956

Configuration: 4×2 rigid ladder-frame forward-control goods chassis
Engine: Dennis 6-cylinder diesel
Capacity: 5,060cc
Max. power: RAC rating 35.74HP; 75bhp at 2,000rpm
Gearbox: Dennis 5-speed plus reverse
Rear axle: 2-speed, spiral bevel
Suspension: Semi-elliptic multi-leaf steel springs
Wheelbases: 162in (4,115mm)
    126in (3,200mm)
Overall length (chassis): 265in (6,731mm) for 162in w/b
Unladen weight: 7,168lb (3,251kg), chassis + scuttle
GVW: 23,000lb (10,433kg)
(Sources: Dennis Bros. publication No. 244C, 1950 and Dennis Bros. publication No. 292C, 1952)

DENNIS CENTAUR ARTICULATED TRACTOR UNIT, 1949–1956

Configuration: 4×2 rigid ladder-frame forward-control articulated tractor unit
Engine: Dennis 6-cylinder diesel
Capacity: 5500cc
Max. power: RAC rating 38.7HP; 87bhp at 2,000rpm
Gearbox: Dennis 5-speed plus reverse
Rear axle: 2-speed, spiral bevel
Suspension: Semi-elliptic multi-leaf steel springs
Trailer coupling: Scammell-type automatic
Wheelbase: 102in (2,591mm)
Overall width: 90in (2,286mm)
Overall height (laden): 95in (2,413mm)
Unladen weight: 7,504lb (3,404kg)
GCW: 34,720lb (15,749kg)
(Source: Dennis Bros. publication No. 336C, 1954)

The Triton

In 1950, the Triton, a 3-ton (3,050kg) payload model, was released, fitted with a Perkins P4 engine and Dennis four-speed gearbox. Before production ended in 1953, 196 were built.

The Stork

The lightweight forward-control 3-ton (3,050kg) payload Stork was introduced in 1952, intended as a competitor to models like the Albion Claymore. The forward frame section was dropped to give a flat walk-through floor. A Dennis 3.14-litre 54bhp 4-cylinder diesel underfloor engine was fitted, mated to a four-speed constant-mesh gearbox. A Perkins P6 was also later offered.

The underfloor engine of the 1954 Stork gave a full walk-through cab. DENNIS ARCHIVES

Many Storks were used as mobile showrooms, such as this 1954 example for Trebor. BOB LOVELAND COLLECTION

DENNIS STORK, 1952–1962

Layout and Chassis
4×2 rigid ladder-frame underfloor-engined forward-control goods chassis with walk-through cab

Engine
Type: Perkins diesel (underfloor)
Block material: Cast iron
Head material: Cast iron
Cylinders: 4 in-line
Cooling: Water, pump-assisted
Bore and stroke: 88.9 × 127mm
Capacity: 3140cc
Max. power (DIN): 54bhp at 2,400rpm
Fuel capacity: 15gal (68ltr)

Transmission
Gearbox: Dennis 4-speed plus reverse
Clutch: 10in single dry plate
Ratios:
    1st: 6.28
    2nd: 3.16
    3rd: 1.74
    4th: 1
    Reverse: 8.14
Final drive: Hypoid

Suspension and Steering
Front: Semi-elliptic multi-leaf springs, 40in (1,016mm) long
Rear: Semi-elliptic multi-leaf springs, 50in (1,270mm) long
Steering: Worm and nut

Brakes
Type: Girling drum on all four wheels, hydraulically operated
Size: 14in (356mm) diameter

Dimensions
Wheelbases: 126in (3,200mm)
    140in (3556mm)
Overall lengths (chassis): 248.5in (6,312mm)
    269.5in (6,845mm)
Overall width (chassis): 76.5in (1,943mm)
Unladen weight (chassis): 3,920lb (1,778kg)
Gross weight: 12,992lb (5,893kg) with 7.00 × 20 tyres;
    11,760lb (5,334kg) with 6.50 × 20 tyres
(Source: Dennis Bros. publication No. 338C, 1954)

Some bodywork designs for the Stork were highly creative, like this 1955 example for Vespa, which combined a mobile showroom with a delivery truck.
BOB LOVELAND COLLECTION

The 3-ton (3,050kg) payload Heron of 1955 marked a return to the lighter end of the market. As with the Stork, many received special-purpose bodywork.
BOB LOVELAND COLLECTION

Many Storks received special-purpose bodies, including a mobile printing unit for the *London Evening News*, a photograph of which featured on the 1954 Dennis brochure. Between 1953 and 1962, 420 Storks were built.

The Heron

The Heron followed on from the Triton as a 3-ton (3,050kg) payload forward-control chassis with the same Perkins P4 engine and four-speed gearbox.

Many of the 277 Herons built between 1955 and 1963 received special-purpose bodies such as travelling showrooms.

This 1958 Bottogas mobile showroom vehicle is typical of the special-purpose bodywork often fitted to Herons.
BOB LOVELAND COLLECTION

DENNIS HERON, 1955–1963

Configuration: 4×2 rigid ladder-frame forward-control goods chassis
Engine: Perkins P4V 4-cylinder diesel
Capacity: 3140cc
Max. power: 55bhp
Max. torque: 134lb ft
Gearbox: Dennis 4-speed plus reverse, synchromesh
Rear axle: Hypoid bevel
Suspension: Semi-elliptic multi-leaf steel springs
Wheelbases: 90in (2,286mm)
105in (2,667mm)
126in (3,200mm)
Overall lengths (chassis): 174.5in (4,432mm)
207.7in (5,275mm)
240in (6,093mm)
Overall width: 84in (2,134mm)
Overall height: 97.5in (2,477mm)
Unladen weight: Chassis cab: 4,312lb (1,956kg)
Gross weight: 12,992lb (5,893kg)
(Sources: Dennis Bros. publications Nos 365C and 104P, 157P, 158P, 159P, 160P, 1956 and data sheets PD101(R)-103(R), drawing Nos 161605, 161295, 163626)

The Hefty

The Hefty replaced the Max in 1957. It was a forward-control 14-ton (14,220kg) two-axle rigid chassis with a Pax-style cab. It was powered by the 120bhp 8-litre O6 engine coupled to a six-speed constant-mesh gearbox driving into a Dennis hub-reduction rear axle.

The Condor

The Condor replaced the Centaur in 1957 and was a 12-ton (12,190kg) GVW heavy-duty 4×2 chassis for tipper, plat-form or tractor use. It used the Dennis 5.5-litre diesel engine, although Gardner 4LW and 5LW engines were also available.

The later Condor II featured a BMC 5.1-litre 6-cylinder 105bhp diesel engine, a four-speed constant-mesh gearbox and an Eaton two-speed rear axle. Four wheelbases were available as well as a short tractor chassis configured for a Scammell coupling. Production ended in 1965 after 127 Condors had been built.

The 12-ton (12,190kg) GVW Condor replaced the Centaur in 1957 but was not a huge success, with only 127 being built between 1957 and 1965. BOB LOVELAND COLLECTION

DENNIS HEFTY, 1957–

Configuration: 4×2 rigid ladder-frame forward-control goods chassis
Engine: Dennis 6-cylinder diesel
Capacity: 8000cc
Max. power: 120bhp
Max. torque: 368lb ft
Gearbox: 6-speed plus reverse, constant mesh
Rear axle: Double-reduction spiral bevel
Suspension: Semi-elliptic multi-leaf steel springs
(Source: unnumbered Dennis Bros. sales brochure, c.1957)

DENNIS CONDOR, 1957–1965

Configuration: 4×2 rigid ladder-frame forward-control truck chassis for articulated or rigid operation
Engine: Dennis Mk II 6-cylinder diesel
Max. power: RAC rating 38.7HP; 87bhp at 2,000rpm
or
Engine: Gardner 5LW 5-cylinder diesel
Capacity: 7000cc
Max. power: 94bhp
Max. torque: 300lb ft

or
Engine: Gardner 4LW 4-cylinder diesel
Capacity: 5600cc
Max. power: 75bhp
Max. torque: 237lb ft
Gearbox: 5-speed constant mesh
Rear axle: Eaton 2-speed spiral bevel
Suspension: Semi-elliptic multi-leaf steel springs
(Sources: Dennis Bros. publication Nos 106P, 152P-156P, 1956)

DENNIS CONDOR II, c.1960–1965

Configuration: 2-axle ladder frame forward-control truck chassis for articulated or rigid operation
Engine: BMC 6-cylinder diesel
Capacity: 5100cc
Max. power: 105bhp

Max. torque: 232lb ft
Gearbox: 4-speed constant mesh
Rear axle: Eaton 16500 2-speed spiral bevel
Suspension: Semi-elliptic multi-leaf steel springs
Wheelbase: 126in (3,200mm) to 210in (5,334mm)
Unladen weight (chassis): 7,750lb (3,515kg)
(Source: Dennis Bros. publication No. 177P)

The Pax III

The Pax III was offered with a wide choice of diesel engines, including the Gardner 4LW and 5LW, Perkins P6, BMC 5.1-litre or a Dennis 4-cylinder petrol engine. It was introduced in 1957 and ran to 1962, with 192 being made.

The Paravan

The Paravan was aimed squarely at the multi-drop urban delivery market, with an underfloor engine that made possible a full flat-floor walk-through cab. To ease entry and exit in tight conditions, the bodywork could be configured to set the up-and-over front passenger door at an angle, so that when opened it did not protrude beyond the rest of the body. Additionally, the load space could be accessed directly from the cab without the driver having to go round to the rear of the vehicle. Its closest competitor was the BMC FG model, which had its doors set facing rearwards at an angle for similar safety reasons.

The Paravan concept was originated by the general manager of Essex Carriers Ltd, who recognized the productivity benefits of such a configuration. Initially, he was unable to find a manufacturer willing to take on the challenge of producing a suitable 3- to 5-ton (3,050–5,080kg) van. However, Dennis came up with a 3-tonner with a body floor height as low as 2ft 6in (760mm). It used a Perkins 4.236 diesel engine mounted vertically above the front axle, with the driver set well forward. Although the engine intruded into the load space, the cowl enclosing it was narrow enough to give adequate space for the driver to move between the cab and the load area. The configuration gave a low enough frame height that only a single step entry was

This view clearly shows the unusual, if logical, shape of the front of the original Paravan. BOB LOVELAND COLLECTION

required. The frame width was kept to a minimum, allowing, in turn, a width of only 6ft 9in (2.06m) to facilitate operation in narrow streets. With a kerb weight of around 3 tons (3,050kg), a similar payload was possible.

The prototypes were bodied by Sparshatts and showed that putting the up-and-over front door at an angle made the body design much more complicated and was in any event not necessary.

The Paravan was launched at the 1958 Commercial Vehicle Show. Two vehicles were then put into service by Essex Carriers. After initial driver resistance, they found them extremely user-friendly, both for the ease of entry and exit and for their manoeuvrability thanks to the set-back front axle.

Paravan was aimed at city-centre delivery services, the angled doors avoiding the need to open them into passing traffic. Although ingenious, it was just too expensive, and few were sold. BOB LOVELAND COLLECTION

DENNIS PARAVAN, 1958–1966

Configuration: 4×2 rigid delivery van chassis
Engine: Perkins 4.236 4-cylinder direct-injection diesel
Capacity: 3867cc
Max. power: 80bhp
Max. torque: 193lb ft
Gearbox: Dennis UH-type 5-speed plus reverse, constant mesh, aluminium casing
Rear axle: Spiral bevel
Suspension: Semi-elliptic multi-leaf steel springs
Wheelbase: 141in (3,581mm)
Overall width: 81in (2,057mm)
Floor height: 30in (762mm)
(Source: Dennis Bros. publication No. 164P, 1958 and publication No. NS1091, 1965)

The Mk II Paravan introduced in 1965 retained the low floor but had a more conventional frontal appearance.
DENNIS ARCHIVES

The 1960 Vendor 30-cwt (1,520kg) van was the forerunner of the Transit, but was just too well engineered to be competitive. DENNIS ARCHIVES

Paravan II was then launched in 1965, promoting the use of more conventionally shaped bodywork but retaining the low entry and ability to access the load space from the cab.

The Paravan was inevitably expensive, and despite its brilliantly effective layout, achieved sales of less than 100, in contrast to the wide success and long production period of the cheaper FG.

The Paravan was an unfortunate example of the right product at the wrong time. It could have been an outstanding success in today's online purchasing lifestyle where parcel delivery vans are ubiquitous, usually with drivers being paid by the parcel, making the rapid entry and exit highly desirable.

The Vendor

The 1960 Vendor was a 30-cwt (1,520kg) payload front-wheel-drive chassis intended mainly for van use. It had a high-grade corrosion-resistant frame, independent front and rear suspension for a low load height – the front using a transverse leaf spring and the rear with rubber springs – and a 2.2-litre 56bhp 4-cylinder Standard-Triumph engine coupled to a three-speed all-synchromesh Dennis gearbox.

It could have changed the world, for it was, in many respects, the forerunner of Ford's Transit, which did not appear until 1965. However, the high-level specification and materials again made it too expensive, and the Vendor sadly never got beyond the prototype stage. Standard-Triumph, however, were so impressed with it that they considered buying the Dennis business!

The small Standard Triumph engine of the Vendor nestles under a large bonnet – perhaps the plan was for bigger engines at a later date, like the Transit?
DENNIS ARCHIVES

DENNIS VENDOR, 1960

Layout and Chassis
4×2 rigid ladder-frame low-floor normal-control van chassis

Engine
Type: Standard Motor Co. petrol
Block material: Cast iron
Head material: Cast iron
Cylinders: 4 in-line
Cooling: Water, pump-assisted
Capacity: 2190cc
Max. power: 56bhp at 4,000rpm
Max. torque: 107.5lb ft at 1,600rpm
Fuel capacity: 10gal (45ltr)
or
Type: Standard Motor Co. diesel
Block material: Cast iron
Head material: Cast iron
Cylinders: 4 in-line
Cooling: Water, pump-assisted
Capacity: 2260cc
Max. power: 57bhp at 3,500rpm
Max. torque: 101.7lb ft at 1,800rpm

Transmission
Gearbox: Dennis 3-speed plus reverse, Porsche synchromesh, combined differential
Clutch: Borg & Beck single dry plate, 9in (229mm) diameter

Ratios:
1st: 4.071
2nd: 2.087
3rd: 1.182
Reverse: 4.07
Final drive: Front wheel drive

Suspension and Steering
Front: Transverse leaf spring and wishbones, hydraulic piston dampers
Rear: Trailing arms and progressive rubber springs, hydraulic piston dampers
Steering: Recirculatory ball and nut
Tyres: 7.50 × 16 8-ply
Wheels: 6.00 × 16 5-stud steel disc

Brakes
Type: Drum, hydraulic actuation, cable-operated handbrake
Size: 12in (305mm) diameter

Dimensions
Overall length (chassis): 200in (5,080mm)
Overall width (chassis): 78in (1,981mm)
Floor height: 19.5in (495mm)
Unladen weight: 3,192lb (1,448kg)
Gross weight: 7,616lb (3,455kg)

Performance
Top speed: 48mph (77km/h)
(Source: Dennis Bros. publication No. 183P, 1960)

The Pax IV

Pax IV was introduced in 1963, both to simplify the Pax range, which ran to over eighty variants, and to reduce production costs. A new fibreglass cab was fitted, which was built in Woodbridge Works and produced in two parts, bonded together to make a full cab. The bottom and scuttle section was moulded from black fibreglass, giving great flexibility to use that part of the cab for fire and other specialized applications.

The Pax IV medium weight goods chassis were available as either a 12/15.5-ton (12,190/15,750kg) GVW tractor unit or a 10/11.25-ton (10,160/11,430kg) GVW rigid. The lower-rated versions used a Moss lightweight rear axle, while the heavier vehicles used a Dennis axle. Three 6-cylinder diesel engine options were available: a 5-litre 89bhp Perkins 6-305, a 5.8-litre 112bhp Perkins 6-354 or a 105bhp BMC 5.1-litre.

Eighty-seven Pax IVs were built between 1963 and 1966.

The Pax IV introduced the new two-piece fibreglass cab manufactured by Dennis. It is seen here fitted to a 1961 vehicle. DENNIS ARCHIVES

DENNIS PAX IV, 1963–1966

Configuration: 4×2 rigid ladder-frame forward-control articulated or goods chassis
Engine: Perkins 6-cylinder 6.305 diesel
Capacity: 5000cc
Max. power: 89bhp at 2,600rpm
Max. torque: 218lb ft at 1,250rpm
or
Engine: Perkins 6-cylinder 6.354 diesel
Capacity: 5800cc
Max. power: 112bhp at 2,800rpm
Max. torque: 260lb ft at 1,400rpm
or
Engine: BMC 6-cylinder diesel
Capacity: 5100cc
Max. power: 105bhp at 2,600rpm
Max. torque: 232lb ft at 1,750rpm
Gearbox: Dennis U-type wide-range 5-speed plus reverse, constant mesh, 260lb ft max. rating

or Dennis UH-type 5-speed plus reverse, constant mesh, 300lb ft max. rating
or Dennis UO-type overdrive 5-speed plus reverse, constant mesh, 300lb ft max. rating
or BMC 4-speed plus reverse, constant mesh
Rear axle: 10-ton (10,160kg) GVW: Moss spiral bevel
or 11.25-ton (11,431kg) GVW: Dennis spiral bevel
Suspension: Semi-elliptic multi-leaf steel springs
Trailer coupling: Scammell-type automatic or fifth wheel
Wheelbase: Tractor: 84in (2,134mm)
    Rigid: 169in (4,293mm)
Overall length: Tractor: 170.25in (4,324mm)
    Rigid: 304.25in (7,728mm)
Overall width: 87.6in (2,225mm)
    Max. GVW: 22,400lb (10,160kg) on 7.50 × 20 tyres
    25,200lb (11,431kg) on 8.25 × 20 tyres
Max. GCW: 26,880lb (12,193kg) on 7.00 × 20 tyres
    34,720lb (15,749kg) on 7.50 × 20 tyres
(Source: undated Dennis Bros. Pax IV brochure incorporating drawing Nos AR986 and AR1114)

This Pax IV from around 1963 is yet another example of an unusually bodied Dennis. BOB LOVELAND COLLECTION

The Maxim

The Maxim was introduced in 1964 to take advantage of the recently revised Construction and Use regulations, which had increased the maximum permitted weight to 16 tons on a 4×2 and 32 tons on an artic. Two- or three-axle tractors were offered, along with two-axle 14/16-ton (14,220/16,260kg) and three-axle 20- and 22-ton (20,320 and 22,350kg) GVW rigids.

A Cummins engine was specified initially, but this proved troublesome and was quickly replaced by a 185bhp Perkins V8, along with a Dennis five-speed gearbox. Unladen weights were very competitive: a typical tractor weighed just under 4 tons (4,060 kg), while even a 6×4 was only 5 tons 8 cwt (5,490kg). This meant that a 30-ton (30,480kg) Maxim could carry almost as much as many competitive 32-ton (32,510kg) chassis.

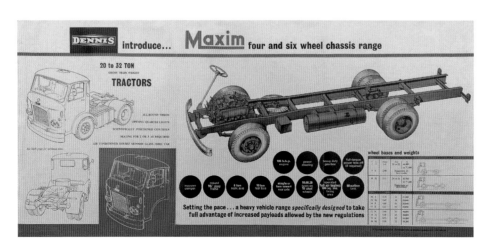

An extract from the Maxim sales brochure of 1964. BOB LOVELAND COLLECTION

Ancient and modern – a posed photo from 1966 showing Whitbread's latest Maxim artic and the horses once used for the same purpose. DENNIS ARCHIVES

The Pax V/Dominant/DB 15.5

The Pax V 4×2 was introduced at Tipcon, the tipper show in Buxton, Derbyshire in 1969. With an unladen weight of around 5.5 tons (5,600kg), it was lighter than the competition, giving around half a ton (500kg) more payload and proving extremely popular. It had a 120bhp Perkins 6-cylinder 5.8-litre diesel engine coupled to a U-type five-speed gearbox. It was also marketed as the Dominant, then in 1970 was rebranded as the DB 15.5.

The DB 15.5 was also offered with a third, non-driven axle conversion by Primrose, either self-steering or trailing. This gave a 20-ton (20,320kg) GVW with a 15-ton (15,240kg) payload. The three-axle version was used by many breweries, as when fitted with 16in wheels on the rear axles it had an exceptionally low deck height.

Some 22-ton (22,350kg) 6×4 Pax Vs were built in the mid-1960s fitted with V8 Perkins engines, a model that subsequently developed into the Maxim.

DENNIS MAXIM THREE-AXLE, 1964–c.1967

Layout and chassis
4×2, 6×2 and 6×4 chassis, all with ladder-frame forward-control fibreglass cab

Engine
Type: Perkins V8-510 diesel
Cylinders: V8
Cooling: Water, pump-assisted
Bore and stroke: 108 × 114.3mm
Capacity: 8360cc
Compression ratio: 17.5:1
Max. power: 170bhp at 2,800rpm
Max. torque: 390lb ft at 1,500rpm
Fuel capacity: 60gal (273ltr)

Transmission
Gearbox: Turner T5C 4001 5-speed plus reverse, synchromesh
Clutch: Single dry plate
Ratios:
    1st: 7.361
    2nd: 4.73
    3rd: 2.79
    4th: 1.66
    5th: 1
    Reverse: 7.361
Final drive: 10-ton-per-axle capacity, 2-speed hypoid bevel, double-reduction, double-drive on 6×4

Suspension and Steering
Front: Semi-elliptic multi-leaf steel springs, 52in (1,321mm) long, with hydraulic lever arm dampers
Rear: Semi-elliptic multi-leaf steel springs, 54in (1,372mm) long, with hydraulic lever arm dampers
Steering: Power, recirculatory ball
Tyres: 10.00 × 20
Wheels: 10-stud steel rims; single on front, twin on rear axles

Brakes
Type: Drum brakes, air actuated
Size: 15.5in (394mm) diameter

Dimensions
Wheelbases: 4×2 tractor: 115in (2,920mm)
    6×4 rigid: 146in (3,708mm), 171.5in (4,356mm) or 189in (4,800mm)
Overall width: 95in (2,413mm)
Overall lengths (chassis): 6×4 rigid: 293in (7,442mm), 333in (8,458mm) or 361in (9,169mm)
Unladen weight: 4×2 tractor: 10,192lb (4,623kg)
6×4 rigid: 12,382–14,000lb (6,045–6,350kg)
Gross weight: 4×2 tractor: up to 67,200lb (30,482kg)
    Rigid: up to 49,280lb (22,353kg)

Performance
Top speed: 4×2 tractor: 52.9mph (85km/h)
0–30mph: 43.5sec
(Source: Dennis Bros. publication No. NS1098, 1966 and publication No. NS1119, 1967)

Some Pax Vs were built as 6×4 low-load-height vehicles, like this mid-1960s vehicle shown here. The Pax lowloader was introduced in 1958 in an attempt to speed up unloading of drinks cases at public houses. They ran on 17in wheels and were bought by a number of breweries.
DENNIS ARCHIVES

The light weight of Pax V models made them popular for carrying high-volume but relatively low weight loads, such as furniture removals or, as seen here, baby food.
DENNIS ARCHIVES

DENNIS PAX V/DB 15.5/ DOMINANT, c.1965–1972

Configuration: 4×2 rigid ladder-frame forward-control fibreglass cab
Engine: Perkins 6.354 6-cylinder diesel
Capacity: 5800cc
Max. power: 120bhp at 2,800rpm
Max. torque: 260lb ft at 1,275rpm
Gearbox: Dennis U-type 5-speed plus reverse, constant mesh
Rear axle: Eaton 18802 2-speed, 10-ton capacity, hypoid bevel or Dennis single-speed
Suspension: Semi-elliptic multi-leaf steel springs, telescopic dampers on front axle
Wheelbases: Tipper: 128in (3,251mm)
    148in (3,759mm)
Platform body: 124–209in (3,150–5,308mm)
Overall width: 95in (2,413mm)
Overall length (chassis): 244–269in (6,198–9,373mm)
Unladen chassis/cab weight: 209in w/b: 8,736lb (3,963kg)
GVW: 33,600lb (15,241kg); later 34,720lb (15,749kg)
Price (chassis/cab): 128in w/b tipper: £2,997
(Source: Dennis Bros. publications Nos NS1129, NS1153 and NS1187 and NS 1198, 1967–1969)

Dennis introduced the DB 15.5 4×2 rigid at the 1969 CV Show. Confusingly, however, it was also sometimes badged as either Dominant or Pax V. DENNIS ARCHIVES

All together, 936 Pax Vs/Dominants/DB 15.5s were built between 1963 and around 1972.

The Defiant

The 24-ton (24,390kg) GVW DB 24T Defiant tractor unit, launched in 1970, was the first chassis to use the then-new Perkins 6.354 5.8-litre 155bhp turbocharged 6-cylinder engine. It was broadly similar to the lower-powered DB 15.5 two-axle rigid truck: both DB models were designed specifically for low unladen weight and the highest possible payload.

Skip loaders were becoming commonplace by 1971, some of which were fitted to Dennis chassis like this Dominant. DENNIS ARCHIVES

DENNIS DEFIANT DB 24T TRACTOR, 1970–

Configuration: 4×2 rigid ladder-frame forward-control fibreglass-cab articulated tractor
Engine: Perkins 6.354 6-cylinder turbocharged diesel
Capacity: 5800cc
Max. power: 155bhp at 2,600rpm
Max. torque: 378lb ft at 1,600rpm
Gearbox: Dennis WM-type 5-speed plus reverse, constant mesh
Rear axle: Eaton 18200 2-speed, 10-ton capacity, hypoid bevel
Suspension: Semi-elliptic multi-leaf steel springs, telescopic dampers on front axle
Wheelbase: 114in (2,900mm)
Overall width: 95in (2,413mm)
Overall height: 101in (2,565mm)
Overall length (chassis): 200.4in (5,091mm)
Unladen chassis/cab weight: 8,736lb (3,963mm) less fifth wheel coupling
GVW: 53,760lb (24,384kg)
Top speed: 57.5mph (93km/h)
(Source: undated/unnumbered Dennis Defiant brochure)

In the case of the DB 24T tractor plus a typical single-axle trailer, this resulted in a highly competitive payload of around 17 tons (17,270kg), about half a ton (500kg) better than the competition, thanks to the 3-ton 18-cwt (3,950kg) unladen weight of the DB 24T. Dennis's own WM five-speed gearbox was fitted, driving an Eaton two-speed rear axle.

LAWNMOWERS

Lawnmower production also resumed after World War II, the 1947 brochure listing many impressive worldwide customers, including British kings George V and VI, three Maharajahs, six Dukes and many others. Indeed, in 1949, the factory produced 452 lawnmowers, as well as 1,096 buses and trucks, 445 municipal vehicles, fifty-seven fire engines and forty-eight trailer or portable pumps.

One reason for the popularity of the Dennis mower was the excellent torque characteristics of its Dennis-built 500cc side-valve engine. The speed of a mower engine normally drops significantly if the blades hit a patch of particularly tough grass. However, the slow-revving Dennis-produced engine had such a flat torque curve that it treated severe conditions with disdain and would cut through almost anything. While Dennis regularly evaluated alternative engines, mainly US brands such as Kohler, they invariably had much peakier torque delivery that could not match the cutting performance of the Dennis. The Dennis engine, therefore, continued to be made at Guildford right up to the 1960s.

It was the proud boast of the company in its seventy-fifth

Mower production is in full swing in this undated photo of the assembly lines. BOB LOVELAND COLLECTION

anniversary publicity material of 1969 that Dennis mowers could be seen on practically every league football and county cricket ground in England, including at Wembley. The mowers were made in four cutting widths, from 20in to 36in (510–910mm), with options for a driving seat on each version.

Between 1946 and 1966, 8,893 mowers were built at Guildford.

FIRE APPLIANCES

The F-Series

The fire engine market was another in which Dennis got off to a good start after the war, with the introduction of the F-series in 1945. The first-numbered of the range was the normal-control F1, a development of the pre-war Light Four. It had a choice of petrol engines, either a 70bhp Dennis unit or a 150bhp Rolls-Royce B80, which put the performance of the F-series on a par with the average family car. It was in production until 1969, and 163 units were built.

The F2–F6 models were also normal-control models with restyled front wings and bonnet, although all subsequent F-series models were forward control.

In response to a post-war government document defining the minimum specification for a fire appliance, Dennis introduced the F7, which shared a similarly styled curved-front cab to the Pax, Max and Jubilant. Importantly for safety, the later F-series models all seated the firefighters inside the vehicle: no longer did they need to cling perilously to a brass rail on the side of the vehicle.

The various F-series models were the fire appliances that made Dennis a household name after World War II. This preserved F12 of 1958 was used by Middlesex. AUTHOR

DENNIS F1 'ONSLOW', 1945–

Configuration: 4×2 rigid ladder-frame with normal-control ash-framed coachbuilt bodywork (typically 'New World' style) with open cab
Engine: Dennis 4-cylinder petrol
Capacity: 3770cc
Max. power: 70bhp
Gearbox: Dennis 4-speed plus reverse
Rear axle: Spiral bevel
Suspension: Semi-elliptic multi-leaf steel springs
Pump: Dennis turbine, 400gal/min (1,820ltr/min) at 120psi, rear-mounted
Unladen weight: 10,080lb (4,572kg), est.
(Source: Dennis Bros. publication No. 196C, 1952)

400/500 GALLON FIRE ENGINES ON THE DENNIS **ONSLOW** CHASSIS

DENNIS BROS LTD GUILDFORD ENGLAND

RIGHT: **One 1952 version of the F1 was marketed as the Onslow, aimed at rural brigades. This had a New World body, only reverting to a Braidwood type if a wheeled escape was carried. The engine was the Dennis 3.77-litre 4-cylinder petrol engine coupled to a four-speed gearbox.** BOB LOVELAND COLLECTION

The double grille of the F101 makes it highly distinctive. Thirty-seven were built between 1955 and 1960. BOB LOVELAND COLLECTION

ABOVE: **This ex-Blackburn appliance is typical of the 101 F28s built between 1959 and 1964.** BOB LOVELAND COLLECTION

The mid-1950s F-series appliances, such as this vehicle for Papua New Guinea, used the front scuttle of the Pax fibreglass cab. DENNIS ARCHIVES

DENNIS F8, 1949–

Layout and Chassis
4×2 rigid ladder-frame forward-control fire appliance

Engine
Type: Rolls-Royce B60 petrol
Block material: Cast iron
Head material: Cast iron or aluminium
Cylinders: 6 in-line
Cooling: Water
Bore and stroke: 88.9 × 114.3mm
Capacity: 4250cc
Valves: Overhead inlet, side exhaust
Max. power: 122bhp at 4,000rpm

Transmission
Gearbox: 4-speed manual
Clutch: Single dry plate
Final drive: Spiral bevel

Suspension and Steering
Front: Semi-elliptic leaf springs
Rear: Semi-elliptic leaf springs

Brakes
Type: Drum, hydraulic actuation with vacuum servo
assistance

Fire Equipment
Pump: Dennis No. 2 rear-mounted, 500gal/min
(2,275ltr/min)
Emergency water tank: 250gal (1,140ltr)
Ladder: Typical 35ft (10.7m)

Dimensions
Wheelbase: 82in (2,083mm)
Overall width: 78in (1,981mm)
Gross weight (max.): 11,200lb (5,080kg)

Performance
0–60mph: 45sec
(Source: Dennis Bros. publication No. 240C, 1950)

RIGHT: **An unusual batch of F44 appliances
was built in the mid-1960s for South
Africa, devoid of a roof and with the
doors stopped at waist level, thus
becoming the last open-topped fire
appliances built by Dennis.** DENNIS ARCHIVES

With relations with Germany restored, Dennis turned
once again to Metz in the early 1950s to provide
turntable ladders like this 100ft (30m) example. It was
powered by an 8-cylinder 165bhp Rolls-Royce B80 petrol
engine. A No. 2 500gal/min (1,800ltr/min) pump could be
mounted amidships. DENNIS ARCHIVES

DENNIS METZ TURNTABLE LADDER, 1954–

Configuration: 4×2 rigid ladder-frame chassis with forward-control coachbuilt cab and 100ft (30m) or 120ft (36m) turntable ladder
Engine: Rolls-Royce B80 8-cylinder petrol
Capacity: 5675cc
Max. power: RAC rating 39HP; 165bhp
Gearbox: Dennis 4-speed plus reverse
Suspension: Semi-elliptic multi-leaf steel springs

Pump: Dennis No. 2, mounted midships
Wheelbase: 186in (4,724mm)
Overall length: 358.25in (9,100mm) with 100ft (30m) escape ladder
Overall width: 90in (2,286mm)
Overall height: 123in (3,125mm) to top of 100ft escape ladder
Gross weight: 17,900lb (8,130kg) approx.
Top speed: 55mph (88km/h)
(Source: Dennis Bros. publication No. 333C, 1954)

DENNIS F7 AND F12, 1949–

Specification as Dennis F8 except for the following:
Engine: Rolls-Royce B80 petrol 8-cylinder
Capacity: 5675cc
Max. power: 160bhp at 4,000rpm
Pump: Typical: Dennis No. 3 1,000gal/min (4,550ltr/min), side- or rear-mounted
Wheelbase: F7: 162in (4,115mm)
 F12: 150in (3,810mm)
Overall width: 90in (2,286mm)
Gross weight (max.): 17,920lb (8,128kg)
0–60mph: 30sec

Most F-series appliances were the then-standard 7ft 6in (2.3m) width, but one model, the 6ft 6in-wide (1.98m) F8, was developed primarily for use in rural areas. It was popular, with 253 being sold between 1951 and 1960. The standard-width F12, of which 354 were built between 1950 and 1961, was also popular.

In the mid-1950s, the F-series saw a significant update, with a new-look cab that shared the same fibreglass front scuttle, doors and roof as the Pax truck range. It also featured for the first time a one-piece windscreen. Most F-series with this cab were 7ft 6in (2.3m) wide; however, a 7ft-wide (2.13m) version was also available.

A subsequent styling update around 1976 saw the grille replaced by one featuring full-width horizontal bars.

The facelifted F-series cab received a full-width grille, as fitted to this Durham appliance. BOB LOVELAND COLLECTION

DENNIS F101, 1955–

Configuration: 4×2 rigid ladder-frame with dual-purpose composite steel and timber bodywork and seating for 6 crew
Engine: Rolls-Royce 6-cylinder C6 diesel
Capacity: 12170cc
Max. power: 170bhp at 2,000rpm
Gearbox: 4-speed plus reverse, constant mesh
Rear axle: Double reduction, spiral bevel gears
Suspension: Semi-elliptic multi-leaf steel springs, telescopic dampers on front axle
Brakes: Hydraulically operated drum brakes with Lockheed continuous flow assistance
Wheelbase: 150in (3,810mm)
Overall length: 309in (7,849mm)
Overall width: 89.5in (2,274mm)
Overall height: 105in (2,667mm) over cab
Gross weight: 20,160lb (9,145kg)
Top speed: 55mph (88km/h)
Pump: Dennis No. 3 1,000gal/min (4,550ltr/min), rear- or midship-mounted
Water tank: 100gal (455ltr)
Power take-off: Rear of gearbox
Ladder: Typical: 50ft (15.25m)
(Source: Dennis Bros. publication, 1955)

Worsening traffic conditions affected fire engine response times, leading to demands for increased performance. These were satisfied in the early 1960s by offering an optional 235bhp Rolls-Royce B81 6.52-litre 8-cylinder petrol engine mated to either an Allison MT640 automatic gearbox or a Turner T5 manual unit. A 185bhp Perkins V8.510 8-cylinder 8.36-litre diesel was also available. Although diesel engine performances were improving, some idea of the benefits offered by the high-power petrol engine can be appreciated by comparing its 0–30mph acceleration rate to that of a similar diesel-powered machine. The diesel managed a not unreasonable 17-second time, but the big petrol engine slashed that to 10 seconds.

This level of power demanded improved braking performance. Dennis responded by introducing optional four-wheel disc brakes in 1962, until then a feature found only on performance cars. They were so successful that by 1967 they became standard fitment on many models.

With the increased numbers of multi-storey buildings appearing by the early 1960s, the brigades needed vehicles with a higher vertical reach. To meet this need, in 1963 Dennis introduced a radical new F-series model, the Delta. Instead of the cab being mounted above the engine in the traditional way, it was set in front of the front axle and lowered, with the engine behind it. This helped to produce a chassis with an extremely low centre of gravity, which was ideal for either a Simon Snorkel hydraulic platform or a turntable ladder.

The last F-Series built was a water tender for the Tyne & Wear Fire Brigade, ending a production run of over twenty years.

DENNIS F-SERIES, 1976–

Configuration: 4×2 forward-control fire appliance chassis with 6-man cab
Applications: Water tender, water tender ladder, hydraulic platform or emergency tender
Engine: Rolls-Royce B81SV 8-cylinder petrol
Capacity: 6520cc
Max. power: 235bhp at 4,000rpm
Max. torque: 358lb ft at 2,500rpm
or
Engine: Perkins V8-540 V8 diesel
Cylinders: V8
Capacity: 8834cc
Max. power: 180bhp at 2,600rpm
Max. torque: 410lb ft at 1,650rpm
Gearbox: Turner T5 400 5-speed manual, synchromesh
or
Engine: Allison MT640 4-speed automatic
Power take-off: Full torque sandwich PTO
Suspension: Semi-elliptic multi-leaf steel springs
Pump: Typical: Dennis No. 2 600gal/min (2,730ltr/min)
First aid tank: Typical: 400gal (1,820ltr)
Wheelbase: Water tender: 150in (3,810mm)
Emergency tender and hydraulic platform: 194.9in (4,950mm)
Overall length (chassis):
Water tender: 278in (7,061mm)
Emergency tender: 383.9in (9,750mm)
Hydraulic platform: 432in (10,973mm)
Overall width:
Water tender: 90in (2,286mm)
Emergency tender and hydraulic platform: 95in (2,413mm)
(Source: Dennis Bros. publication Nos NS1256 and NS1501, 1971/1977)

The Delta chassis was specifically designed to accept hydraulic platforms, such as this early 1980s example for Cleveland County Fire Brigade. DENNIS ARCHIVES

The D-Series

The D-series was launched in 1968. It shared a similar fibreglass-fronted cab as the F-series of the time, although twin headlights were fitted to the F-series where the later D-series had to make do with single items. The unique selling point for the D-series was its narrow cab width of 7ft (2.13m). This made it ideal for rural brigades, helped by its short wheelbase and maximum GVW of 10 tons (10,160kg). The usual engine was the 6-cylinder 180bhp 4.2-litre Jaguar petrol engine more often seen in the XJ saloon car. This was mated to a five-speed synchromesh

gearbox. Drum brakes were fitted all round. A No. 2 600gal/min pump was installed at the rear along with a 400gal (1,800ltr) water tank.

In the mid-1960s, Glasgow Brigade faced a significant problem in providing fire cover to the planned Anderston commercial centre, a large complex spread over 25 acres (10ha). This had three levels and numerous tower blocks imposing restrictions on the overall height, width, length and weight of fire appliances. After much investigation, the only British chassis found capable of adaptation to meet these limits was the D-series. The 'top hamper' of the

DENNIS DELTA, 1963–

Application: Hydraulic platforms and turntable ladders
Engine: Perkins V8-640
Capacity: 10800cc
Max. power: 215bhp at 2,600rpm
Gearbox: Allison MT640 fully automatic
Length (body): 375.6in (9,540mm)
Width: 98in (2,490mm)
Height (over cab): 93in (2,362mm)
Wheelbase: 196.9in (5,000mm)
GVW (max.): 35,487lb (16,260kg)
Working height: Typical: 72ft 2in (22m)
Working reach: Typical: 41ft (12.45m)
(Source: various)

Ever wondered what the inside of a fire engine looks like? Most have at their heart an emergency water tank of a few hundred gallons capacity to provide an initial water supply for immediate use until the appliance can be coupled up to a hydrant. BOB LOVELAND COLLECTION

THE GLASGOW 'SCOOSHER'

New concept in Fire Fighting Engineering

DENNIS

The Anderston Commercial Centre being constructed in the heart of Glasgow is the largest of its kind in the United Kingdom, with a site area of over 25 acres basically constructed in three decks with numerous tower blocks and other buildings. The Glasgow Fire Service found themselves present-with a major problem.

The maximum permitted weight load on the Podium Deck of 7½ tons.

Projecting balconies, receding flat roofs, high rise buildings and openings into areas below the Podium Deck.

Restrictions on overall height, width and length.

The design of a fire appliance which would be suitable for both normal city work and the Commercial Centre.

The Scoosher was developed for Glasgow. Once seen as the future of fire fighting, it remained unique to them.
RICHARD NORMAN

unique body developed for Glasgow featured a rotatable articulated boom manufactured by Simon Engineering. This carried a water pipe to a monitor mounted on top of the boom together with a window breaker and an infra-red monitor to probe for fire sources. All this equipment was controlled by a panel at ground level.

Additionally, the boom could lift loads of up to 300lb (135kg) and raise a fireman up to 30ft (9.1m). It also carried a 45ft (13.4m) Lacon ladder.

In western Scottish children's slang, a 'scoosher' is an old term for a water pistol. The same word was also used by Glasgow firefighters to describe a quick hose-down with a jet of water. So, because of its ability to project a powerful jet of water over a considerable distance, Glasgow's new D-series soon earned the nickname 'Scoosher'.

RED IS THE COLOUR

Ever since the first horse-drawn, steam-powered fire engines, their traditional colour had been red. However, the increasing usage of sodium lighting began to cause problems at night, for red appeared black under these lights, so a fire engine failed to stand out to other road users. Following a fatal road accident in 1966, there were several experiments and research into the optimum fire engine colour, yellow eventually being selected. Coventry specified yellow fire appliances for a period, as did West Sussex for a batch of sixteen D-Series appliances between 1968 and 1972. While the logic was that yellow, like red, was bright and easily seen in daylight conditions, under sodium lighting it appeared not yellow but white – better, perhaps, but not ideal. Eventually, the Home Office decided that enough was enough, and ruled that fire engines must be red.

This 1968 D-series operated by the West Sussex brigade initially wore a yellow livery, which at the time was thought to aid visibility. The D-series was only 7ft (2.1m) wide, making it a popular choice for rural brigades. AUTHOR

DENNIS D-SERIES, 1968—

Configuration: 4×2 rigid ladder-frame fire appliance chassis with fibreglass-fronted, ash-framed aluminium-panelled bodywork
Engine: Jaguar XK 6-cylinder twin-overhead-camshaft petrol
Capacity: 4200cc
Max. power: 180bhp at 4,000rpm
Max. torque: 240lb ft at 3,100rpm
or
Engine: Perkins T6.354 6-cylinder turbocharged diesel
Capacity: 5800cc
Max. power: 180bhp at 4,000rpm
Max. torque: 240lb ft at 3,100rpm

Gearbox: Dennis 5-speed constant mesh (later Turner 5-speed or Allison 4-speed automatic)
Rear axle: Dennis spiral bevel
Suspension: Semi-elliptic multi-leaf steel springs, hydraulic dampers on front axle
Pump: Dennis No. 2: 600gal/min (2,730ltr/min)
Water tank: 400gal (1,820ltr)
Wheelbase: 129in (3,277mm)
Overall length: 254.3in (6,460mm)
Overall width: 83.9in (2,130mm)
Gross weight (typical): 17,360lb (7,874kg)
Top speed: 68mph (109km/h)
0–30mph: 16sec
(Source: Dennis Bros. publication Nos NS1140R, NS1223R and NS1257, 1968/1977)

ENGINE DEVELOPMENTS

One of the new developments in this period was the 7.58-litre O6 diesel engine introduced in 1940, which gave 100bhp and was offered in both double- and single-deck chassis, such as the revived and updated Lance and Lancet.

The O4 was followed in 1940 by the O6 shown here, the pair becoming the first successful diesel engines produced by Dennis. Although late to the market, they gained a strong following. BOB LOVELAND COLLECTION

DENNIS MERCURY MD300 MK II AIRTUG

Configuration: 4×4 rigid steel-plate welded and bolted body
Engine: Perkins V8-510 V8 diesel
Capacity: 8400cc
Max. power: 163bhp at 2,500rpm
or
Engine: Cummins V8
Max. power: 185bhp
Gearbox: Allison CRT3531-1, 3-speed in both forward and reverse
Axles: Centrax hypoid bevel hub reduction
or Kirkstall Forge spiral bevel hub reduction
Tyres: 15.5 × 25 12-ply
Brakes: Twin-calliper disc brakes on both axles, air-operated
Cab: 4-man
Wheelbase: 108in (2,743mm)
Overall length: 222.25in (5,645mm)
Overall width: 96in (2,438mm)
Overall height (over cab): 90in (2,286mm)
Unladen weight: 40,000lb (18,144kg)
Drawbar pull (max.): 30,000lb (13,608kg)
(Source: Dennis Mercury MD300 brochure, 1970)

Both were available with a five-speed overdrive gearbox, giving them a good turn of speed, and the Lancet, in particular, sold well in a market hungry for social travel. The 7.58-litre engine was later increased in capacity to 8 litres and was followed by a 5.1-litre diesel in 1948 and a 5.5-litre in 1953.

TUGS AND TRACTORS

Dennis acquired the Mercury Truck and Tractor Company of Gloucester in 1964, further diversifying the Dennis product range. Mercury was primarily a manufacturer of small machines for industrial use, although they had developed a range of heavier aircraft tractors with drawbar pull ratings of up to 20,000lb (9,070kg). Design and production of the Mercury products were transferred to Guildford in 1965. Some notable sales successes were achieved, including in 1970 a £350,000 order from the UK Ministry of Technology for a batch of military versions of the MD300 30,000lb (13,600kg) drawbar pull aircraft tractor for use at Royal Air Force stations around the world.

The MD300 model with its 163bhp Perkins V8 engine also achieved some fame as a frequently seen pushback tractor for Concorde, at that time probably the world's most high-profile aircraft type.

The Dennis Mercury product range was developed to span a wide range of capacities, from the MD20 with a drawbar pull of 2,000lb (900kg) right up to the 40,000lb-capacity (18,140kg) MD400. This was designed at Guildford in 1970 and was intended to haul jumbo jets and similar aircraft. The MD400's designer sadly lost his life in a road accident before the design was finalized or all the parts procured. A couple of Experimental Department staff, one of whom was a young Richard Norman, were then given the job of turning the incomplete collection of parts into a running vehicle for display at the Earl's Court Mechanical Handling Exhibition. They achieved their objective, but not without some difficulty, not least because the engine for the beast, a V8 from a Leyland coach, was not delivered on time, so to get the tug to its launch the two engineers borrowed a lawnmower engine from the lawnmower line to power the hydraulics for the steering.

After the show, and completion of this tug, it was featured in the promotional material for the machine and was later sold to Dan Air for operation at London Gatwick airport.

With the prototype out of the way, a heavily revised production version was developed, using much thicker steel plate and simplifying the build. Several were built at Guildford before the Dennis Mercury operation was sold

The profile of the Dennis Mercury Division was given a real boost when the MD300 Airtug was chosen by the British Aircraft Corporation for the ground handling of Concorde. The MD300 was also widely used both by airlines and, in modified form, by the Royal Air Force. BOB LOVELAND COLLECTION

and production transferred to the new owner's premises in Halifax.

Other products included the Haulmajor Terminal Tractor, or dock-spotter, developed in 1971 at Guildford. The use of such vehicles, with their elevating fifth wheels, was increasing rapidly to move unaccompanied trailers around ports and distribution centres. This was driven by the growth of containerization and roll-on, roll-off services, with a move away from the old traditional 'crane and sling' operations that needed hundreds of frequently striking dock workers. The Haulmajor HM155 tractor was claimed

This picture shows a production MD400 being manoeuvred near the North Gate entrance to Woodbridge Works. Note the alternative standing driving position for increased visibility. The driver in this photo is the Dennis Mercury design section leader of the time, Dennis Howes, who went on to increasingly senior roles within the company. RICHARD NORMAN

The 1971-designed Haulmajor was an elevating fifth-wheel tractor designed for ports and transport depots. All production took place at Halifax after the tug and tractor business was sold to Marshalls. RICHARD NORMAN

DENNIS MERCURY HAULMAJOR HM155 TERMINAL TRACTOR, 1971–

Configuration: 4×2 rigid ladder-frame forward-control tractor unit with elevating fifth wheel
Engine: Perkins T6.354 6-cylinder turbocharged diesel
Capacity: 5800cc
Max. power: 155bhp at 2,600rpm
Max. torque: 376lb ft at 1,600rpm
Gearbox: Allison Torqmatic powershift, 3 forward and reverse speeds
Rear axle: 56,000lb (25,402kg) capacity spiral bevel, hub reduction
Suspension: Front: semi-elliptic springs, telescopic dampers
Rear: direct-mounted to structure
Steering: Twin steering positions, full hydrostatic power
Overall length: 194in (4,927mm)
Overall width: 97.5in (2,476mm)
Top speed: 7.5mph (12km/h) laden, 27mph (43km/h) unladen
(Source: Dennis Mercury Haulmajor HM155 data sheet NS1255, 1972)

to be able to pull a 60-ton (60,960kg) trailer up a 1:5 (20 per cent) slope such as the loading ramp of a ship. As Richard Norman recalls, however, the high fifth-wheel height made the stability of the vehicle and its load questionable! It featured a Perkins T6.354 155bhp engine coupled to an Allison Torqmatic powershift transmission.

Before any sales of the Haulmajor could take place, Dennis was taken over by Hestair, as described in Chapter 4.

MIKE HAWTHORN

In 1931, Leslie Hawthorn, a motorcycle racer from Mexborough in Yorkshire, moved his family, including his two-year-old son, John Michael, to Surrey to be closer to Brooklands. As Leslie also ran the Tourist Trophy Garage in Farnham, it was almost inevitable that John Michael, or Mike as he became known, also became involved in motor sport. However, even promising racing drivers need an income, and on leaving school in 1946, Mike joined Dennis as an apprentice. He commuted to Woodbridge Works on his 1939 250cc Triumph motorbike, or occasionally his mother's Fiat 500. Ron Foster, an apprentice at the same time, recalls Mike arriving in the Fiat 'like a bat out of hell!'

Mike worked for a time in the lawnmower section, and it seems that he enjoyed giving them some stick as he drove them to the paint shop. In his book, *Challenge Me the Race*, he recounts that:

> One day I decided to drive one of the Dennis lorries, of which there were plenty; this one was partly assembled ready to go to the bodybuilder. Unfortunately, I hadn't noticed that the body panels were stacked loosely on the back – I had to stop suddenly while accelerating down the yard and one of the panels came off and landed at the supervisor's feet...

Shortly after completing his apprenticeship, Mike's racing became his full-time occupation, and the rest is history, with him winning the Formula 1 World Championship in 1958. He retired shortly afterwards, and, sadly, on 22 January 1959 was killed while driving his Jaguar 3.4-litre saloon on the A3, almost exactly outside Dennis's Woodbridge Works factory.

Mike was not the only Dennis Apprentice to enjoy success on the race track: they included John Cooper, of Mini and Formula 1 fame, and Alan Brown, who drove Coopers for nine years in Formula 1.

AMBULANCES

Dennis had been reasonably successful in their early days with ambulance sales, and it was a market to which they regularly returned.

The Heron chassis formed the basis of the AV-series ambulances of the mid-1950s. Either the 60bhp Perkins P4V diesel or 78bhp Rolls-Royce B40 petrol engine was fitted, coupled to a four-speed synchromesh gearbox that drove into a chassis-mounted differential to provide a 21in (530mm) floor height. Gregoire variable-rate rear suspension was installed. The AV series met with some market success but was up against established competitors, and lacked enough unique features to stand out against them successfully. Only 334 were built between 1955 and 1966.

As with fire engines, Dennis also bodied other manufacturers' chassis, notably the Karrier 'Walk-thru' 1.5-tonner of the early 1960s.

Conversely, in 1959 Dennis used the AV-series chassis as a basis for the AG-series light van, the attraction being the low load height. Chassis were bodied by several companies including Appleyard of Leeds, Lawler Motors of London and Sparshatts of Portsmouth.

This unusually coloured 1959 AV4 ambulance was used by the City of Sheffield. BOB LOVELAND COLLECTION

In the early 1960s, Dennis made use of their ambulance body technology by working with other chassis manufacturers, particularly Karrier. BOB LOVELAND COLLECTION

The chassis of the AV4 ambulance. BOB LOVELAND COLLECTION

DENNIS AV-SERIES AMBULANCE, 1954–

Configuration: 4×2 rigid ladder-frame low-floor ambulance chassis
Engine: Perkins P4 4-cylinder diesel
Max. power: 60bhp at 3,000rpm
or
Engine: Rolls-Royce B40 4-cylinder petrol
Max. power: 78bhp at 3,750rpm
Gearbox: 4-speed plus reverse, synchromesh
Rear axle: De Dion type, hypoid bevel differential

Suspension: Front: semi-elliptic multi-leaf steel springs with telescopic dampers
Rear: Gregoire variable rate system, lever-type hydraulic dampers
Wheelbase: 105in (2,667mm)
Overall length (chassis): 177.5in (4,509mm)
Overall width: 78.5in (1,993mm)
Floor height: 21in (533mm) unladen, 18in (457mm) laden
Unladen weight (chassis): 2,632lb (1,194kg)
Unladen weight (bodied): 4,928lb (2,235kg)
(Sources: Dennis Bros. publication No. 339C, 1954, publication No. 102P, 1956 and publication No. 368C, 1956)

The AG-series van was produced from 1959, based on the AV ambulance chassis. It is not recorded how many were sold. BOB LOVELAND COLLECTION

Dennis's next attempt at the ambulance market was the FD4, launched at the 1968 Commercial Vehicle Show. The design of the FD4 was inspired by a government-sponsored draft ambulance specification, which called for front-wheel drive and very low floor height.

The FD4 offered its patients an extremely low loading height of less than 20in (500mm), thanks to an ingenious drive system. Rather than a propeller shaft taking the drive from the Borg-Warner Type 35 fully automatic gearbox to the axle, it used a Morse Hi-Vo chain drive to drop the drive down from the gearbox output. A short prop-shaft then linked this to a chassis-mounted Salisbury differential, which drove via constant-velocity joints out to the front wheels.

Sophisticated independent suspension was provided all round, initially by using rubber springs and later by variable-rate coil springs. Front-wheel location was by wishbones, with the rear using trailing arms. Wheels of only 14in diameter were used at the back to minimize the load-bed height and wheel-arch intrusion into the patient area, with 16in wheels on the front axle. A 2.8-litre 140bhp Jaguar 6-cylinder petrol engine gave excellent performance. Two spare wheels – one each of the different-sized front and rear wheels – were housed under the reinforced plastic bonnet.

The FD4 had a long front overhang of 4ft (1.22m), made necessary by the front-wheel-drive configuration; however, the trade-off was excellent manoeuvrability, echoing the Ace range of three decades previously.

The working party that produced the 1967 draft specification for the government had noted caustically that 'In our view the needs of the seriously ill or injured persons … are not being adequately met by [any of] the vehicles at present in use.' But despite the FD4 more than meeting the requirements of the draft specification, unlike any current UK competitor, sales were negligible. Indeed, only three were produced, one of which was very quickly written off while under evaluation by the Rutland Ambulance Service. The remaining vehicles saw service with St John Ambulance. The FD4 was inevitably expensive – at £3,800 for a fully kitted vehicle – and cost, it seems, took priority over care even in those days.

The FD4 sold in small numbers but deserved greater success, being the first British purpose-designed ambulance since the bonneted Daimler of the early 1950s. It was an object lesson into not always believing the customer knows best: after Dennis put so much effort into developing a vehicle that exactly and uniquely met the NHS's much-researched requirements, the customer changed their minds! DENNIS ARCHIVES

DENNIS FD4, 1968–

Layout and Chassis
4×2 front-wheel-drive ladder frame low-floor ambulance
Body: Hardwood frame, aluminium panelling, fibreglass roof

Engine
Type: Jaguar XK petrol
Cylinders: 6 in-line
Cooling: Water
Bore and stroke: 83 × 86mm
Capacity: 2792cc
Valves: Double overhead camshaft
Compression ratio: 8.0:1
Max. power: 140bhp at 5,500rpm
Max. torque: 150lb ft at 4,000rpm
Fuel capacity: 12gal (54.5ltr)

Transmission
Gearbox: Borg Warner Type 35 3-speed automatic
Clutch: Borg Warner torque convertor
Final drive: Morse Hi-Vo chain drive and Salisbury differential unit to front-wheel drive shafts

Suspension and Steering
Front: Independent with wishbones and coil springs, lever-type dampers
Rear: Independent with trailing arms and coil springs, lever-type dampers
Steering: Marles cam and roller
Tyres: Front 6.00 × 16, rear 165 × 14 radial ply

Brakes
Type: Lockheed hydraulically actuated, vacuum-assisted two-leading-shoe drums
Size: 10in (254mm) diameter

Dimensions
Wheelbase: 120in (3,048mm)
Overall length: 216in (5,486mm)
Overall width: 79in (2,007mm)
Overall height: 91.5in (2,324mm)
Unladen weight (bodied): 6,104lb (2,769kg)

Performance
Top speed: 70mph (112km/h) approx.
0–30mph: 9.0sec
(Sources: Dennis Bros. publication No. NS1154, 1968 and *Commercial Motor* magazine, 13 June 1969)

DECLINING SALES

With the generally limited sales success of the various niche Dennis models and the uncompetitive pricing of their more mainstream 'me-too' offerings, both truck and bus sales began a steady decline, with fire appliance sales again becoming predominant. Here, engineering innovation kept the products at the top of their game, and at least this was in a market that was not at that time so price-sensitive.

So, in the early 1960s, Dennis fortunes were declining, with a shrinking number of orders to fill the large Woodbridge factory, and the company lost money in 1965. By this time, front-engined deckers such as the Loline had been made obsolete by rear-engined competitors with even lower floor lines that were suitable for one-man operation, which of course reduced operating costs substantially. With the inevitable demise of the Loline, the decision was made to cease bus production at Guildford.

This proved to be the right decision because, on the operating side, potential sales were being made more difficult by the formation in 1968 of the government-owned National Bus Company, responsible for some one-third of the entire 75,000-strong British bus fleet. The various passenger transport authorities, which were again effectively government-owned, ran a further 11,000 or so buses, so almost half of the British bus fleet was effectively nationalized.

On the manufacturing side, mergers again resulted in the formation and nationalization of the British Leyland Motor Corporation, which then enjoyed a monopoly supply situation. This left Bristol as the only, and by comparison, tiny, independent bus supplier. Finally, in July 1969, the two nationalized concerns announced the formation of a joint company, Leyland National, to produce initially a new single-decker, the National bus, and later a double-decker, Titan. Development of the National was underwritten by £1.6 million of publicly funded investment, a sum of which companies such as Dennis could only dream.

To make matters worse, the Dennis truck range had failed to make real sales headway. In 1967, Dennis therefore decided to also withdraw from the truck market and concentrate on municipal vehicles and fire appliances, where their sales were still healthy. Both of these product lines were, of course, relatively low volume, leaving the company with too little production to be viable.

Between 1969 and 1972 company rearrangements, the installation of John King as the new chairman, and even a company name change to Dennis Motor Holdings, failed to keep the business viable. Although turnover in 1968 had increased slightly to £3.94 million from £3.56 million in 1967, profits fell from £181,500 to £105,200. Despite cost-cutting measures, including 150 redundancies and the sale of many of the Dennisville houses, the weakened company became a target for takeover – indeed, in 1969 it was almost bought by rival truck manufacturer Seddon.

The company was eventually purchased by the Hestair group in 1972, despite strong opposition from the Dennis board. Although this was the end of Dennis as a family-led affair, it was far from the end for the business, as the next chapter reveals.

CHAPTER FOUR

THE EARLY HESTAIR ERA: 1972–1985

HESTAIR RATIONALIZATION

Hestair had been formed in 1970 by the David Hargreaves takeover of the former Heston Airport Company. Hestair was primarily an industrial investment business, and as such had a diverse portfolio of business interests ranging from agricultural equipment to toy making to employment agencies. Along their investment path, Hestair had acquired Eagle Engineering of Warwick, manufacturers of tankers and refuse bodies, and Leeds-based Yorkshire Vehicles Ltd, makers of tankers and road-sweeper bodies. One of the Yorkshire Vehicles employees was John Smith, who later rose to become the managing director of Dennis Specialist Vehicles.

Hestair took over Dennis in 1972, calling the newly formed business Dennis Motors Ltd. The new company inherited annual losses approaching £1 million on a turnover of £12 million.

When Hestair took over Dennis, they were keen to stay in the vehicle business, and scotch any rumours that Dennis products had no future. To underline that, this cartoon appeared in the September 1972 edition of *Teamwork*, the in-house newspaper of the Hestair Group Fire Division, which was aimed at fire brigade personnel.

RICHARD NORMAN

Hestair's solution was to embark on a dramatic rationalization programme. An early move was to sell the sprawling Woodbridge Works site, renting back less than half of the buildings. Lawnmower production was moved from Guildford to Hestair's farm machinery division in Kent.

The Dennis Mercury tug and tractor division was sold to Marshalls, the Yorkshire quarrying and paving company. Marshalls already owned Reliance, a manufacturer of small tractor units, and Dennis Mercury, with its range of heavier tractors, was a natural fit. Dennis Mercury production was moved to the Reliance site in Halifax, and the company was rebranded as Reliance Mercury.

Guildford gearbox and axle production were also ended, leaving Woodbridge Works to concentrate on vehicle assembly rather than component manufacture.

Integration of Hestair's vehicle interests was a logical step, and the Dennis products together with those of Eagle and Yorkshire Vehicles were combined into the Vehicle Division of Hestair. Bodies for the division's refuse vehicles and street sweepers were produced at the Warwick factory of the newly formed Hestair Eagle. Dennis in Guildford continued to make the chassis for these vehicles until 1985, when they too moved to a new Dennis Eagle factory in Warwick.

Initially, Hestair continued to target the Dennis customer base of local authorities because of their regular demand for fire appliances and specialist trucks. Production for all other markets, including haulage, was all but abandoned.

R-SERIES – RECOVERY IN THE FIRE MARKET

However, this left the company producing only around 300 vehicles a year, which was not enough to sustain the business financially. Some relief was provided by a contract to body Thornycroft Nubian aircraft crash tenders for the Ministry of Defence.

The once-innovative Dennis fire engine range, however, was becoming uncompetitive, having been starved of investment. While the F-series was always a premium product, its high-quality materials and low-volume production made it uncompetitively expensive. Market leadership had therefore passed to cheaper truck-derived ERF and Dodge models. To regain the market, Dennis fought back and introduced the R-series in the mid-1970s, the R standing for 'Retained' (fire stations).

This was a lower-cost version of the F-series, with a full fibreglass cab and fewer options, at least initially, although

An order from the RAF to body a batch of Thornycroft Nubian airfield crash tenders was probably instrumental in keeping the company afloat during the dark days of 1974. DENNIS ARCHIVES

some vehicles were built with the more powerful Perkins V8-640 diesel engine. This new model, no doubt also helped by ERF announcing their withdrawal from the fire market, saw the Dennis share of the fire engine market increase dramatically, from 20 per cent in 1974 to 40 per cent by 1978.

Two thoroughbreds together: superstar racehorse Red Rum meets his namesake R-series fire engine at a ceremony at Southport fire station on 17 February 1979. DENNIS ARCHIVES

A 1980s Foambird foam tender for an unidentified customer.

BOB LOVELAND COLLECTION

MIDDLE EASTERN LIFELINE

The need to increase production led the company to focus on export markets, primarily the Middle East, which had grown rich on the dramatic oil price rises of the early 1970s. Iraq, in particular, needed vehicles urgently, specifically tankers, as they had found out to their cost in the

---

DENNIS R133, 1975–1979

Configuration: 4×2 rigid ladder-frame forward-control fire appliance chassis
Engine: Perkins V8-640
Capacity: 10500cc
Max. power: 218bhp (163kW)
Gearbox: Allison MT640 fully automatic
Cab: Fibreglass
Emergency water tank: 400gal (1,820ltr)
Pump: 500gal/min (2,275ltr/min)
Top speed: 75mph (120km/h)
0–42mph: 19sec
(Source: various)

1973 Yom Kippur conflict where their military progress overland was hampered by lack of fuel and water supplies. By the mid-1970s, Dennis were selling hundreds of tankers to Iraq. Ironically, these very successful products were, in fact, largely designed before the Hestair takeover. Perhaps with better marketing of these new models, Dennis could have avoided losing their independence.

At that time, Dennis trucks featured an in-house-manufactured fibreglass cab. However, this was not acceptable in the Middle East due to concerns over fibreglass degradation in the high desert temperatures. A redesign was therefore carried out to fit a modified proprietary cab. This was sourced from Motor Panels in Coventry — themselves to become allied to Dennis via the Mayflower takeover some decades later. Notwithstanding the enforced buying-in of the cab, much manufacturing was still carried out in house in typical Dennis fashion, even the fuel and water tanks being rolled in Woodbridge Works.

It is easy to dismiss such high levels of in-house manufacture as a management whim. It was, however, fundamental in ensuring that Dennis could continue to manufacture vehicles to order within reasonable time frames without being at the mercy of suppliers who would invariably put Dennis's low-volume needs at the bottom of their build

One of hundreds of Deltas delivered to a Middle East country in 1977. DENNIS ARCHIVES

Ogle Design were brought in to provide styling input on the new steel cab; this is one of their proposals. GARY AVERY

schedules. Not only that, but these were the dark days of the British motor industry when it was all too frequently beset by industrial action, which often delayed deliveries even further, to the extent that Dennis probably regularly incurred penalty charges from customers. Indeed, the delays experienced with getting cabs from Motor Panels was a crucial driver in the subsequent decision to invest heavily in a new in-house-manufactured steel cab.

All the income – and profit – from the Middle East allowed the revitalized company to develop new modern products for the home market. By 1976, the company was well on the way to financial recovery, recording a turnover of £15 million and pre-tax profit of £1.5 million for the year. The Middle Eastern business also gained the company the Queens Award for Export in 1977 on the back of £12.7 million in exports that year, compared to only £500,000 five years earlier. In 1977, the company name changed yet again, this time to Hestair Dennis, in line with the parent company's naming policy for all of its subsidiaries.

RE-ENTRY INTO THE UK TRUCK MARKET

New Steel Cab

In the late 1970s, the European truck market was facing the introduction of ECE R29, legislation demanding specific frontal impact standards to be achieved. The trusty fibreglass cab was not going to comply with R29, so Dennis engineers developed a new steel cab.

Unlike the bought-in cab used as a stopgap on the Middle Eastern vehicles, this was entirely designed in house. The new cab made much use of simple folded steel panels with few costly pressings. This resulted in a total cost to develop the new cab, including the necessary jigs, spot welders, paint booths and stoving ovens, of under £1 million. (Compare this to the cost of at least £10 million incurred by Leyland, for example, in bringing their C40 cab range to market in the same era.) The new cab was engineered so expertly that there was no evidence of the lack of tooling in the cab's appearance, which was devised by respected design house Ogle. Indeed, the new cab bore more than a passing resemblance to the Leyland Ergomatic cab, which in contrast was of all-pressed components.

The new steel cab was produced with variants to suit the three main product ranges of trucks, municipal and fire vehicles. Manufacture of the cab initially took place at Guildford but was moved to the Duple factory at Blackpool around 1985.

The Delta 16 Series

The new range of trucks launched in 1980 and fitted with the new steel cab retained the name of Delta, but this time also identified as the 16 Series. This was Dennis's 'truck for the eighties', as it was described in its sales brochure. As ever, the company promoted heavily the almost bespoke nature of the product. The brochure invited the potential customer to 'choose the combination of performance and economical running which best suits your particular

DUPLE COACHBUILDERS OF BLACKPOOL

Duple Coachbuilders was a long-established company originally from Hornsey in London. As the business developed, it moved to a new site in Hendon, north London. Along the way, it took over several competitors, notably Willowbrook of Loughborough in 1958, followed by Burlingham of Blackpool in 1960. By 1968, most production was taking place at Blackpool, with the Hendon site finally closing in 1970. Although highly successful in the 1970s, most Duple products gradually became uncompetitive. By the time of the takeover by Hestair in 1983, Duple's losses for that financial year were estimated at around £1.4 million on a turnover of some £20 million.

The real reason that Hestair bought Duple was to acquire Duple Metsec. Duple had bought Metsec, a West Midlands company previously named Metal Sections, in the early 1980s. Metsec were makers of, unsurprisingly, metal sections, which they sold for general use. Spotting that some companies bought these sections to make bus body frames, Metsec had decided to develop their own body kits. These became quite successful in export markets, particularly Hong Kong. This was a market of growing importance to Hestair, to the extent that a fully staffed office was eventually set up in the territory as well as an extensive parts and service operation. The purchase of Duple Metsec reduced Hestair's dependency on sourcing bodies from Alexander, who traditionally worked closely with Hestair's closest competitor, Volvo. This relationship no doubt arose because the Volvo chassis plant at Irvine was close to Alexander's Falkirk operation, unlike the Guildford chassis factory, which was over 400 miles (650km) away.

DENNIS DELTA 1600 SERIES, 1980–1984

Configuration: 4×2 rigid ladder-frame forward-control truck chassis with steel cab
Engine: Perkins T6.354.4 6-cylinder turbocharged and intercooled diesel
Max. power: 155bhp at 2,600rpm
Max. torque: 365lb ft at 1,700rpm
or
Engine: Perkins V8-540 or V8-640 diesel
Gearbox: Eaton 542 5-speed manual
Rear axle: Eaton 1800 series single reduction, single speed; 2-speed optional
Suspension: Semi-elliptic, multi-leaf, with telescopic dampers
Wheelbase: 3,250–5,700mm (128–224.4in)
Overall width (cab): 2,489mm (98in)
Unladen weight (chassis): 4,945–5,140kg (10,902–11,332lb)
GVW: 16,260kg (35,847lb)
Top speed: 64mph (102km/h)
Price (1980): Chassis/cab: £14,795
(Source: *Truck* magazine, October 1980)

requirements.' It also urged the buyer to 'come to Guildford to discuss your requirements and see your vehicle being built to your specification.'

Unlike the earlier Delta, which was primarily for export, the new Delta 16 Series marked the return of Dennis to the

The Delta 1600 marked the return of Dennis to the UK truck market. BOB LOVELAND COLLECTION

mainstream UK truck market. The Delta was, however, never intended to compete directly with the relatively high-volume offerings of the major established producers. David Hargreaves, Hestair's chairman, was reported in *Truck* magazine in October 1980 as saying that 'the plans for the new truck put the production rate at between fifty and one hundred a year.' Not only that, every vehicle would be built to order, the usual lead time being quoted as eight weeks. As he told *Truck* magazine, 'Unlike the volume producers we never have a vehicle on the line for which there is not already a customer.'

Respected commercial vehicle journalist Pat Kennett tested the Delta 1600 Series, writing in *Truck* magazine in October 1980 that 'cab furnishing is of a high order, certainly up to the standard of the newly popular deluxe four-wheelers,' and that it was 'an impressive vehicle to drive' and 'from a maintenance point of view, just about the best in the class'. Praise indeed, particularly when the same edition of the magazine reported on a competitive European 16-tonner, the Magirus 168M, finding during their test that 'the truck's gear lever broke' and 'the mirrors collapse along the sides of the cab at motorway speeds'!

FIRE APPLIANCE DEVELOPMENTS

The RS/SS

In 1979, the RS (Retained, Steel) range was introduced featuring both the new steel cab and a new, stiffer, chassis.

The RS/SS range was introduced in 1980; this is a copy of the specification sheet at that time. AUTHOR

This SS was used by Gulf Oil at their Milford Haven plant from the early 1980s. BOB LOVELAND COLLECTION

DENNIS RS/SS, 1979–

Layout and Chassis
4×2 rigid ladder-frame fire appliance chassis
Engine
Type: Perkins V8-540
Cylinders: V8
Cooling: Water
Bore and stroke: 108 × 120.7mm
Capacity: 8840cc
Max. power: 180bhp (134kW) at 2,600rpm
or
Type: Perkins TV8-540
Max. power: 215bhp (160kW) or 240bhp at 2,600rpm
or
Type: Perkins V8-640
Bore and stroke: 117.6 × 120.7mm
Capacity: 10480cc
Max. power: 215bhp (160kW) at 2,600rpm
or
Type: Perkins T6.354.4
Capacity: 5800cc
Cylinders: 6 in-line
Bore and stroke: 98 × 127mm
Max. power: 159bhp (119kW)
or
Type: Perkins Phaser
Capacity: 6000cc
Cylinders: 6 in-line
Bore and stroke: 100 × 127mm

Max. power: 180bhp (134kW) or 210bhp (157kW)
or
Type: Cummins 6CT/6CTA
Cylinders: 6 in-line
Capacity: 8270cc
Bore and stroke: 114 × 135mm
Max. power: 211bhp (157kW) or 240bhp (179kW)
Transmission
Gearbox: Turner T5-400 5-speed manual or ZF S6-65 manual
or Allison MT643 automatic or ZF 5HP500 automatic
Final drive: Eaton
Suspension and Steering
Front and rear: Semi-elliptic steel springs, telescopic dampers
Brakes: Full air
Cab: All steel, 6–8 crew capacity, front tilt or fixed double
Dimensions
Wheelbase: 149.6in (3,800mm)
Overall length (body): 288.75in (7,334mm)
Overall width: 90in (2,286mm)
Overall height: 121in (3,072mm) to top of ladder
GVW (max.): 25,749lb (11,700kg)
Fire Equipment
Pump: Godiva 500–1,000gal/min (2,275–4,550ltr/min) output
Emergency water tank: 400gal (1,820ltr)
(Source: Dennis fire range brochure and operator's handbook, publication No. 1839, *c.*1983)

Unusually for the era, it had a fixed cab rather than the tilt cab, which was then in vogue. This was not Dennis being slow to respond to market forces; it was because fire sales believed that few fire stations had the headroom to tilt an extended crew cab.

Later, a lower-cost vehicle was also developed, intended to have fewer options and therefore called the 'Standard Specification' or SS. After the SS was presented to London Fire Brigade, they placed a large order but stipulated a tilt cab. This was then added to the SS specification to match competitive practice. To address the headroom issues, only the front portion of the cab tilted.

The folded-steel-sheet construction of the cab endowed it with excellent strength, an important feature, since fire appliances, inevitably, are sometimes involved in serious collisions. Indeed, sales literature of the time included photographs of one appliance on its roof following a crash, with the cab structure completely intact having protected the crew very effectively. Small wonder that the firefighters preferred Dennises!

Both RS and SS models offered anti-lock brakes for the first time, using the Girling Skidcheck system more commonly seen on high-performance cars.

By this time, diesel engine performance had advanced to such a level that petrol engines were generally no longer specified. The RS initially used the Perkins V8 diesel, but from 1987 a new option was offered, the 8.3-litre Cummins C-series, rated at 240bhp.

Most vehicles were 4×2s, although some export customers took three-axle vehicles.

The RS/SS range was nothing if not versatile. Depending on the users' requirements, pumps from 500gal/min (2,275ltr/min) to 1,000 gal/min (4,550ltr/min) could be fitted to a typical water tender. The model was also available as a pump escape, a foam or emergency tender or even a control centre.

RS and SS models were the cornerstones of the fire appliance range. Dimensionally, the two models were identical, and with a gross vehicle weight of only 11.5 tons (11,700kg), their performance was impressive. They were deservedly popular with the fire brigades not only in the UK but around the world, enjoying a sixteen-year production run of over 1,750 vehicles.

The DF

For applications where a higher gross weight was needed, Dennis offered the DF. Sharing the same cab and engine power options of the RS/SS range, the DF had a GVW of 16 tons (16,260kg). It was slightly wider than the RS/SS range, at 8ft (2.44m), and was intended primarily for specialist bodies such as foam tenders carrying up to 1,500gal (6,800ltr) or a range of hydraulic platforms and turntable ladders.

The Firebird variant carried up to 1,000gal (4,550ltr) of water, while the Waterbird carried even more water, at 1,800gal (8,200ltr). The DF was particularly popular with overseas customers, including buyers in Hong Kong, Brunei, Abu Dhabi and Kenya.

DENNIS DF, 1979–

As Dennis RS/SS with the following exceptions:

Water capacity: Firebird model: up to 1,000gal
   (4,550ltr)
Waterbird model: up to 1,800gal (8,200ltr)
Foam capacity: Foam tender: up to 1,500gal (6,820ltr)
Wheelbase: 150–210in (3,810–5,334mm)
Overall width: 97.25in (2,472mm)
Overall height (over cab): 104in (2,640mm)
GVW: 35,847lb (16,260kg)
Unladen weight (chassis): 4,945–5,140kg (10,902–11,332lb)
GVW: 16,260kg (35,847lb)
Top speed: 64mph (102km/h)
Price (1980): Chassis/cab: £14,795
(Source: *Truck* magazine, October 1980)

The DS

To meet the needs of brigades operating in restricted locations, the company offered the DS. With a GVW of only 13.3 tons (13,500kg) and a narrow width of only 7ft (2.13m), 6in (150mm) less than the RS/SS, this compact appliance still managed to package a tilt cab for up to eight firefighters, a 400gal (1,800ltr) water tank and a 500gal/min (2,275ltr/min) pump.

DENNIS DS, 1979–

As Dennis RS/SS with the following exceptions:

Pump: 500gal/min (2,275ltr/min)
Emergency water tank: 400gal (1,820ltr)
Wheelbase: 130in (3,280mm)
Overall length (body): 261.25in (6,636mm)
Overall width: 84in (2,134mm)
Overall height (over cab): 101in (2,565mm)
GVW (max.): 21,826lb (9,900kg)
(source: Dennis fire range brochure, *c*.1979)

The F127

Completing the range was the F127 chassis, launched in 1984. It was a dedicated low-profile chassis-cab to accommodate aerial equipment such as turntable ladders and hydraulic platforms. At only 7ft 9in (2.36m) high, it was almost 12in (300mm) lower than the DF. The low cab height was achieved by designing a special three-person version of the steel cab, which was set forward of the front axle. Overall dimensions were 8ft 2in (2.49m) wide and 31ft (9.5m) in length.

BACK TO BUSES

The Dominator

In 1975, with the Iraq tanker contract coming to an end, something was needed in its place. Dennis management, and particularly the managing director, John Smith, felt the time was right to re-enter the bus business after a break of almost a decade. At that time, British Leyland, while dominant in the market, were intent on forcing their standard products, the Leyland National single-deck and Titan double-deck, onto customers. This did not sit well with traditionally conservative bus operators. The popular Daimler Fleetline had just gone out of production, and the bus industry was, therefore, seeking an alternative rear-engined double-decker.

To investigate this market opportunity, Dennis purchased a sixteen-year-old Daimler double-decker from West Yorkshire PTE, replacing the engine with a Gardner 6LXB and the transmission with a Voith fully automatic unit. This 'mule' was then given to various operators for evaluation, the first being Leicester City Transport in January 1976, where Geoffrey Hilditch was the youngest-ever general manager of a bus company. Mr Hilditch was the ultimate 'hands-on' manager, who delighted in experiencing his fleet from behind the steering wheel. He was no lover of British Leyland or their products, and by contrast, had rated the Dennis Loline as one of the best-engineered buses, putting his money firmly in the same location as his mouth by taking a large number. This included the last five Lolines from the production line.

The feedback gained from the test bus, dubbed the 'clockwork orange' as it remained in its West Yorkshire livery, duly resulted in the launch by Dennis in August 1977 of the Dominator. Among the first customers was Mr Hilditch and his Leicester operation, who took a total of 143 Dominators over the years, the last still being in service as late as 2005.

The principal drivetrain for the Dominator was the Gardner 6LXB 180bhp engine mounted transversely at the rear, coupled to a Voith DIWA transmission and drop-centre rear axle. Later, several alternative engines were also offered, such as the Gardner 6LXCT, Cummins L10, and Rolls-Royce Eagle 220bhp 6-cylinder. Two wheelbases were offered to suit body lengths from 28ft (8.5m) to 36ft (11m).

THE MAXWELL TRANSMISSION

Some Dominators were fitted with the innovative UK-designed and manufactured Maxwell automatic gearbox, which had several significant benefits to both the manufacturer and operator. Its inherent flexibility made it easier to install in a range of drivetrain configurations than most competitive transmissions, and in the case of the Dominator simplified maintenance by removing the need for an angle drive.

A further maintenance benefit was the ability to quickly change clutch packs, always a slow task requiring transmission removal. In the case of the Maxwell transmission, however, a clutch pack could be replaced in under four minutes with the gearbox still in situ. The Maxwell transmission also had weight advantages, being over 300lb (150kg) lighter than the Dominator's alternative Voith transmission plus Dennis angle drive.

Despite the maintenance and packaging benefits, however, the transmissions gained a reputation for unreliability, leading the manufacturer to abandon the project.

This 1977 photo is of Leicester's first Dominator. DENNIS ARCHIVES

DENNIS DOMINATOR, 1977–1996

Layout and Chassis
4×2 rigid rear-engined welded steel-fabricated chassis for double- and single-deck 8.5m–11m bus bodywork
Engine
Type: Gardner 6LXB diesel
Block material: Cast iron
Head material: Cast iron
Cylinders: 6 in-line
Cooling: Water
Bore and stroke: 120.6 × 152.4mm
Capacity: 10450cc
Compression ratio: 14.14:1
Max. power: 188bhp (140.2kW) at 1,850rpm
Max. torque: 562lb ft (762Nm) at 1,000rpm
or
Type: Rolls-Royce Eagle 220 diesel
Cylinders: 6 in-line
Max. power: 180bhp (134kW) at 1,850rpm
Max. torque: 580lb ft (800Nm) at 1,050rpm
or
Type: DAF DK 1160V diesel
Cylinders: 6 in-line
Max. power: 180bhp (134kW) at 1,850rpm
Max. torque: 531lb ft (720Nm) at 1,400rpm
Fuel capacity: 227ltr (50gal)
Transmission
Gearbox: Voith D851 3-speed or D854 4-speed automatic with integral retarder
or Maxwell 4-speed automatic with integral retarder and built-in bevel box:

Transfer box: Drive from gearbox via helical-geared transfer box to a right-angle spiral-bevel box
Final drive: Standard height model: GKN D65 (later D66) 10.8-ton (10,970kg) capacity straight beam offset-drive hub-reduction axle
Low-height model: Dennis 10-ton (10,170kg) capacity drop-centre double reduction
Suspension and Steering
Front: Semi-elliptic leaf springs 50in (1,270mm) long, with piston-type dampers or full air suspension
Rear: Semi-elliptic leaf springs 62in (1,575mm) long, with telescopic dampers or full air suspension
Steering: Integral power
Tyres: 11R × 22.5
Wheels: 7.5 × 22.5
Brakes
Type: Full air-operated drum brakes, Girling twin wedge
Size: 394mm (15.5in) diameter
Dimensions
Track: 2,095mm (82.5in) front, 1,829mm (72in) rear
Wheelbase: 9.6m body: 4,953mm (195in)
    10.3m body: 5,639mm (222in)
Overall length (body): 8,500–11,000mm (334.6–433in)
Overall width: 2,500mm (98.4in)
Unladen weight (chassis): 6,180–6,540kg (13,625–14,418lb)
GVW (max.): 16,260kg (35,847lb), later 16,800kg (37,037lb)
Performance
Top speed: 43mph (69km/h) approx.
(Source: Dennis Dominator brochures and data sheets)

One Dominator from the South Yorkshire fleet had the distinction of being probably the first double-decker to be fitted with Girling Skidcheck antilock braking. This much impressed operators and trade press alike when it was demonstrated at a Dennis test day in 1981.

Right from the start, the Dominator was marketed as either a double- or single-decker, with wheelbases to suit. The single-deckers were less popular than the double-deckers, selling mainly to Darlington and Hartlepool corporations, who between them took around thirty.

Despite the proliferation of variants offered, Dennis had only limited success in re-establishing a niche in the UK bus market with the Dominator. They were popular with some municipal operators such as Leicester, but there was lim-

ited success in breaking into the larger passenger transport executives, with the notable exception of South Yorkshire. To put this into perspective, the average annual production of Dominator was around 100, against about 400 a year for the Leyland Olympian.

The modest success of the Dominator against well-established competitors was repeated in the coming years with other 'me-too' products produced by the company. Dennis bus and coach products really only came to the fore when they offered unique benefits that could not be obtained from rival and more established manufacturers.

One notable Dominator was produced as a trolleybus and shown at the 1984 Commercial Vehicle Show before entering trials with South Yorkshire PTE. It was powered

The 1977 introduction of the Dominator brought Dennis once again into the PSV world. This extract from a contemporary brochure shows the low chassis and rear 'pod'. BOB LOVELAND COLLECTION

One of Leicester's first Dominator chassis about to leave Woodbridge Works in 1977 en route to the bodybuilders. DENNIS ARCHIVES

by 600 volt overhead electric lines but also had a diesel engine driving an alternator to allow it to be operated 'off the wires'. This intriguing hybrid was hoped to be the precursor to more general reintroduction of trolleybuses into the UK, the last of the traditional trolleybuses having ceased operating in 1972. A 1-mile (2km) private test track

THE DENNIS DOMINATOR

A new dimension in durability

This Dominator brochure dates from 1981. BOB LOVELAND COLLECTION

What better way for Dennis to turn up to Downing Street to collect their 1977 Queen's Award for Export than in a Dominator? DENNIS ARCHIVES

The Jubilant was launched in 1978, proving highly successful in the difficult operating environment of Hong Kong. DANNY CHAN

was set up near Doncaster racecourse, with testing starting in July 1985. However, the project never got beyond this initial testing stage, and the sole test vehicle lay idle for some years before being passed to the Sandtoft Trolleybus Museum.

Overall, 970 double-deck and 37 single-deck Dominators were built, the last single-deck in 1980, with the double-deck continuing until 1996.

The Jubilant

The front-engined Jubilant double-decker was launched in 1978 and was developed specifically for Hong Kong. This was then effectively a new market for Dennis but one that was to play a significant role in the company's future, as the Jubilant became a great success in this notoriously arduous location. It had a vertical front-mounted Gardner 6LXB engine, with either a Voith three-speed fully automatic

Jubilants are still in Hong Kong over forty years later, as this picture taken at a March 2019 bus rally demonstrates.
PAUL BROMLEY

The first four Jubilant front-engined bus chassis are shown here being despatched to the bodybuilder in 1977, before being shipped to Hong Kong. DENNIS ARCHIVES

DENNIS JUBILANT, 1978–1982

Engine: Gardner 6LXB
Max. power: 180bhp (134kW)
or
Engine: Mercedes Benz 407
Max. power: 233bhp (174kW)
Gearbox: Voith DIWA D851
Wheelbase: 4,800mm (189in)
(Source: Dennis bus brochure, 1981)

transmission or four- or five-speed semi-automatic units from Self-Changing Gears Ltd.

Production ceased in 1982, after a total of 395 had been built, many with bodies from Duple Metsec.

The Condor and Dragon

Eventually, larger overseas chassis were also produced: the Condor and Dragon, launched in 1982, were 6×2 22-ton (22,350kg) chassis derived from the Dominator design and

capable of carrying 128-seat bodywork. Sales were substantial, with over 1,000 being in operation with KMB alone by 1992. Indeed, the level of Hong Kong business helped Dennis to survive a significant downturn in the UK bus market in the 1980s. Dragon and Condor, which were identical vehicles, the name differing only at the request of their operators, remained in production until 1999, when they were replaced by the low-floor Trident 3.

Later vehicles were fitted with full air-conditioning, a welcome feature in Hong Kong's hot and humid climate.

A small number of Dragons were also sold into Africa: ten to Malawi and twenty to Kenya, many of which eventually returned for further service in the UK.

Altogether, 1,650 Dragons and Condors had been built, before production ended in 1999.

Dennis Dragons and Condors performed sterling service for many years in the arduous conditions of Hong Kong, latterly equipped with welcome air-conditioning, unlike this 1982 example. Note the typical Hong Kong bamboo scaffolding in the background. DANNY CHAN

Rivalry between Hong Kong operators extended to not wishing to operate vehicles of the same name, hence China Motor Bus took their three-axle deckers as Condors, while KMB called theirs Dragons. The number of passengers on this air-conditioned Condor is not unusual at peak hours! DANNY CHAN

DENNIS DRAGON/ CONDOR, 1982–1999

Configuration: 6×2 rigid welded-frame rear-engined double-deck bus chassis for 10m–12m body lengths
Engine: Cummins LT10 or LTA10
or Gardner 6LXC or 6LXCT
or Cummins L10
Gearbox: Voith D851 or ZF 4HP500 automatic
Suspension: Semi-elliptic leaf springs or full air
Wheelbases: 5,926mm (233.3in)
    6,726mm (264.8in)
Overall lengths (bodied): 11,000mm (433in)
    12,000mm (472.4in)
Overall width: 2,500mm (98.4in)
Unladen weight (chassis): 8,400–8,470kg (18,519–18,673lb)
GVW (max.): 23,000kg (50,706lb)
Capacity: up to 120 seats (some 3+2 configuration) plus 50 standees
(Source: Dennis Dragon data sheet)

export. It had a high-floor bolted-construction straight frame, with either a vertical front- or mid-mounted engine, the potential options for which included the Perkins 6.354, Gardner 6LXB and ADE 407 or 409. The last two – Atlantis Diesel Engines – were designed by Mercedes and built in South Africa, and were effectively a mandatory fitment in vehicles destined for South Africa. Transmissions were by ZF, Voith, Allison or Self-Changing Gears, while the suspension used 'extra-heavy-duty' leaf springs. Weightwise,

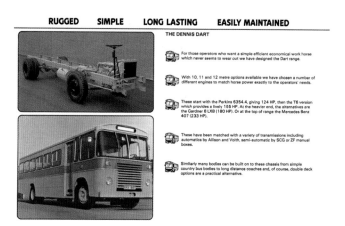

The Dart
One little-known model launched in 1978 resurrected the Dart name and was a simple, rugged chassis intended for

This brochure describes the export Dart, which appeared in 1978. Most were built in South Africa, but this example ended up with the West Midlands Fire Service. RICHARD NORMAN

DENNIS DART EXPORT CHASSIS, 1978–

Engine: Perkins 6.354.4 or T6.354.4,
or Gardner 6LXB
or Mercedes 407 or 409 (ADE engines)
Gearbox: ZF manual, Allison, Voith or SCG
Lengths: 10,000mm (393.7in)
    11,000mm (433in)
    12,000mm (472.4in)
(Source: Dennis bus brochure, 1981)

16-tonne (15.7-ton) and 18-tonne (17.7-ton) versions were offered.

Dennis had a joint venture operation in South Africa, where Darts were assembled from UK-supplied kits with ADE engines and fitted with local Busan bodies. The joint venture foundered when the substantial devaluation of the local currency, the rand, made the business unprofitable.

The Lancet

Another old name, Lancet, was resurrected in 1981. This came about as a result of earlier success in selling refuse-collection vehicles to Maidstone Corporation, previously a

Bedford user. Maidstone Corporation ran a fleet of Bedford buses and wanted to retain commonality of parts with their new dustcarts, so persuaded Dennis to produce a Bedford bus lookalike. The resulting vehicle was suitably basic, with leaf springs and a Wadham Stringer Vanguard body, but was competitively priced at £22,592 for a Perkins T6-354 engine, ZF gearbox variant. Ironically, in the end Maidstone never actually bought any Lancets. However, Dennis went on to produce them for other customers, with a

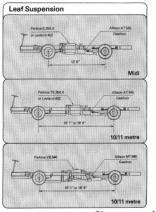
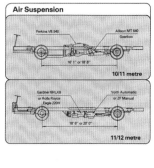

Choose your Lancet and win.

The Lancet was available in a host of different guises, although none was really successful. RICHARD NORMAN

The 1981 Lancet was intended as a competitor to Bedford and Ford lightweight buses, but never really broke into that market, selling less than 100 in almost a decade. BOB LOVELAND COLLECTION

DENNIS LANCET, 1981–1990

Layout and Chassis
4×2 rigid ladder-frame mid-engined chassis

Engine
Type: Perkins T6.354.4 6-cylinder turbocharged diesel
Capacity: 5800cc
Bore and stroke: 98.4 × 127mm
Max. power (DIN): 145bhp (108kW) at 2,600rpm
Max. torque: 367lb ft (498Nm) at 1,450rpm
or
Type: Perkins 6.354.4 6-cylinder turbocharged diesel
(standard on 3,800mm w/b)
Capacity: 5800cc
Bore and stroke: 98.4 × 127mm
Max. power: 124bhp (92.4kW) at 2,800rpm
Max. torque: 270lb ft (366Nm) at 1,300rpm
or
Type: Leyland 402 6-cylinder turbocharged diesel
Max. power: 140bhp (104.4kW) at 2,600rpm
Max. torque: 310lb ft (420Nm) at 1,600rpm
or
Type: Cummins 6BT 5.9 6-cylinder turbocharged
diesel
Max. power: 160bhp (119kW) at 2,500rpm
Max. torque: 394lb ft (534Nm) at 1,700rpm
or
Type: Perkins V8-540 diesel
Max. power: 163bhp (121.5kW) at 2,200rpm
Max. torque: 410lb ft (556Nm) at 1,700rpm
or
Type: Rolls-Royce Eagle 220H diesel
Fuel capacity: 227ltr (50gal)

Transmission
Gearbox: Allison AT545 or MT 643 automatic
or Voith automatic
or ZF HP500 automatic
or ZF6-80 6-speed or Eaton manual
Retarder: Telma and Ferodo options
Final drive: Single-reduction spiral bevel; 2-speed optional

Suspension and Steering
Front and rear: Semi-elliptic multi-leaf or full air
Steering: ZF integral power
Tyres: 10R × 22.5
Wheels: 10-stud 6.75 × 22.5 steel rims; single front, twin
rear

Brakes
Type: Full air S-cam drums, spring parking brake
Size: 394mm (15.5in) diameter

Dimensions
Track: 2,094mm (82.4in) front, 1,810mm (71.25in) rear
Wheelbases: 3,860mm (152in)
    4,902mm (193in)
    5,639mm (222in)
    6,096mm (240in)
Overall length (bodied): 9,000–12,000mm (354.3–
472.4in)
Overall width: 2,500mm (98.4in); 2,286mm (90in)
optional
Unladen weights: 3,925–4,210kg (8,653–9,281lb)
Gross weights: 11,000kg (24,250lb)
    13,000kg (28,660lb)
    16,000kg (35,274lb)

Price
Chassis (1983): £22,592
(Source: Dennis Lancet brochure and data sheet, *c*.1981)

wide variety of options, including engines from Perkins and Leyland. Gardner and Rolls-Royce installations were also engineered but never fitted. Power ratings from 92kW to 134kW (120–180bhp), manual or automatic transmissions from Allison, Voith and ZF, leaf spring or air suspension, alternative radiator positions and 13-tonne (12.8-ton) and 16-tonne (15.7-ton) GVW ratings were all offered.

Bodies were built by several companies, including Jonkheere and Van Hool, some of which formed the basis of special-purpose vehicles such as mobile libraries. However, the Lancet was up against established competition, particularly from the Bedford YMQ range, limiting sales. As a result, Lancet production ceased in 1990 after only

ninety-two had been sold, several of which were exported to customers in Bermuda and Cape Town.

The Dorchester

In the early 1980s, Dennis were approached by the Scottish Bus Group, previously a loyal Leyland user, who were seeking a heavyweight coach chassis fitted with the 10.45-litre Gardner 6HLXCT engine. This was a package Leyland did not wish to supply, preferring to fit their own TL11 engine to their popular heavyweight Tiger coach. The resulting product was the Dennis Dorchester, a single-deck coach and bus chassis. One unusual feature of the Dorchester was

This photo shows the Tillingbourne Lancet undergoing tilt testing. RICHARD NORMAN

that the right-hand chassis rail was in two sections, with the front portion of the rear section cranked outwards to provide space for the big horizontal Gardner engine.

The Dorchester was offered with a vast range of options including transmissions from ZF, Voith and Self-Changing Gears, although the last option was never fitted. Air suspension was standard; a leaf spring installation was designed but found no takers. The model was also offered with low- and high-floor body options, three overall lengths to suit bodies 10m, 11m and 12m (32ft 8in, 36ft and 39ft) long with bus and coach options, as well as left- or right-hand drive.

Dennis introduced the Dorchester at the 1982 NEC Show and subsequently held roadshows around the UK. These displayed both an unbodied Dorchester chassis and a Berkhof-bodied Dorchester demonstrator as well as one of the Western Scottish Plaxton Paramount 3200-bodied vehicles. As well as Plaxton and Berkhof, potential body-builders included Alexander's, Wadham Stringers, Reeve Burgess and Caetano. Duple was reportedly reluctant to

DENNIS DORCHESTER, 1982–1988

Layout and Chassis
4×2 rigid ladder-frame chassis with horizontal Gardner engine and air suspension, for 10m, 11m or 12m bodywork

Engine
Type: Horizontal Gardner 6HLXCT turbocharged diesel
Cooling: Water, hydraulic fan drive
Bore and stroke: 120.6 × 152.4mm
Capacity: 10450cc
Max. power: 230bhp (171.5kW) at 1,900rpm
Max. torque: 673lb ft (915Nm) at 1,400rpm
or
Type: Rolls-Royce Eagle, Gardner 6HLXB
Fuel capacity: 363ltr (80gal)

Transmission
Gearbox options: ZF S6.80 6-speed manual
or SCG GB300 4- or 5-speed semi-automatic pneumocyclic
or SCG GB400 GB 4- or-5-speed semi- or fully automatic hydrocyclic with integral retarder
or Voith D851 3-speed or D854 4-speed automatic with integral retarder
Final drive: Single-reduction spiral bevel

Suspension and Steering
Front: Full air with 2 airbags, anti-roll bar and 2 telescopic dampers
Rear: H-frame located by 2 parabolic leaf springs with 4

airbags and 4 telescopic dampers
Steering: ZF integral power
Tyres: 295/80R × 22.5 or 11R × 22.5
Wheels: Spigot-mounted

Brakes
Type: Full air-operated S-cam drum brakes, spring-operated parking brake
Size: 394mm (15.5in) diameter
Retarder: Telma, Voith and Ferodo options

Dimensions
Track: 2,056mm (81in) front, 1,842mm (72.5in) rear
Wheelbases: 4,953mm (195in)
    5,639mm (222in)
    6,096mm (240in)
Overall lengths (bodied): 10,000mm (393.7in)
    11,000mm (433in)
    12,000mm (472.4in)
Overall width (chassis): 2,486mm (98in)
GVW (max.): 16,260kg (35,847lb)

Performance
Top speed: 75mph (120km/h) approx.

Price
Chassis (1983): £34,700
(Sources: Dorchester brochures and specification sheets, 1982)

The World Famous Dorchester

The Dorchester

DENNIS

DD 230

The name says it all....

The brochure for the 1983 Dorchester clearly relied heavily on the implied association with the upmarket hotel of the same name. RICHARD NORMAN

body the Dorchester chassis, but were left with little option when they were bought by Dennis's parent company, Hestair, in June 1983. Nevertheless, only five Dorchester chassis ever went to Blackpool to be bodied by Duple.

The Western Scottish wing of the Scottish Bus Group took their first eight Plaxton Paramount 3200-bodied

The Dorchester chassis was unusual in having a two-piece right-hand sidemember. RICHARD NORMAN

Dorchesters in March 1983. Despite their earlier pressure on Dennis to produce the Dorchester, the only other company within the Scottish Bus Group to take the model was Central Scottish Motor Traction. Several independents operated Dorchesters, including Tillingbourne from Cranleigh, who took two Wadham Stringer bus-bodied vehicles. Only one Dorchester was exported; this went to Rand Coach Tours in South Africa.

The fate of the Dorchester range was sealed when Leyland Bus, realizing their error of omission, quickly introduced a Gardner-engined Tiger chassis, pricing it below the Dorchester. Leyland, of course, benefited from a reliable dealer network; the lack of a Dennis network had always been an area of concern for operators, who traditionally buy from dealers rather than directly from the manufacturer. This is not least because most dealers take their customers' older vehicles in part-exchange for new replacements. Dennis tried to persuade several dealers to stock their chassis. However, the main chassis suppliers of the time – Leyland and Bedford – guarded their dealers jealously, threatening to withdraw their support from any dealer who dared to handle any new Dennis chassis. This issue continued to hamper Dennis coach sales until Bedford's demise left one dealer group, Yeates, without a manufacturer, allowing Dennis a sales outlet for the first time.

Dorchester production finally ceased in 1988, with only sixty-seven finding homes.

The Falcon

In 1981, the Dominator was followed by a close derivative, the Falcon. This was intended primarily for bus use, although some express coaches were produced, as were a few double-deckers. Dennis hoped it would replace the sturdy and efficient rear-engined Bristol RE chassis, which had recently been dropped by Leyland.

With typical Dennis ingenuity, the front half of the Falcon H chassis was almost identical to that of the Dominator. The rear frame, however, was upswept over the rear axle, featuring a complex drive arrangement to minimize the rear overhang resulting from the longitudinally mounted horizontal Gardner 6HLXB engine. This took the drive

DENNIS FALCON H, 1981–1993

Configuration: 4×2 rigid ladder-frame chassis with rear-mounted horizontal engine for single- and double-deck bus and coach applications
Engine: Gardner 6HLXB 6-cylinder diesel
Max. power: 170bhp (126.8kW) at 1,850rpm
Max. torque: 536lb ft (727Nm) at 1,000rpm
or
Engine: Rolls-Royce Eagle 220H 6-cylinder diesel
Max. power: 180bhp (134kW) at 1,850rpm
Max. torque: 590lb ft (800Nm) at 1,050rpm
Gearbox: Voith D851 3-speed or D854 4-speed automatic with integral retarder
or Self-Changing Gears RV68 4- or 5-speed semi-automatic with integral transfer gears
Final drive: Helically geared transfer box from gearbox
Dennis 10-ton (10,160kg) drop-centre double reduction axle
or Eaton 18000 single reduction
Suspension: Semi-elliptic multi-leaf springs with piston/telescopic dampers
or Full air with telescopic dampers
Wheelbase: 4,953mm (195in)
5,639mm (222in)
Overall length (chassis): 9,533mm (375.25in)
10,219mm (402.3in)
Overall width: 2,500mm (98.4in)
Unladen weight (chassis): 5,890–6,250kg (12,985–13,779lb)
Gross weight (max.): 16,260kg (35,847lb)
(Source: Dennis Falcon H data sheets)

DENNIS FALCON V, 1981–1993

Configuration: 4×2 rigid ladder-frame chassis with rear-mounted vertical engine for single- and double-deck bus and coach applications
Engine: Perkins TV8.640 V8 turbocharged diesel
Max. power: 260bhp (194kW) at 2,400rpm
or
Engine: Perkins V8.640
Capacity: 10450cc
Max. power: 215bhp (160kW) or 206bhp (154kW)
or
Engine: Mercedes OM 421 V6
Max. power: 188bhp (140kW)
Gearbox: Voith D854 4-speed or D851 3-speed automatic gearbox with integral retarder
or ZF S6.80 or ZF S6.90 6-speed manual synchromesh gearboxes
Rear axle: Eaton 23000 Series
Suspension: Full air, with telescopic dampers
(Source: Dennis Falcon data sheets)

from the engine, over the top of the Eaton rear axle and into a Voith transmission and then, via a transfer box, back into the rear axle input flange.

The driveline was simplified in the later HC model, with the Voith D851 three-speed automatic transmission being coupled directly to the same Gardner engine. The output was then taken via a short propeller shaft directly into an Eaton single-reduction rear axle. This then meant all major components were shared with the Dominator double-decker chassis, simplifying maintenance requirements.

Subsequently, the Falcon V was introduced, the V denoting its vertical engine installation. Double-deckers used Mercedes-Benz V6 OM 421 engines, with a Perkins V8 engine in the coach version. At that time, the concept of timetabled express countrywide inter-urban coach services under the National Express banner was growing. National Express had a high-specification operation, Rapide, and as a nationalized operation were keen to use British-built coaches for this high-profile service, approaching Dennis to request a suitable vehicle. National Express demands were high, for they wanted to see this coach in service within months. Dennis rose to the challenge and very quickly designed a 12m (39ft 4in) chassis based on the Falcon to meet the Rapide specification. This Falcon V Rapide chassis featured a 260bhp (194kW) turbocharged Perkins TV8-640 engine

RAPIDE WOES

The first two Falcon V Rapide coaches were handed over to National Express in September 1982, entering service with Western National. To meet the unrealistically tight timetable demanded by the customer, the Falcon Rapides came straight off the drawing board with virtually no testing before they entered service. Unsurprisingly, several problems surfaced in operation, including overheating and fuel starvation. Structural issues were also experienced with the Goldliner body, which, probably because it was designed for a mid- rather than rear-engined chassis, experienced distortion at the front. This resulted in the power-operated plug door opening inadvertently, in turn activating the interlock on the accelerator and bringing the vehicle to a halt.

The Perkins V8 engine had the fuel system nestled between the two arms of the V, an arrangement that was liable to lead to fuel being sprayed onto the hot turbocharger in the event of a fuel system leak. Exacerbated by the inevitably higher under-bonnet temperatures experienced in a rear-engined coach as compared to a front-engined truck, this was probably responsible for several fires on Falcon Rapides. Such events did little to enamour the Falcon Rapide to the operators who ran National Express services – in fact, National Express withdrew all their Falcon Rapides during 1985 after only three years in service.

mounted vertically at the rear, mated to a Voith D854 fully automatic four-speed gearbox. A front-mounted radiator was fitted, as was full air suspension. In this specification, a Falcon V Rapide was priced at £42,090 at a time when the Dorchester chassis cost £34,700. The Rapide chassis was bodied with a version of the Duple 'Super Goldliner' bodywork.

Falcons were built between 1981 and 1993, sales totalling around 120. This low sales volume demonstrated once again how Dennis was unable to make significant inroads into the bus and coach market with copycat products lacking any real reason for operators to pick them over tried and tested brands.

The Domino

In the mid-1970s Greater Manchester Passenger Transport Executive operated several Seddon midibuses, which were used to provide a shuttle service between the city's Piccadilly and Victoria railway stations, their small size and excellent manoeuvrability being particularly valued. The Seddon Pennine 4 midibus was a 25/27-seater, built to big-bus standards, but Seddon bus production had ceased in 1983, leaving Manchester unable to replace their ageing fleet.

Knowing Dennis's reputation for the production of robust, reliable vehicles, Greater Manchester PTE approached the Guildford firm with a view to them producing a replacement for their Seddons. Sensing an opportunity, David Hargreaves, Dennis's managing director, agreed to do so, but only if Manchester would order at least

fifty. In the event, Manchester purchased only twenty, with a further fourteen going to South Yorkshire PTE before production ceased in 1985.

In truth, the Domino, with its heavy Dominator-derived chassis frame, Perkins 6.354 engine, Maxwell transmission, big 22.5in wheels and air suspension, was probably just not an attractive proposition to a marketplace by then facing the prospect of deregulation.

The 425 Integral Coach

When Duple were designing their high-floor Caribbean coach body, they realized that the market was moving towards rear-engined high-floor integral coaches, built by the likes of Neoplan, Bova and Setra. They knew that they needed to develop their own integral coach, but were concerned at the cost of designing and developing their own running gear. The company therefore approached German manufacturer Neoplan, who at the time were keen to break into the UK market. A deal was agreed whereby Neoplan would supply Duple with a Neoplan Cityliner underframe on which to develop their new body. Duple would then take twenty-five Neoplan underframes in the first year, building up subsequently to fifty per year.

A Cityliner underframe was duly delivered to Duple towards the end of 1982, with Duple completing the prototype Caribbean Integral by the spring of 1983, showing it both at the Brighton and Blackpool coach rallies. No further progress was made with the project, however, not least because in mid-1983 Hestair announced their purchase of Duple.

This Duple 320 coach was Dennis's first experimental Cummins engine installation. The original Mercedes engine was removed and a Cummins L10 substituted. The experience gained with this 'mule' installation was instrumental in Dennis selecting the Cummins C-series as the Javelin power unit.
RICHARD NORMAN

At this time, Cummins was almost unknown in the UK bus and coach industry, and the relatively staid industry looked on the firm with some suspicion. This was despite the corporate Cummins publicity machine spending heavily on promotion, taking potential customers to visit the parent US plant, and offering free engines for trial. Dennis engineers, however, felt that Cummins engines were worthy of further investigation, and eventually the Mercedes engine was removed from the prototype Duple integral coach and a Cummins L10 power unit installed for evaluation.

The experience gained with this L10 mule led to the decision in 1984 to develop a high-spec, high-power integral coach, which duly became the iconic Duple 425 model; the number 425 referring to the drag coefficient of the body, which was the result of much wind tunnel testing.

Duple was responsible for the 425's body design, with the Dennis team looking after the running gear as well as building and testing the prototypes.

Initially, the plan was to make the body structures at the Duple Blackpool factory and transport them to Guildford, where the running gear would be fitted. The body framework would then be driven back to Blackpool to be completed by Duple. This process was in fact only used for the prototypes and the first twelve production vehicles, because Hestair had sold off a large part of the Dennis Woodbridge Works site, leaving insufficient space for

425 production. The decision was therefore taken that the 425 running gear should also be installed at Blackpool. A team of Dennis engineers and fitters was accordingly transferred to Blackpool for a period to oversee and advise on the assembly of the running gear.

The 425 was only offered in one length – 12m (39ft 4in) – and only in a high-floor configuration. Styling of the body was done by John Worker, while the structure was built from Cromweld 3CR12 stainless steel for corrosion resistance. It was one of the first coaches constructed to meet the then-proposed, and now mandatory, roll-over strength requirements. The roof and lower panels were fibreglass, while the rest of the structure was clad with galvanized steel.

At first, the standard engine was the Cummins LTA10 turbocharged diesel engine rated at 290bhp, with a no-cost option of a DAF engine being offered subsequently. The transmission was either a ZF six-speed (later seven-speed) manual gearbox or a ZF five-speed auto box. A Telma retarder was fitted. The Rockwell rear axle and rear suspension were carried over from the Dorchester. In addition to the finite element analysis of the frame structure, Dennis subcontracted the design of a new independent front air suspension for the 425 to Alan Ponsford of Capoco Design. Unlike the Dorchester, the radiator package was mounted at the rear beside the engine.

Because Dennis were regarded in law as the chassis man-ufacturer, most 425s were registered as Dennises, or later as Hestairs. All used a Dennis chassis numbering system with an SDA prefix (for Single-Deck Air suspension). This chassis numbering terminology was then used on all chassis types for many more years.

The 425 was launched at the 1984 NEC Show to much interest, not least for its integral construction. The wind-cheating shape, together with the unusually high gearing purposely specified by Dennis and the efficiency of the L10 endowed the 425 with class-leading fuel economy. This was recorded by *Commercial Motor* magazine in their October

The 425 was a fully integral vehicle, and this photo illustrates the integrated structure.
RICHARD NORMAN

BELOW: **The 425 premium coach was originally a Duple project. This photo shows the 1986 prototype vehicle.**
RICHARD NORMAN

1987 Scottish Route road test as an 'incredible' 18.08mpg (15.65ltr/100km) at a time when competitor vehicles were achieving at best 11mpg (25.73ltr/100km).

Full production of the 425 did not begin until 1987, at which point the coach market in the UK was at a low level due to the privatization of the National Bus Company. The production run of 425s, therefore, ended up fairly limited, believed to number only 136. Many, however, remained in service long after production effectively ceased in 1989 with the demise of Duple as a coach and bus bodybuilder. The 425 design rights were sold to Plaxton, who are believed to have subsequently produced around a dozen vehicles at their Carrosserie Lorraine factory in France. Sadly, their lack of chassis expertise precluded any further chassis development, and the project soon fizzled out.

CHANGE IN THE AIR

With a proliferation of models, none of which were best-sellers in their field, profits by the end of the 1970s were again declining: in 1978, the Special Vehicles Division lost £988,000 on a turnover of £25.2 million. Matters were not helped when John Smith, the Hestair Dennis managing director who had done so much both to secure those huge export orders and build the foundations for future success by taking the company back into bus manufacture, fell foul of the law in Iraq in 1979. He was on a visit to sell a left-hand-drive version of the Dominator when he was arrested for alleged bribery, and remained incarcerated there for nine long years.

Eventually, management changes at Hestair prompted a much-needed review of the vehicle-building activities of the group. During 1984, Hestair management decided, wisely, to focus each plant on their most successful products. Thus the Guildford factory became responsible for two key chassis markets, bus and fire. The Guildford fire engine bodybuilding business was no longer considered particularly profitable due to the costly and unique requirements of each fire brigade, and in 1985 was transferred to Carmichaels in Worcester. John Dennis, the grandson of one of the founders of the company, at that time the Dennis sales manager, left and set up his own fire appliance bodybuilding operation, John Dennis Coachworks, close to the Dennis factory. Municipal vehicle operations were centralized at the Hestair Eagle plant at Warwick.

This review was indeed overdue. Although sales were increasing, profitability was not: in 1984, Hestair Special

DENNIS 425 INTEGRAL COACH, 1984–1989

Engine: Cummins LT10
Max. power: 290bhp (216kW)
or
Engine: DAF DK-SB
Max. power: 310bhp (231kW)
Gearbox: ZF 7-speed manual plus Telma Focal 190 retarder
or ZF 5-speed automatic
Rear axle: Rockwell R150.6 single-reduction hypoid
Suspension: Front: air, independent double wishbone with telescopic dampers
Rear: 4-bag air using H frame located by Weweler mountings
Overall length: 11,990mm (472in)
Overall width: 2,500mm (98.4in)
Overall height: 3,390mm (133.5in)
Unladen weight: 10,500kg (23,148lb)
Capacity: up to 63 seats and 14cu m (494cu ft) of luggage
(Source: various brochures/specification sheets)

Vehicles made a profit of only £1.6 million on a turnover of £53 million. Sadly, the Hestair restructure was accompanied by job losses: some 450 at Guildford, representing over half the workforce.

The ensuing reduction in the size of the Guildford operation allowed Hestair to withdraw from a large part of the site. The assembly lines were relocated into No. 11 shop, originally built during World War II to assemble Churchill tanks. Chassis frames were built up in an adjacent workshop, also erected hastily during World War II to produce large numbers of the legendary Dennis trailer pumps.

To reflect the new-found focus of the much smaller company, in 1985 the company was renamed Dennis Specialist Vehicles, usually shortened to DSV.

It took some time for the effects of this major restructure to take effect, not least because it coincided with a drastic drop in bus sales due to the uncertainties following deregulation and privatization. In 1986, the Guildford factory produced just 350 chassis across all their product types, and the future looked very uncertain.

CHAPTER FIVE

HESTAIR – THE RENAISSANCE PERIOD: 1985–1988

NEW PRODUCTS, NEW THINKING

Hestair's restructure of their vehicle-building interests set the scene for a remarkable and rapid expansion of Dennis in the bus and coach market. This success was driven by the introduction of several innovative product launches such as Javelin, Dart and Trident, which over a ten-year time frame brought Dennis to a position of market leadership in the UK.

In large part, this success was the result of efforts of the engineering team, led by the then newly promoted but highly experienced chief designer, Richard Norman. He brought innovation to the design of new products, echoing the early years where the company's success was the result of offering unique vehicles not available elsewhere.

For some time previously, development of new Dennis bus and coach products had generally been customer-led. A typical example was the Dorchester coach, where the engineers were given a very clear brief from sales to design a mid-engined coach fitted with a Gardner 6HLXCT engine. So that is precisely what the customer got – an excellent, sound, chassis in the Dennis (or indeed Leyland) tradition. There was no in-depth analysis of what the customer really needed, or what product could be designed given the available technology, that would not just meet, but exceed, their expectations.

This approach was by no means unusual. Many companies proudly proclaim that they listen to 'the voice of the customer', and clearly that is an essential starting point for any successful new product design. However, the customer, although expert in their own business, rarely has either the knowledge or expertise to envisage a product that may not at that time even exist, so naturally tends to think in terms of current technology. In contrast, a good design engineer knows what is possible, both today and in the future. Innovative and successful new products, therefore, need to combine both market understanding and engineering inspiration. Dennis's new chief designer therefore quietly began to put forward proposals that could lead, rather than follow, the market's perceived requirements.

THE JAVELIN – INNOVATION AGAINST THE ODDS

New Engine

The first opportunity to implement this approach came in early 1986 when Richard spotted an article in an American trade magazine. This revealed that a compact and efficient 8.3-litre 6-cylinder Cummins engine had just been launched in the USA. At that time, most engines fitted by Dennis were either Gardner or Perkins. However, a relationship with Cummins had been initiated with the Integral 425, which adopted the Cummins L10 engine, and also with some trials of the same engine in the Dominator. Cummins advised that they had no plans to market their new engine in the UK or Europe, but agreed to supply drawings and specification sheets. It was immediately apparent from these that the new C-series engine was very compact for its power rating and would ideally suit a mid-engined coach.

From working on the earlier Dennis coach products, Richard fully appreciated the importance of maximizing luggage capacity to meet increasing customer expectations. High-floor, rear-engined European integral coaches were starting to appear in the UK with what seemed at the time to have cavernous centre luggage lockers, typically with 10cu m (350cu ft) of useable volume. This contrasted with the rear boot and series of small lockers shoehorned around the power unit of a typical mid-engined Leyland, Volvo or Bedford coach of the time. The ill-fated Volvo C10M integral, which had a horizontal 10-litre engine positioned mid-wheelbase but close-coupled to the rear axle to provide a through-locker forward of the engine showed what could be achieved within the scope of a mid-engined design, although the bulk of the C10M's horizontal engine itself provided a significant restriction to luggage locker space.

Early studies soon demonstrated that the new compact Cummins C-series 6CTA engine would fit vertically under the floor of a typical low-height 3.2m (10ft 6in) coach body. The vertical engine allowed for packaging of the engine ancillaries such as the fuel tank, air cleaner and alternator around the power unit, leaving ample clear space for luggage under the saloon floor. With the power unit positioned mid-wheelbase but as close as possible to the rear axle, a large through-locker forward of the engine, together with a full-width rear locker, was possible. This would give, on a 12m (39ft 4in) coach, a class-leading total capacity of over 10cu m (350cu ft) of luggage within a 3.2m-high (10ft 6in) body, making such a coach a very competitive product compared to the 3.5m (11ft 6in) high-floor continental coaches.

A further benefit would be to improve weight distribution. Rear-engined coaches tend to overload the rear axle, while traditional mid-engined coaches tend to overload the front axle. In both instances, legal laden weights could easily be exceeded in service, leaving operators liable for fines or, in the worst case, the loss of their operator's licence. In contrast, Richard's proposed coach provided a very well-balanced design with a high degree of loading latitude.

Green Light

Up to this point, design of the proposed new coach had been an unofficial 'what-if' exploratory exercise by the engineering team. Richard, however, realized that this was potentially a 'eureka' moment for a new product opportunity for the business. At that time, however, there was considerable market uncertainty in the wake of deregulation, and there were conflicting views at Dennis board level as to the direction future products should take in the recently reorganized company. Coach products were, however, clearly not top of the agenda.

More in hope than expectation, the Chief Designer then prepared a proposal entitled 'Proposed Lancet with Cummins' C-Series Engine – A Middleweight Coach Chassis with High Luggage Capacity'. Although aware it would not bear much resemblance to the Lancet in its final form, he thought that it would stand more chance of consideration in that guise!

The first approach was to discuss the proposal with Sales: the response, perhaps quite rightly, was 'forget coaches: to sell coaches you need a dealer,' and Dennis had been consistently prevented from entering the coach dealer networks by their major competitors.

The eventual go-ahead for the project came in a typically Dennis way, particularly considering that the long-term consequences of that decision probably led to the renaissance of the company and onwards to the leadership of the

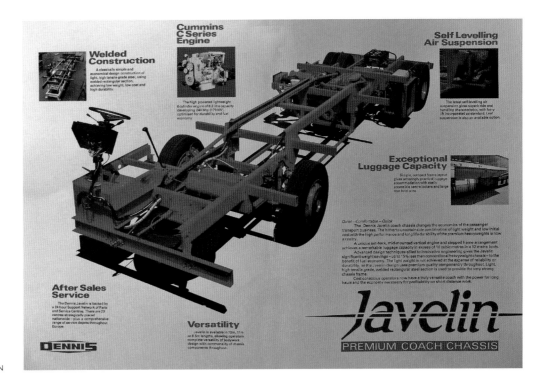

This brochure extract shows the innovative centre chassis frame of the Javelin. RICHARD NORMAN

UK bus market. One day, an engineering meeting to review potential new projects was taking place in the Guildford offices, involving Don Plumley, the engineering director at that time, Alan Ponsford of Capoco Design, and Richard Norman. On passing the room and seeing the assembled engineers, Steve Burton, the recently appointed managing director, poked his head around the door to enquire what was new, and what new product Dennis could be exhibiting at the Commercial Vehicle Show that autumn. Some possibilities that had been on the table were discussed, including the proposal for the new coach. Steve Burton, always a dynamic decision-maker, decided there and then to go ahead. He had a harder job later, selling the idea to the Hestair board, but the decision was made.

The other significant approval received was for the vehicle to feature a welded frame structure. This was a major departure for Dennis with its long history of bolted construction frames. The adoption of a modular, semi-integral welded structure proved very successful and it was later used for all subsequent Dennis bus and coach chassis. The proposed coach frame was particularly novel, with the main centre module chassis rails raised to just below floor level and two shallow box sections tying the front and rear modules together at a low level. This provided the maximum possible unobstructed luggage space.

And so the concept of Javelin, as it was later named, was born. The next challenge was to find a suitable bodybuilder. Although Duple was part of the Hestair group, they were reluctant to put engineering resource into what they considered would be a very low-volume product. At the RAI Bus and Coach Show in Amsterdam, discussions were held with Van Hool, Jonckheere and Berkhof, who had bodied the first Dorchester chassis. They all showed polite interest but declined an involvement.

Perhaps all success stories need an element of luck. Dennis's came when Bedford's parent company, General Motors, announced that it was pulling out of bus, coach and truck manufacturing in the UK. Bedford's mid-engined coach could have been a significant competitor to the Javelin. Fortunately for Dennis, however, David Brown (of Artix articulated dump truck fame), who subsequently bought the Bedford Dunstable factory and its product portfolio, elected not to continue coach and bus production. At around the same time, Ford also pulled out of producing their similar chassis. Bedford's demise left W. S. Yeates, their principal coach dealer, without a chassis brand to sell, so they were keen to link up with Dennis at last. It also left both Duple and Plaxton without one of their leading suppliers of chassis on which to body. The timing could not have been better: with significant assured orders, Duple was soon working on adapting their new 320 body to the Javelin chassis, and Plaxton were not far behind.

The chassis was designed for both bus and coach use, initially with 3.2m-high (10ft 6in) bodywork, a high-floor option being introduced later. It also complied with the European 'Tempo 100' requirements, making it suitable for operation on the continent.

The standard gearbox offered on the Javelin was the well-proven six-speed ZF S6-80 manual, with ZF HP500 four- and five-speed automatics as alternatives. One of the many areas where the Javelin differed from competitor vehicles with manual transmissions was in the use of a substantial

The massive luggage space made possible by the Javelin's chassis design is evident in this view. RICHARD NORMAN

rod linkage rather than the usual and frequently imprecise cable gearshift. Although this unconventional mechanism raised some eyebrows, the rod gearshift performed excellently and was well liked by drivers.

The radiator was mounted alongside the engine on most versions, with a hydraulically driven cooling fan. However, the shortest 8.5m (27ft 9in) coaches, as well as all bus chassis, featured a radiator mounted in front of the engine. This radiator location proved troublesome on some of the Ministry of Defence vehicles operating in Germany, where snow and ice built up in front of it, causing overheating.

Positive Reception

The Javelin was launched at the 1986 Show to a positive reception by the industry. With its light weight, and modern high-power free-revving diesel engine well matched to high overall gearing, the Javelin gave good performance with excellent fuel economy. *Commercial Motor* magazine published a road test of a 12m (39ft 4in) Duple-bodied Javelin in August 1987 and reported that the fuel consumption over their arduous Scottish test route was the best-ever recorded for a 12m coach, at 11.9mpg (23.78ltr/100km). Operators were also quick to see the benefits. In its first full year in production, the Javelin took 18 per cent of the UK market, with lead customers including Go Whittle and Buddens Coaches. Over the first eighteen months of production, over 350 Javelins were manufactured.

The Javelin was offered in a range of body lengths, from 8.5m to 12m (27ft 9in to 39ft 4in), the shorter bodies being particularly popular with smaller operators. Sales were boosted substantially by orders from the UK Ministry of Defence (MoD), who had traditionally bought Leyland Tiger coaches for transporting service personnel around both in the UK and elsewhere. However, in 1991, Volvo, who had taken over the Leyland Bus operations, announced the end of Tiger production, probably because it took sales from their own Volvo B10M. The MoD was keen to continue to buy British and turned to Dennis for the supply of Javelins. Their first vehicles were given dual-purpose Wadham Stringer bodies capable of being used as ambulances. These had doors in the rear panel, allowing them to carry stretcher-borne patients. Later MoD orders reverted to more conventional coach bodies, mainly from Plaxton. In total, the MoD operated over 400 Javelins, many of which were leased from Ryders.

One of the first companies to use Javelins on National Express services was Selwyns of Runcorn in Cheshire with a fleet of five Plaxton Premiere-bodied vehicles. First Group later also took several Plaxton Expressliner-bodied

Javelin sales were boosted significantly by purchases from the MoD. Many vehicles were kitted out to cope with conflict; this one is shown with riot screens protecting the side windows. RICHARD NORMAN

Javelin GX coaches for use on National Express services operated by First Cymru and First Wessex. Some of these vehicles were reported to have clocked up over 1 million miles (1.6 million km) in only three and a half years without significant problems.

In 1993, Stagecoach took fifty 11m (36ft) Plaxton Premiere Interurban-bodied Javelins, built on low-specification chassis with leaf suspension and de-rated engines.

UK service support was by Dennis's traditional 'man in a van' augmented by contracts with repair agencies around the country. To provide European support, the company introduced a new network for the Javelin under the name of EuroCare Assistance. This operated twenty-four hours a day, 365 days a year, with on-the-road support being provided by 6,000 specialist repair centres backed up by the Cummins European service network. However, this was never seen by the operating industry as being as effective as a full manufacturer-managed service organization. Ultimately, Javelin sales were therefore limited by the lack of a formal Dennis service network in mainland Europe.

The stylish Neoplan Transliner body was fitted to a number of Javelin GXs. This is one of several operated by Ellison's. Note the engine bay cooling intake grille on the front bumper, looking like an afterthought – which is exactly what it was, Neoplan having ignored Dennis's bodybuilder guidance! NEIL JENNINGS

By 1992, the dealer network had expanded considerably, with W. S. Yeates now joined by others, including DSB Sales Ltd of Loughborough, AVE Berkhof and Salvador Caetano. Other bodybuilders using the Javelin chassis included Caetano (who had taken over Wadham Stringer), Berkhof and Marcopolo. Anticipating that a Neoplan-bodied Javelin could be successful as a premium coach, in 1994 Dennis developed a new version, the GX, with a 290bhp version of the Cummins C-series fitted. However, despite its typically stylish Neoplan appearance, the GX Transliner was not a huge success.

Caetano and others took advantage of legislation relating to the transport of schoolchildren, and in 1999 introduced a Javelin fitted with their Cutlass body specifically for school transport, with seventy seats in a three-plus-two configuration. Initial sales were to Translinc in Norfolk, the Javelin being selected based on its fuel economy – vital on highly competitively priced school operations.

Export sales of Javelin were limited, although there were a few sales of a three-axle version that was developed for New Zealand.

The Javelin proved to be generally very reliable. The only cloud that appeared on the horizon with some early vehicles was brake judder. This problem was initially put down to the use of non-asbestos brake linings, which had caused similar problems for other manufacturers. How-

ever, it was soon realized that the problem was more fundamental and was the result of thermally induced brake drum ovality caused by rapid heating of the drum during prolonged braking from high speed, such as on an exit slip from a motorway. In the short term, the solution was to specify a Telma retarder to reduce the amount of heat generated by the brakes. The ultimate cure, introduced at the first significant model update, was a move from drum to disc front brakes.

With that exception, Javelin proved remarkably trouble-free during its long history, with over 2,500 being made before the last Javelin was registered in 2012. By then sales had declined considerably, and the industry was being faced with ceaseless and expensive engineering activity to revise vehicle designs, not least to comply with ever-changing and increasingly stringent emissions legislation. At that point, the company (ADL as it was then) took a hard-nosed business decision that the cost and engineering resource involved in taking Javelin to Euro 4 was not justified. However, the Javelin had indeed served to put Dennis back on the map and gave them new credibility as they progressively introduced other new and innovative products.

During the development of the Javelin, a good working relationship arose between Plaxton and Dennis personnel, a relationship that resulted in Plaxton becoming the lead

DENNIS JAVELIN, 1986–2004

Layout and Chassis
4×2 rigid welded-steel fabricated chassis structure for
8.5m–12m bodywork

Engine
Type: Cummins C-series at levels from pre-Euro 1 to Euro
3
Block material: Cast iron
Head material: Cast iron
Cylinders: 6 in-line
Cooling: Water
Bore and stroke: 114 × 135mm
Capacity: 8270cc
Valves: Overhead
Max. power: Euro 1
Bus and 8.5m coach: 211bhp (157kW) at 2,400rpm
Option of 240bhp (179kW) as for 10m–12m coaches
10m–12m coach: 240bhp (179kW) at 2,400rpm; Option
of 211bhp (157kW) as for bus model
GX: 290bhp (216kW) at 2,200rpm
Max. torque: Euro 1
Bus and 8.5m coach: 590lb ft (800Nm) at 1,500rpm
10m–12m coach: 645lb ft (874Nm) at 1,500rpm
GX: 825lb ft (1,118Nm) at 1,400rpm
Fuel capacity: All models except GX: 360ltr (80gal)
GX: 435ltr (95gal)

Transmission
Gearbox: Bus: ZF S6.80 or S6.85 6-speed manual,
synchromesh
Coach: ZF S6.80 or S6.85 6-speed synchromesh, ZF 5HP-
500 5-speed automatic with integral retarder, or Voith
D854 4-speed automatic with integral retarder
Retarder: Optional Telma Focal 191 with manual
gearboxes
Clutch: All models except GX: 15in (380mm) diameter
single dry plate
GX: 420mm (16.5in) diameter single dry plate
Final drive: All models except GX: Eaton 18100 single-
reduction spiral bevel
GX: Eaton 23120 single-reduction spiral bevel

Suspension and Steering
Front: Bus and 8.5m coach: 3-leaf taper-leaf springs with
anti-roll bar and telescopic dampers; option of full air on
8.5m coach
Coach: full air, 2 airbags, axle located by two quarter-
elliptic springs and panhard rod, two telescopic dampers,
ferry lift; option of taper-leaf springs and anti-roll bar

Rear: Bus and 8.5m coach: 3-leaf taper-leaf springs with
anti-roll bar and telescopic dampers; full air option on
8.5m coach
Coach: 4 airbags, H-frame located by 2 twin-leaf parabolic
springs, 4 telescopic dampers; option of taper-leaf springs
and anti-roll bar
Steering: ZF integral power
Tyres: 8.5m coach: 10R × 22.5. All other models:
275/80R × 22.5 tubeless
Wheels: One-piece spigot mounted; single front, twin rear.
8.5m coach: 6.75 × 22.5 All other models: 7.5 × 22.5

Brakes
Type: Front disc, rear S-cam drum, full air-operated
(early vehicles had drum front brakes). Exhaust brake on
manual transmission vehicles, optional Telma electric
retarder
Size: 394mm (15.5in) diameter drums

Dimensions
Track: 2,117mm (83.3in) front, 1,830mm (72in) rear
Wheelbases: 8.5m: 4,000mm (157.5in)
　　　10m: 5,000mm (196.9in)
　　　11m: 5,640mm (222in)
　　　12m: 6,250mm (246in)
Overall lengths (body): 8,500mm (334.6in)
　　　10,000mm (393.7in)
　　　11,000mm (433in)
　　　12,000mm (472.4in)
Overall width: 2,500mm (98.4in)
Unladen weight: 4,895–5,760kg (10,792–12,698lb)
　　　GVW (max.): 8.5m: 11,500kg (25,353lb)
　　　10m and 11m: 14,500kg (31,967lb), later 16,800kg
(37,037lb)
12m: 16,170kg (35,648lb), later 16,800kg (37,037lb)
Capacity: 8.5m: max. 39 seats, up to 4.0cu m (141.25cu ft)
luggage
　　　11m: max. 57 seats, up to 7.2cu m (254.25cu ft) luggage
　　　12m: max. 61 seats, up to 10.1cu m (256.75cu ft)
　　　luggage (70 seats with 3+2 configuration)

Performance
Top speed: Bus: 58mph (93km/h) approx., coach 76mph
(122km/h) approx.

Price
1987: 12m chassis: £29,538
　　　12m bodied: £65,000 approx.
　　　*c.*1997: 12m Neoplan Transliner GX (bodied): £152,500
(Source: Javelin brochures and data sheets,
1986/1993/1996, Neoplan brochure, 1997)

SEASIDE BODYBUILDERS

It is no coincidence that Plaxton and other bodybuilders set up factories in coastal areas. The reason is simple – availability of labour. Coastal towns tend to have seasonal peaks of employment, with everyone busy in the summer tourist months but with much less work available in the colder autumn and winter months. This fitted well with the bodybuilders' labour requirements, which were also seasonal but with their busy period in the winter rather than summer months. This is because coach orders tended to be cyclic, with many operators placing orders for delivery in the following spring, which then needed to be built over the autumn and winter period. A further reason to prefer coastal locations is that they often contained a ready pool of artisans experienced in the skills of boatbuilding, which could readily be transferred to bus and coach body manufacture.

bodybuilder for several Dennis products – something we will return to later.

Operator acceptance of Cummins engines via first the 425 and later the Javelin was crucial in developing one of Dennis's next, and most successful model of all time, the Dart.

DART – THE BIRTH OF THE MIDIBUS

There have been many accounts of how the Dart midibus came about. These have ranged from it being the result of a customer survey to individuals claiming the credit for the concept. The actual events behind the origins of what was to become Britain's bestselling bus have probably never been published. However, Dennis's chief designer, Richard Norman, who was closely involved from the outset, has confirmed the real story, which demonstrates that truth is at times indeed stranger than fiction.

Gap in the Market

One early result of deregulation of the bus industry in the mid-1980s was the explosion of minibus services. The highly manoeuvrable and compact van-derived minibuses were successful in providing frequent services that could penetrate housing estates, so bringing the bus services to

the customer. These converted vans, however, were never designed for the rigours of bus operation and soon suffered from transmission, clutch and brake problems. Additionally, the success of the minibuses generated more passengers than the small van-based products could cope with, and there was soon a need for higher capacity.

Bedford had spotted this opportunity and as early as 1978 had developed prototypes of the Bedford JJL, a 24-seat midibus. For whatever reason, this did not continue to production: if it had, the Dennis story might well have been entirely different.

In the mid-1980s, however, the only manufacturer to attempt to provide a more durable midibus was MCW with their Metrorider. This shared the front-engined, centre-entrance layout of the van-based minibuses, but used more suitably rated components along with integral frame construction. Soon after launch, the 7m (23ft) Metrorider was stretched to 8.4m (27ft 7in) to provide yet higher capacity, as it was becoming apparent that there was an ever-increasing gap in the market between the minibuses and full-size single-deck buses. However, with such a relatively costly specification, and competing directly with the van-based units on price, the profitability of the Metrorider was questionable. MCW's parent group announced the closure of the company in 1989; the Metrorider design was bought by Optare, rebranded as their Metro-Rider, and continued in production until 2000.

Even Leyland, traditionally a maker of heavyweight buses, had recognized the midibus potential, and in 1987 introduced their Swift model. This was a mid-engined vehicle using the same Cummins B-series engine and Allison transmission combination as eventually used on the Dennis Dart. It was, however, fundamentally a high-floor chassis derived from the Roadrunner truck, which limited its acceptability as a passenger chassis.

It had become clear that the midibus market was one where, given the right ingredients, a competitive product could be introduced that should command a higher price than a van-based bus, making it financially viable to manufacture in typical bus market volumes.

Product cost was seen as key to this sector, and Dennis looked at many solutions to provide a competitive small bus. These included utilizing a set of Ford truck components and incorporating them in a Duple-built integral frame. The high cost of this, however, when compared to the market expectation at that time of a list price equating to 'a bum on a seat for £1,000', meant the project foundered. At a project development meeting in 1987, the Dennis quest for the holy grail of a small, low-cost bus was officially abandoned when chairman David Hargreaves decided that the engineering team would waste no further time on the project. Instead, he decreed, the very limited Dennis engineering resources should be redeployed towards both a new fire engine and a full size single-deck bus with a side-mounted Cummins C-series engine to replace the Falcon H.

From Fire Engine to Midibus

This made some sense: following Hestair's closure of the fire engine body manufacture, there was a strong feeling among fire brigades that Dennis would, in future, concentrate on buses and coaches at the expense of fire appliances. It was therefore considered by Dennis management that a new fire product launch was necessary to restore confidence within the fire market. Having learned from the company's history, David Hargreaves promoted a company policy that new products should be high on USPs (unique selling points) rather than simply 'me-too' offerings.

This was particularly relevant with the fire appliance product, which in essence was a high-performance truck with a crew cab. With truck power ratings increasing rapidly at that time, the traditional performance advantage provided by a Dennis fire engine was being eroded. Dennis, therefore, set out to design a dedicated fire engine that would once again move the company well ahead of the converted trucks. The internal project code for this model was F88 (**F**ire 1**988**), which later became the Rapier. At that time, 19.5in wheels, smaller than the more usual 22.5in ones, were appearing in Europe for lighter-weight trucks. These were proposed for F88 to reduce height and weight, together with a new 8-tonne (7.87-ton) capacity rear axle. A feature of this smaller wheel size was that it could still accommodate a decent-sized brake to cope with the high stopping performance needed from a fire engine.

While chief designer Richard Norman was laying out the rear axle and suspension for the F88 on the drawing board, he realized that this was a missing link for a new mid-sized bus. Those small wheels could give a low floor height with minimum saloon intrusion, but still be big enough to fit a brake that could withstand the rigours of bus duty cycle. Not only that, but the compact 8-tonne rear axle would allow a suitable floor height through to the rear of the bus. Soon, there was no longer a front-engined fire engine and pump driveline on the drawing board but a rear-engined bus with a low floor line. This, then, was the origin of what was soon to become the highly successful Dart midibus: conceived from Dennis's future fire engine development.

Dennis had made a previous attempt at a midibus with the Domino. This had a transverse engine and used the ill-fated Maxwell transmission to achieve the short rear overhang regarded as essential for a manoeuvrable midibus. However, it was based on high-cost heavyweight components, needing 22.5in tyres to carry the resulting weight. As such, it did not provide a cost-effective platform to compete in the newly deregulated market.

The other missing link to a viable midibus was a compact, low-cost transmission with an integral retarder. Coincidentally, Renk, the German manufacturer better known for their big main battle-tank transmissions, announced the launch of a suitable small gearbox with an integral retarder. Renk planned to build the unit, designated the OTR, under licence from a Swedish company. The key was simplicity, and this very compact transmission coupled to the new compact 6-cylinder Cummins B-series engine would provide a reasonable 2.4m (7ft 9in) overhang in a simple 'T' drive layout ideal for a midibus.

In the newly privatized industry, low cost was seen as a critical factor, so a simple leaf-spring suspension was chosen, fitted with patented Weweler rubber cushions in place of the more conventional steel shackles to mount the springs. This introduced a small degree of compliance between the axles and chassis that improved the isolation from road inputs and eliminated any 'shackle rattle'.

With these essential ingredients in place, an outline proposal was prepared to take to senior management. Initially, there was guarded interest from the sales team, who after a close look at the costs formed the view that there was potential to sell around 250 per year. This was not an unreasonable assessment for the time, given that there was no established market for this size of bus, and also given typical Dennis annual production volumes at that time. The board, however, could see the potential, and at a meeting at the Hestair headquarters in Buckingham Gate, London on 10 February 1988, David Hargreaves made the decision to go ahead with the project. It was also decided at the meeting that initially the bodywork would be kept within the group and exclusive to Duple.

To free up the necessary engineering resource to develop this new model, the F88 fire engine project was postponed and the new DM88 (**D**ennis **M**idi 1988) project started instead, with a target to launch at the NEC show in October of that year. Such a timescale would be impossible today with the increased levels of technical complexity and legislative requirements.

The layout of DM88 provided what was for that time an exceptionally low frame height with a two-step entrance alongside the driver, a width of only 2.3m (7ft 7in) and an initial overall length of 9m (29ft 6in) for the launch model. What no one could have known, or even foreseen, at the time was that this was the start of a product that, as the Dart midibus, would go on to revolutionize the UK bus industry by single-handedly creating a new 'midi' market sector and put the Dennis brand at the forefront of UK bus manufacturing. To produce a completely new prototype chassis and an all-new body in eight months was an exacting target. In fact, the body was launched at the show on a dummy frame as there was insufficient time to get a representative chassis frame to Duple. The DM88 was the first Dennis chassis frame to use computer-aided design, and the learning curve for this new method added to the pressures and frustrations of achieving the target date.

Early in the design stage, it became apparent that Renk would not be proceeding to production with the OTR transmission. The Allison AT545 gearbox was the fallback, with which Dennis had some operating experience in previous Lancet variants. The increased length of this unit meant a small increase in the rear overhang, but by this stage, the merits of the overall package were very apparent and work on the project continued unabated. Interestingly, Cummins and Allison already had experience of this engine and transmission package, for it was a very familiar and well-regarded sight in the USA, albeit in the much smaller Dodge Ram pickup.

An integral retarder was not available with the Allison transmission, which was a concern, although there was reasonable confidence that the foundation brakes alone would give adequate service. This may well have been the case.

This is the chassis of the step-frame Dart. RICHARD NORMAN

Early in the trials, Dennis had experienced rapid brake wear, but the resulting exercise to evaluate different lining types and optimize the front-to-rear brake balance showed promising results. However, the pressure to get the chassis into volume production meant that the safe option of an axle-mounted Telma electric retarder had to be adopted.

Dennis had been initially reluctant to move to such a retarder, as previous experience on a Lancet had shown that the rotor inertia generated unacceptable axle noise. However, with the help of Telma, their Focal retarder was developed and fitted to the Dart. Axle noise did indeed prove a problem that varied in intensity with variations in axle build tolerances. Rear-axle noise issues dogged the Dart until ground crown-wheel and pinion gears together with a new purpose-built low-inertia retarder were introduced quite some time later.

The all-welded chassis was comprised of three welded modules, the front containing the front axle, steering and controls, while the rear encompassed the engine, gearbox and rear axle. A relatively simple centre module was interposed between them, which made it possible for additional body lengths to be made available subsequently. The chassis was 2.3m (7ft 6in) wide, enabling the Dart to access narrow streets unsuitable for full-width buses.

Successful Launch

Dart's October 1988 NEC Motor Show launch generated considerable interest, with the striking John Worker-styled Duple Dartline bodywork with its distinctive curved front profile drawing a lot of comment. Although more expensive than the 'bread van' conversions, at around £51,000 for a complete vehicle, the Dart was only approximately two-thirds the price of a conventional single-decker. It was soon apparent that this would fill the need for a durable small bus with a traditional 'big bus' layout. Operators were rightly conservative in their choice of vehicle types and initially took only small numbers for trial, the first customer being Southampton. However, this very soon converted into sizeable fleet orders.

London Buses had shown great interest in the Dart from the outset but demanded a shorter vehicle, possibly to avoid paying their drivers the rate for longer buses. Thanks to the three-module design of the Dart chassis, Dennis was able to quickly shorten the simple centre module to produce an 8.5m-long (27ft 10in) frame. Within a couple of years, 500 of these 8.5m Darts were in service in London. The 8.5m chassis also found favour with many operators elsewhere, and later a longer 9.8m (32ft 2in) chassis was also made available, capable of providing over forty seats.

DENNIS DART, 1989–2005

Layout and Chassis
4×2 rigid welded modular frame, rear-engined midibus chassis for 8.5m, 9m and 9.8m single-deck bodies

Engine
Type: Cummins B-series Euro 1 (later Euro 2) turbocharged diesel; alternative 150PS CNG-powered version
Block material: Cast iron
Head material: Cast iron
Cylinders: 6 in-line
Cooling: Water
Bore and stroke: 102 × 120mm
Capacity: 5900cc
Max. power (DIN): Euro 1: 130bhp (97kW) at 2,500rpm
Euro 2: 130PS (96kW) at 2,500rpm
Max. torque: Euro 1: 336lb ft (457Nm) at 1,500rpm
Euro 2: 347lb ft (470Nm) at 1,500rpm
Fuel capacity: 134ltr (29.5gal)

Transmission
Gearbox: Allison AT545 4-speed fully automatic
Retarder: Telma Focal 90 electric
Final drive: Eaton 08.18 single-reduction hypoid, 8,000kg (17,736lb) capacity

Suspension and Steering
Front: 3-leaf taper-leaf springs 1,500mm (59in) long, two telescopic dampers; anti-roll bar on 9.8m w/b model

Rear: 3-leaf taper-leaf springs 1,700mm (67in) long, 2 telescopic dampers
Steering: ZF 8090 integral power
Tyres: 245/70 R 19.5 low-profile tubeless
Wheels: Spigot mounted, 6.75 × 19.5 steel

Brakes
Type: Wabco Perrot Simplex air wedge drums, air operated; spring parking brake
Size: 360mm (14.2in) diameter

Dimensions
Track: 1,870mm (73.6in) front, 1,765mm (69.5in) rear
Wheelbases: 8.5m body: 3,775mm (148.6in)
    9m body: 4,300mm (169.3in)
    9.8m body: 5,115mm (201.4in)
Overall lengths (body): 8,500mm (334.6in)
    9,000mm (354.3in)
    9,800mm (385.8in)
Overall width (chassis): 2,301mm (90.6in)
    Unladen wt. (chassis): 3,420kg (7,540lb)
    GVW: 10,000kg (22,046lb)
Capacity: up to 60 passengers

Performance
Top speed: 47mph (76km/h) with 4.88:1 rear axle
    56mph (90km/h) with 4.11:1 rear axle
(Source: Dennis Dart data sheets, 1993 and 1996)

This 1991 Dart wears the original Duple Dartline body as produced by Carlyle and was one of the first built for Hong Kong.
DANNY CHAN

The demise of Duple's bodybuilding activities soon saw other bodybuilders being needed for Dart. Plaxton were initially not interested, for their research had indicated a likely market potential of only forty per year, even less than Dennis's own estimates. Eventually, Carlyle, the Birmingham bodybuilder, took over the Dartline body design and production in 1989, the rights later being acquired by Marshalls of Cambridge in 1992 following Carlyle's collapse into receivership. It was then revised and relaunched as the Marshall Capital body in 1996, running until 2002, when Marshalls themselves went into administration. A new company, MCV, then took up the bodies' design and production.

Other bodybuilders also took up the challenge, one of the earliest being Wadham Stringer, followed by Wrights. Eventually, Reeve Burgess, a subsidiary of Plaxton, developed an aluminium-framed body, the Pointer, which became an instant success. This led Plaxton themselves to undertake subcontract assembly at Scarborough, making a mockery of their earlier pessimistic forty-a-year forecast! Eventually, the small Reeve Burgess factory in Derbyshire was closed down, with all further production taking place at the sprawling Scarborough plant.

Other bodybuilders included East Lancs and Northern Counties. Some of the East Lancs E2000 bodies were built to a full 2.5m (8ft 2.5in) width in response to customer requests, which made them look slightly unbalanced on the narrow 2.3m-wide (7ft 7in) Dart chassis. Alexander of Falkirk remained aloof from the rush to body Darts and only relented in 1991 when asked by Stagecoach to produce a suitable body on the promise of significant orders. Their

Other bodybuilders like Northern Counties soon began to body Darts, like this Warrington vehicle shown undergoing tilt testing. GARY AVERY

resulting body, the Alexander Dash, was shown at the 1991 Coach and Bus Show, accompanied by Stagecoach orders on both the Dart chassis and also on Volvo's newly announced B6 chassis.

With the Dart selling well and having created a new market sector, it was only surprising that competitors had taken so long to try to break into that sector. The Volvo B6 was launched in 1991, a full three years after the first showing of the Dart. Possibly as a result of its reputation suffering after early service problems, the B6 never achieved the level of sales of the Dart, with only just over 600 finding homes in its seven-year production life to 1999. In comparison, by 1994, 2,000 Darts had been sold.

The Dart also did well in export sales. In 1991, China Motor Bus in Hong Kong took twenty air-conditioned Carlyle-bodied Darts. Rival operator KMB took Darts with locally assembled Duple Metsec bodies a couple of years later, as did fellow Hong Kong operators Citybus and KCRC. Darts also saw service in Macau, Singapore and Malaysia. Some of the Singaporean and Malaysian vehicles were locally built at the joint Dennis-UMW plant set up in 1996. Closer to home, Berkhof also bodied several Darts for Dutch operator NZH.

A small number of Darts were built around 1995 with compressed natural gas-powered engines, largely at the request of customers, principally Southampton Citybus, who took ten. The vehicles used a US-developed Cummins Westport engine fed by roof-mounted gas tanks. The fuel systems proved somewhat unreliable, however, and no further CNG-powered vehicles were produced.

Overall, almost 3,500 step-frame Darts were sold, together with over 9,000 of the succeeding Dart SLF/SPD and to date over 8,500 Enviro 200/300 models: sales totalling over 21,000 and making it, without doubt, Britain's most successful, if not most famous, bus. That accolade, of course, goes to London's iconic Routemaster, total sales of which were under 3,000!

GOODBYE HESTAIR, HELLO TRINITY HOLDINGS

However, even while Dennis were enjoying their initial success with the Dart and other models, by the late 1980s their owners, Hestair, were concentrating on other interests, in particular SOS, their employment agency, which ended up providing 80 per cent of Hestair's profits. Whether they would have been quite so uninterested in the Dennis business if they had foreseen its future dramatic renaissance and the resulting high number of sales, is a matter of conjecture.

CHAPTER SIX

UNDER NEW OWNERSHIP – TRINITY HOLDINGS: 1989–1998

A NEW BROOM

In 1989, the senior managers of Hestair's Vehicle Division bought Dennis from Hestair for £27 million. Geoff Hollyhead, the chairman of the Vehicle Division, led the team, and was appointed chairman and CEO of the new business, renamed Trinity Holdings Ltd. The other directors of the new company were Steve Burton, managing director of Dennis Specialist Vehicles; Brendan Geary, financial director of Dennis Eagle; and Richard Owen, managing director of Dennis Eagle.

Trinity Holdings comprised three divisions: Dennis Eagle, making refuse vehicles, road sweepers and tankers; Duple, makers of bus and coach bodies; and Dennis Specialist Vehicles (DSV), producers of fire engines and bus and coach chassis.

At that time, Dennis Eagle was the major UK-owned designer and producer of refuse vehicles and European leaders in the design and manufacture of complete refuse vehicles, with more than 3,000 of their Phoenix models having been sold worldwide.

The coachbuilding side of Duple was not in a good way. The coach market had been changing rapidly in the previous few years with an upsurge in demand for long-distance express and holiday travel. Duple were slow to recognize this change, and by the time they introduced suitable new models, continental competitors had taken around one-third of the British market.

Duple therefore soon became a Trinity Holdings casualty, the bus and coach bodybuilding business being sold to Plaxton. Production ended at the Duple Blackpool factory, which was then repurposed to produce the new steel cabs for the fire appliances and refuse collection vehicles. The successful Duple Metsec body kit-building business in the West Midlands was, of course, retained. Dart bodywork production was moved from Blackpool to the Carlyle Works in Birmingham, while production of the Duple 300 series bodies and 425 Integral transferred to Plaxton.

DENNIS MOVES AGAIN – SLYFIELD WORKS

In November 1990, Dennis Specialist Vehicles moved from Woodbridge Works to a new 115,000sq ft (10,700sq m) factory at Slyfield industrial estate on the outskirts of Guildford. This finally vacated the remaining buildings on the old Dennis site at Woodbridge Hill, which then remained empty for several years before being demolished.

Most of Woodbridge Works was demolished following its sale by Hestair. The remaining part, however, which was only vacated by Dennis in 1990, remained standing for many years afterwards. BOB LOVELAND COLLECTION

The new Slyfield site soon saw several amendments and additions. At first, fabrication of chassis modules took place in one corner of the Slyfield factory. However, with no separating walls, dust and detritus from the fabrication area inevitably found its way into the adjacent vehicle assembly lines: hardly a way to ensure high standards of cleanliness when installing things like hydraulic systems!

A separate frame shop was therefore soon erected on the site. This contained several bays where each module was welded together, and 'marry-up' bays where the three modules were integrated into one complete chassis frame. The building also contained a paint shop where the completed frames were cleaned up, the gaps between frame components sealed where necessary, and then the finished structure finally painted.

Another significant change to free up space for additional vehicle assembly was to move parts and service operations out of Slyfield and into a new-build 40,000sq ft (4,000sq m) rented facility about quarter of a mile (0.5km) away. This facility, Opus Park, was to continue in use for several years until the new ADL parts and service headquarters was established at Skelmersdale in Lancashire. Opus Park was then vacated, and a satellite parts and service facility was re-established in the main Slyfield factory.

Another development was the building of a test centre for the quality department. It contained a £750,000 chassis dynamometer or 'rolling road' to test every production chassis, bringing to an end the road testing that had been

such a familiar sight in the Guildford area. The test centre incorporated sophisticated equipment to identify slow leaks from vehicle air systems, addressing and resolving an 'early life' issue commonplace on many new chassis.

Initially, the Slyfield factory had a large stores area with aisles of tall racking accessed by high-reach stacker trucks. Further production space in the main factory was gained by significantly reducing the size of the stores area. This is not as radical as it sounds, for the industry as a whole was by then embracing the concept of 'just in time' deliveries with enthusiasm, meaning that much less stock needed to be carried. After the stores closure, engines, for example, were delivered by the trailer load, sequenced to match the chassis build schedule precisely. This meant that the engines could be forklifted directly from the trailer onto the production line.

EXPANDING THE FAMILY

In September 1991, Trinity bought the design rights to Shelvoke municipal vehicle products from the official receiver, and the following year made two further additions to the Trinity fold: Carmichael Fire & Bulk, a £900,000 purchase from the receiver, and Reliance Mercury, the tug and tractor maker, also bought from the receiver. Both of the latter purchases reversed earlier Hestair actions, for some products of both of these companies had their origins in Dennis designs. This time, however, design and produc-

Fire and bus chassis assembly were kept separate in the Slyfield factory; this view from the early 1990s shows the fire assembly lines.
GARY AVERY

tion of these vehicles remained in Worcester and Halifax, respectively.

At that time, the Carmichael factory at Worcester was continuing to make dedicated airfield fire rescue vehicles capable of high speeds over rough terrain and delivering up to 4,000gal/min (18,000ltr/min) of foam onto an aircraft fire. Major customers included almost every UK airport as well as many Royal Air Force stations. Fire appliance bodies were also manufactured and fitted to Dennis chassis as well as other brands. Within nine months of being bought by Trinity Holdings, the order book stood at £10 million, which included a sixty-vehicle deal for RAF airfield crash tenders.

The Reliance Mercury range was extensive, from the smallest model, with a drawbar pull of 2,000lb (910kg), up to the mighty RM400 airtug. The MD400 was a 40,000lb (18,140kg) drawbar pull vehicle, the origins of which dated back to the 1971 model designed at Guildford when Dennis previously owned Mercury.

In the same year, 1992, Trinity Holdings was successfully floated. It was valued at £90 million, the prospectus claiming that it was Europe's largest specialist vehicle producer making dedicated products for niche markets. Dennis held 40 per cent of the British fire engine market, and the Dart was Britain's biggest-selling bus, also with a 40 per cent market share.

In 1993, Trinity entered a joint venture with UMW, a Malaysian company, to build step-entrance Darts, Lances and Javelins, including a unique three-axle version for New Zealand. The joint venture used Guildford-supplied chassis kits and body kits from Duple Metsec. Production started in 1995, although it was not a financial success for Dennis due to a significant devaluation of the Malaysian currency in 1997. As a result, Dennis withdrew from the joint venture in 1998.

In December 1995, Trinity purchased the aircraft and cargo handling division of ML Holdings, which comprised Douglas Equipment and Schopf. Douglas Schopf produced a wide range of specialist vehicles, one of their areas of expertise being drawbarless aircraft tractors, the use of which was increasing. Drawbarless tractors are much lighter and more manoeuvrable than conventional pushback tractors. Rather than relying on the substantial ballast weights of conventional aircraft tractors to provide the traction to move heavy aircraft, drawbarless tractors pick up the nosewheel of the plane. The weight of the aircraft itself therefore provides the necessary traction.

Over time, Douglas Schopf merged with Reliance Mercury. All production was centralized at the Douglas plant at Cheltenham, with the Reliance Mercury brand eventually being abandoned in favour of Douglas Schopf.

Product innovation continued apace under Trinity; some of the significant projects will be discussed later.

FIREFIGHTING EXCELLENCE – RAPIER AND SABRE

The Rapier

With Dart design work completed, thoughts returned to fire engines. The previous F88 studies had identified the twin requirements of high performance and light weight. Initially, the engine considered was the Perkins Phaser 210Ti, although this quickly changed to the 240bhp 8.27-litre Cummins 6CTA, a compact unit giving high power with low weight. This was mated to an Allison World Series MDCR five-speed fully automatic transmission driving into an 8 tonne-capacity rear axle. This combination of reliable yet lightweight components ensured that the desired 19.5in wheels could be fitted. This contributed to keeping the centre of gravity of the vehicle as low as possible, enhancing road-holding and giving the crew easier entry and exit, thus increasing their efficiency.

Borrowing principles developed on racing cars, the Rapier featured a welded square-tube spaceframe chassis. This gave light weight as well as being far stiffer than a conventional bolted ladder frame construction, providing the basis for the vehicle's outstanding road behaviour. Coil-sprung independent front suspension was fitted, rather than the traditional truck leaf spring and beam axle arrangement. This enabled the engine to be mounted lower than with a standard beam axle, lowering the centre of gravity even further. The stiff frame, together with the advanced suspension design, provided exceptional ride and handling characteristics – features greatly acclaimed by the fire crews.

Initially, a modified RS/SS cab was fitted, but by 1994 a new design of six-man crew cab was installed, which could tilt to 42 degrees. The new cab shell was made of 'Cromweld' stainless steel. Learning from experience gained with the earlier cab, which, like many competitor cabs of the era, experienced significant corrosion issues, Cromweld was particularly suited to fire engine cabs, which can be subjected to aggressive mixtures of water and chemicals. However, like many grades of stainless steel, the surface of any unpainted parts could take on a rust-like patina under certain conditions. This phenomenon led more than one Brigade to raise entirely unfounded concerns about their new cabs starting to corrode. The cab was successfully tested by the Motor Industry Research Association (MIRA) to ensure that it met the stringent requirements of the ECE R29 Frontal Impact Regulation, and also that it met the 10-tonne (9.84 ton) roof crush-loading requirement. Seat-belt anchorages for every crew member were also tested and approved to EC Directive 90/629/EEC.

Analysis of accident records showed that more firefighter injuries resulted from getting into and out of cabs than in fighting fires, often by tripping on poorly located steps or jumping from a high cab to the ground. This point was therefore given particular attention in the design of the new cab, resulting in broad and strong steps – two on the Rapier, three on the later Sabre – which were wider at the bottom than at the top, increasing their visibility to the crew. Also, wide-opening doors helped a fully kitted firefighter to exit the cab quickly and safely.

The Rapier was first marketed in 1991, and by 1994 had sold around 100 units at a time when average annual UK sales of all fire engines were around 250 a year. Export orders were received from Holland, Hong Kong and the Czech Republic, with Holland being a particularly strong market.

In 1994, the Rapier was the well-deserved winner of a British Design Award.

Towards the end of the Rapier's production run, it was becoming increasingly difficult to obtain some components,

particularly the independent front suspension and brakes. These were sourced from the Renault Midliner, a truck that was at the end of its production life. A re-sourcing exercise could have probably overcome this, but by then sales were reducing, primarily due to the sophisticated Rapier being just too expensive for increasingly cash-strapped brigades, together with the payload limitations (*see* below). The decision was therefore taken to cease production.

The Rapier was fitted with independent suspension at the front to keep the centre of gravity low, aiding both handling and ease of entry and exit. GARY AVERY

This early Rapier with the original RS/SS-based cab saw service with Surrey Fire Brigade. GARY AVERY

DENNIS RAPIER, 1991–

Layout and Chassis
4×2 rigid welded tubular space-frame fire appliance chassis with steel cab

Engine
Type: Cummins 6CTA turbocharged and aftercooled diesel
Block material: Cast iron
Head material: Cast iron
Cylinders: 6 in-line
Cooling: Water
Capacity: 8270cc
Valves: Overhead
Max. power (DIN): 240bhp (179kW) at 2,400rpm
Max. torque: 651lb ft (884Nm) at 1,500rpm
or
Type: Cummins 6CT turbocharged diesel
Max. power (DIN): 211bhp (157kW) at 2,400rpm
Max. torque: 560lb ft (759Nm) at 1,500rpm

Transmission
Gearbox: Allison MDCR World Series 5-speed automatic, side-mounted PTO
Final drive: Hypoid

Suspension and Steering
Front: Coil springs, double-wishbone independent suspension with telescopic dampers

Rear: Coil springs located by trailing taper-leaf springs, telescopic dampers
Steering: ZF 8095 integral power
Tyres: 265/70 R 19.5 radial tubeless
Wheels: Spigot-mounted wheels, 6.75 × 9.5

Brakes
Type: ABS and ASR
Front: Air over hydraulic discs
Rear: Simplex full-air wedge drums
Size: Front discs 354mm (14in) diameter, rear drums 360mm (14.2in) diameter

Cab
Capacity: 6 persons
Tilt: 42-degree hydraulic tilt

Dimensions
Wheelbase: 3,600mm (141.75in)
Overall length: 6,450mm (254in)
Overall width: 2,330mm (91.75in)
Overall height (over cab): 2,420mm (95.25in)
GVW (max.): 11,000kg (24,250lb)

Performance
Top speed: 75mph (120km/h) approx.
(Source: Dennis Rapier specification sheet)

The Sabre

Excellent though the Rapier was, it was inevitably expensive. Also, its relatively light gross weight limited the amount of equipment that could be carried to deal with the increasingly common road traffic collisions. In 1995, it was therefore joined by a simpler machine – internally codenamed F94, later to become Sabre – replacing the long-running RS/SS series. It shared the new Cromweld steel crew cab and Cummins engine of the Rapier but used a more conventional ladder-frame chassis. Coil-spring suspension was used at the rear to ensure the best possible handling, with leaf springs at the front, although full air suspension was an option. Sabre maximum gross vehicle weight was initially 14.5 tonnes (14.27 tons), later increasing to 16.26 tonnes (16 tons) to enable ever more collision-extrication equipment to be carried.

The Dennis Sabre was well regarded by fire brigades the world over as a high-performance, effective appliance. ADL

DENNIS SABRE, 1995–2007

Layout and Chassis
4×2 rigid ladder-frame forward-control chassis with steel cab for fire appliance bodywork

Engine
Type: Cummins C-series Euro 1 (later Euro 2, then 3) turbocharged, intercooled diesel
Block material: Cast iron
Head material: Cast iron
Cylinders: 6 in-line
Cooling: Water
Bore and stroke: 114 × 135mm
Capacity: 8270cc
Valves: Overhead
Max. power (DIN): Euro 1: 250bhp (186kW) at 2,400rpm
Euro 3: 260bhp (191kW) at 2,400rpm
Max. torque: Euro 1: 660lb ft (895Nm) at 1,300rpm
Euro 3: 782lb ft (1,060Nm) at 1,200–1,600rpm
Fuel capacity: 29gal (130ltr)

Transmission
Gearbox: Allison MD World Series 5-speed automatic with integral PTO drive
Power take-off: Chelsea type 275 suitable for 2,275ltr/min (500gal/min) pump
Options: type 855 for 3,410ltr/min (750gal/min) or 4,555ltr/min (1,000gal/min)
Final drive: Eaton 10-24 single-reduction hypoid

Suspension and Steering
Front: Semi-elliptic multi-leaf springs with telescopic dampers

Rear: Coil springs located by trailing taper-leaf springs with telescopic dampers
Steering: ZF 8095 integral power
Tyres: 275/70 R 22.5 low profile
Wheels: 10-stud spigot-mounted, 7.5 × 22.5

Brakes
Type: Disc front, Girling S-cam drum rear, spring parking brake; category 1 ABS system
Size: 438mm (17.25in) diameter front, 410mm (16in) diameter rear

Cab
6-crew capacity, 42-degree tilt
Standard cab: 2,937mm (115.6in) long
ML cab: 3,137mm (123.5in) long
10-crew capacity XL cab: 3,337mm (131.4in) long

Dimensions
Wheelbases: 3,800mm (149.6in)
  4,000mm (157.5in)
  4,200mm (165.4in)
Overall width (chassis): 2,360mm (93in)
Overall height (over cab): 2,714mm (106.9in)
Unladen weight (chassis): 5,800kg (12,787lb) with standard cab
GVW: 13,000kg (28,660lb), later 14,500kg (31,967lb)

Performance
Top speed: 72mph (116km/h)
(Source: Dennis Sabre specification sheets, 1995 and 2003)

As well as specifying all the extra kit that needed to be carried in fire engine body lockers, fire brigades were steadily increasing the amount and size of equipment such as breathing apparatus carried in the cab. Some brigades also wanted to carry extra firefighters, so to cater for these requirements, the cab was available in a range of lengths. The longest of these, the XL, could carry up to ten crew members and was popular with the West Midlands Fire and Rescue Service.

The biggest version of the Sabre, the XL, could carry all ten of these firefighters, nearly twice as many as most appliances. ADL

The prototype Sabre is now converted for use as a towed dynamometer by ADL. AUTHOR

DENNIS SABRE HD, 2003–2007

Specification as for standard Sabre with the following exceptions:
Engine: Cummins ISCe Euro 3
Max. power: 220kW (300PS)
Max. torque: 829lb ft (1,125Nm) at 1,400rpm
Power take-off: Chelsea type 858 suitable for 2,270ltr/min (500gal/min) or 3,000ltr/min (660gal/min) pump
Options: type 277 for 2,000ltr/min (440gal/min) or Webster for 4,000ltr/min (880gal/min)
Final drive: Dana 11-26 single-reduction hypoid
Wheelbases: 4,200mm (165.4in)
    4,572mm (180in)
    5,200mm (204.75in)
Unladen weight (chassis): 5,880kg (12,963lb) with ML cab
GVW: 16,800kg (37,037lb)
Top speed: 63mph (101km/h)
(Source: Dennis Sabre HD specification sheet, 2003)

The original Dennis development Sabre still exists today, albeit in a very different role. As part of the proving programme for any new vehicle, rigorous cooling tests need to be carried out. In these, the test vehicle cooling system needs to be subjected to prolonged operation at maximum load to ensure that the cooling system can cope. This test is performed by towing a dynamometer behind the test vehicle, which applies an appropriate and substantial load to the test vehicle. When the Sabre development chassis was no longer required for its original purpose, it was converted to a towed dynamometer and is still in use today.

BUS AND COACH DEVELOPMENTS

The Lance
The Lance was intended as an economical full-size single-deck chassis to replace the Falcon. It was unveiled at the 1991 Coach & Bus Show and featured the 6-cylinder Cummins 6CT diesel engine mounted longitudinally at the rear, driving forwards through a ZF Ecomat transmission to the rear axle. The chassis, available in 10.6m (34ft 9in) and

One of KMB's Lances in service in Hong Kong.
DANNY CHAN

DENNIS LANCE, 1991–2000

Configuration: 4×2 rigid welded modular frame, rear-engined chassis for 10.5m, 11m and 11.5m body lengths
Engine: Cummins C-series Euro 1 (later Euro 2) 6-cylinder turbocharged diesel
Max. power: 211bhp (157kW) then 180kW (245PS)
Capacity: 8270cc
Gearbox: ZF 4HP500 or 5HP500 automatic, integral retarder
Rear axle: Eaton 11.28 single-reduction hypoid
Suspension: Both axles: 2 airbags located by trailing taper leaf springs and panhard rod, telescopic dampers
Wheelbases: 10m body: 5,050mm (198.8in)
    11m and 11.5m body: 5,850mm (230.3in)
Overall lengths (body): 10.5m (413.3in)
    11m (433in)
    11.5m (452.75in)
Overall width (chassis): 2,486mm (97.9in)
Unladen weight (chassis): 5,410–5,580kg (11,927–12,302lb)
GVW (max.): 16,800kg (37,037lb)
Top speed: 49mph (79km/h)
(Source: Dennis Lance data sheet, 1993)

11.6m (38ft 1in) lengths, was designed to the prevailing DIPTAC disabled-access standards, with a low floor line, although it still featured a step-entry, the full low-floor Lance SLF not arriving until 1993. Bodies usually fitted were the Alexander PS or the distinctive curved-front Plaxton Verde, although a number were also bodied by Northern Counties.

As well as the UK builds, Lances were also made in Malaysia by UMW-Dennis.

Some export sales took place, with vehicles going to Hong Kong, Malaysia, New Zealand, Poland and Singapore. In 2000, Singapore, in fact, took the last twenty Lances ever to be built. These had been kitted at Guildford and destined initially for UMW-Dennis assembly. Following the demise of that operation, they were eventually sold to Trans Island Bus Services in Singapore for local manufacture, eighteen having Duple Metsec bodies and two with Volgren bodies.

Lance production ended in 2000.

The Lance SLF

Even as the Lance was launched, the pressure was increasing for buses to be fully accessible to wheelchair users, meaning that step-free entrances were going to be required. During 1992, London issued a tender for the supply of their first-ever low-floor single-deckers. The contract was awarded to a joint venture partnership between Dennis and Scania for chassis and Wrights/Alusuisse for bodies. This resulted in the Dennis Lance Super Low Floor, or SLF, design. Achieving a no-step entry was at that time simply not possible with a conventional beam front axle. Lance SLF, therefore, like contemporary European vehicles, used independent front suspension, in this case, the ZF RLE66 system. Such suspension, with its proliferation of links and pivots, is not particularly well suited to arduous bus duty and is also much more expensive than a conventional beam axle. Unfortunately, many completed Lance SLF chassis were stored in the open and unprotected at Wrights for some time before being bodied. This resulted in water ingress into the suspension struts and consequent early-life failures.

Only around 105 Lance SLFs were built before the model ceased production in 1996, many of which went to London operators. The Wrights Pathfinder body was fitted to most, the rest being bodied by Berkhof with their Excellence 1000NL body. The British Airports Authority bought thirty of these for use as staff shuttles at Heathrow Airport.

The Dart SLF

The future requirement for step-free access on buses meant that even midibuses like Dart would need to comply. Experience with the Lance SLF had underlined to the Dennis engineering team that independent front suspension was not an ideal way to achieve the necessary low floor levels. No alternatives were evident, however, until the team discovered that Kirkstall, the then-suppliers of the Dart front axle, were able to forge an axle beam with a deeper 'drop' or swan neck at the ends. This would lower the centre portion of the beam far enough to be able to drop the floor line to provide a step-free entry. It could also give a gangway between the wheel arches wide enough to allow a wheelchair to pass. This front axle configuration duly made it into production as part of the DM94 project (Dennis Midibus for 1994), which became known as the Dart SLF. The rest, as

DENNIS LANCE SLF, 1993–1996

Configuration: 4×2 rigid welded modular frame, rear-engined low-floor chassis
Engine: Cummins C-series Euro 1 turbocharged diesel
Capacity: 8270cc
Max. power: 211bhp (157kW)
Max. torque: 604lb ft (819Nm)
Gearbox: ZF 4HP500 or 5HP500 automatic, integral retarder
Rear axle: Eaton 11.28 single-reduction hypoid
Suspension: Front: ZF RLE66 independent with kneeling facility, 2 airbags and one telescopic damper per side
Rear: 2 airbags located by trailing taper leaf springs and panhard rod, 4 telescopic dampers
Brakes: Lucas discs front, GKN S-cam drums rear, air operated; spring brake for parking
Wheelbase: 5,950mm (234.25in)
Overall length (body): 11,000mm (433in)
    11,500mm (452.75in)
Overall width (chassis): 2,411mm (95in)
Unladen weight (chassis): 6,240kg (13,757lb)
GVW (max.): 16,800kg (37,037lb)
Top speed: 49mph (79km/h)
(Source: Dennis Lance SLF data sheet, 1993)

The ultra-low chassis of the Dart SLF, on view here outside the Slyfield factory. RICHARD NORMAN

Few operators in the UK did not include Dart SLFs in their fleet. The shorter 8.5m (27ft 11in) versions were particularly suited to shuttle operations, while the longer models saw much service in slightly less restricted conditions. This 2002 model is operated by Safeguard, a Guildford operator. AUTHOR

they say, is history, with sales being tremendously successful and continuing for many years. Even when replaced by the Enviro 200 range many years later, the Dart SLF chassis continued essentially unchanged under the revamped body.

The Dart SLF's novel chassis design meant that the bodywork needed to be specially created. Some years earlier, Dennis engineers and sales teams had developed a good working relationship with their opposite numbers at Plaxton while developing the Javelin. This relationship was taken a stage further for the Dart SLF, with Plaxton becoming the lead bodybuilder and developing an optimized body-to-chassis interface for the new model. Plaxton, therefore, had a clear advantage in being first to market with a Dart SLF body – moreover a body that was set up to take maximum advantage of the Dart SLF chassis.

Other bodybuilders were left to fit their bodies as best they could. Some took up the challenge: Marshall and their successors, MCV, bodied Dart SLFs, while Caetano proved reasonably successful with their Nimbus body. Indeed, Caetano carved a small market niche of their own when they produced a 2.36m-wide (7ft 9in) version, the Slimbus, which sold to Jersey as well as several mainland UK operators. East Lancs produced their Spryte body, and they too got in on the narrow-body act, selling around thirty to Guernsey's Island Coachways. Wright developed a version of their Crusader body for the SLF, although sales numbered only around 150 between 1996 and 2000. Alexander also produced a version of their ALX200 body.

Unsurprisingly, however, Plaxton Pointer versions of Dart SLF were much better received than any of their competitors, most of which eventually fell by the wayside.

Overall, 9,200 Dart SLFs were sold before the model was replaced, in name at any rate, by the Enviro 200 in 2006.

The Dart SLF was launched at the 1995 Coach & Bus Show along with some competitive new low-floor models, including the similar-sized Volvo B6LE. With the Dart SLF continuing the sales success of the step-entry Dart, it was inevitable that other manufacturers would seek to take a slice of the midibus market. Perhaps the most successful of these was Optare with their Solo, introduced in 1998, although sales never reached the levels of the Dart SLF. DAF Bus also produced their SB120, which was uncannily similar to the Dart. The SB120 had more success due to the close relationship between DAF and Arriva.

The expected sales opposition from Volvo, by then Dennis's arch-rival in sales volume, never really materialized. Volvo's mistake with their B6 and B6 midibus models was to use an independent front suspension, which, just as the Dennis team had forecast, needed frequent maintenance. The end result was that Volvo models sold in their hundreds, Dart SLFs in their thousands.

The SLF was available only at one chassis width, to suit a nominal 2.44m-wide (8ft) body. Body lengths grew considerably, with the shortest SLF now measuring 9.2m (30ft 2in) and the longest 10.7m (35ft 1in), accompanied by an increase in GVW from 10 tonnes (9.84 tons) to 11.5 tonnes

DENNIS DART SLF, 1995–2001

Layout and Chassis
4×2 rigid welded modular frame, rear-engined low-floor chassis for 8.5m (from 1998), 9m, 10m and 10.5m body lengths

Engine
Type: Cummins B-series Euro 2 turbocharged and intercooled diesel
Block material: Cast iron
Head material: Cast iron
Cylinders: 6 in-line
Cooling: Water
Bore and stroke: 102 × 120mm
Capacity: 5900cc
Max. power:
8.5m, 9m and 10m bodies: 130PS (97kW) at 2,500rpm
10.5m body: 145PS (107kW) at 2,500rpm
Max. torque: 8.5m, 9m and 10m bodies: 336lb ft (456Nm) at 1,500rpm
10.5m body: 369lb ft (500Nm) at 1,500rpm
Fuel capacity: 220ltr (48gal)

Transmission
Gearbox: Allison AT545 4-speed fully automatic
Retarder: Telma Focal 5750 electric
Final drive: Eaton 08-18 single-reduction hypoid, 8,000kg (17,636lb) capacity

Suspension and Steering
Front: 2 airbags located by trailing taper leaf springs and panhard rod, two telescopic dampers, fast-kneel facility
Rear: 2 airbags located by trailing taper leaf springs and panhard rod, two telescopic dampers
Steering: ZF 8095 integral power
Tyres: 245/70 R 19.5 low-profile tubeless
Wheels: Spigot-mounted, 6.75 × 19.5 steel

Brakes
Type: Perrot Simplex air-wedge drums, air operated; spring parking brake
Size: 360mm (14.25in) diameter

Dimensions
Wheelbases: 8.5m: 3,900mm (153.5in)
9m: 4,400mm (173.25in)
10m: 5,200mm (204.75in)
10.5m: 5,805mm (228.51in)
Overall lengths (body): 8,500mm (334.6in)
9,000mm (354.3in):
10,000m (393.7in)
10,500m (413.3in)
Overall width (chassis): 2,360mm (92.9in)
Unladen weight (chassis): 3,840–4,140kg (8,466–9,127lb)
GVW: 8.5m and 9m: 11,000kg (24,250lb)
10m: 11,500kg (25,353lb)
10.5m: 12,000kg (26,455lb)
Capacity: up to 60 passengers

Performance
Top speed: 47mph (76km/h) with 4.88:1 rear axle
59mph (95km/h) with 4.11:1 rear axle
(Source: Dennis Dart SLF data sheets, 1996/1999)

(11.32 tons), which allowed seating for up to forty-four passengers. In 10.7m form, the Dart SLF provided virtually the same seating capacity as a full-size single-decker but at a much lower price – around £80,000 rather than the typical £100,000 for the full-size bus.

In 1998, Dennis were watching the sales success of the Optare Solo, which was available in shorter lengths than the Dart SLF, and jointly with Plaxton decided to introduce a cheaper 8.5m (27ft 11in) version of the Dart SLF, known as Mini Pointer Dart or MPD. This had some success in taking business from the Solo, for the Solo was at that time only available in 2.5m-wide (8ft 2.5in) form against the 2.4m (7ft 10in) of the MPD, so giving the MPD greater route availability. Subsequently, of course, Optare fought back with the 2.33m-width (7ft 7in) Slimline version of the Solo.

As emissions standards continued to tighten to Euro 3 level in 2001, the 5.9-litre 6-cylinder Cummins B-series was replaced by the 4-cylinder 3.9-litre ISBe engine in the shorter-length Dart SLFs. This engine developed the same power output as its predecessor, but made both Dennis's and operators' engineers apprehensive, as the 4-cylinder B-series Cummins that was used previously in the Marshall minibus had a reputation for vibration. According to Cummins, however, the engine used by Marshall was an old industrial rather than automotive unit, and the 4-cylinder ISBe in Dart SLF did indeed prove much smoother. Matters were probably helped by the Dennis design team paying very close attention to optimizing the engine mount geometry, an issue that seemed to have been overlooked in the Marshall vehicle.

As well as being used for bus duties, the step-free entry of the Dart SLF made it attractive for other roles needing easy access. In 1999, Durham County Council saw the potential for use as a mobile library, where the easy access

DENNIS DART SLF, 2001–2006

Specification as for earlier model with the following exceptions:
Engine: Cummins ISBe 4-cylinder Euro 3 turbocharged and intercooled diesel; Cummins ISBe 4-cylinder Euro 4 from approx. 2005
Max. power: 130PS (97kW) or 150PS (112kW)
Gearbox: Allison S2000 4-speed, fully automatic from approx. 2002
Brakes: Wabco Pan 19.1 375mm (14.75in) diameter air disc brakes from approx. 2003

DART SLF EXPORTS

Export sales of the Dart SLF were greater than had been enjoyed by the earlier step-frame Dart. In 1996, Berkhof bodied five Dart SLFs for use by NZH in Holland, while in 2001 Arriva Nederland put a batch of fifty Alexander-bodied SLFs into service, also in Holland. The Arriva vehicles were not well received by their drivers and were returned a couple of times to have additional sound insulation fitted. Spain also became a market for the SLFs, with local bodybuilders Hispano, Unvi, Castrosua and PIC all producing vehicles for Spanish operators. Marcopolo also bodied SLFs for operation in Portugal, as did Caetano and Camo. Gibraltar saw Dart SLFs fitted with the Caetano Slimbus bodies in service around their tricky road system, while an unusual sale in 1999 was of two Pointer Darts to Iceland.

Darts were popular in Hong Kong. This one was operated by New Lantao Bus on Lantau Island, the largest of the territory's islands. DANNY CHAN

One European country where much sales effort was expended for little return was Malta. By the mid-1990s, the Maltese bus fleet was long overdue for renewal. Four SLFs were supplied to one Maltese operator, Paramount, in 1997 in what Dennis hoped would be the forerunner of further business. These were unique vehicles, being the only modern Darts ever to be fitted, at Malta's insistence, with manual gearboxes. The much-promised fleet renewal failed to arrive until 2002, thanks to protracted wrangling between the Maltese government and their bus operators. Despite all the hard work by the sales team, the eventual orders were not for Dart SLFs but Chinese King Long 6113s.

Farther afield, a joint Plaxton and Dennis sales visit in January of 1998, of which the author was part, persuaded British Columbia Transit in Canada to purchase Dart SLFs for use in the Olympic winter sports resort of Whistler, and elsewhere. The initiative for this activity came from one of BC Transit drivers who had the ear of his management and who, while visiting relatives in the UK, had seen for himself the sterling performance of the Dart and Dart SLF. The sales visit resulted in an order for ninety Dart SLFs, which were delivered from 1999. These were not well received in operation, so further orders were not forthcoming. In truth, though, some at least of the operational issues seemed to have been self-inflicted by BC Transit, such as the apparent fitment of incorrect air filter elements, leading to dirt-laden air reaching the engine with consequent rapid wear. Realistically, adopting the lightweight Dart SLF was probably just a step too far for BC Transit, who at that time were more used to typically hefty North American bus models.

Hong Kong was also a successful Dart SLF market, with all the major operators there taking Dart SLFs into their fleets. Some of the Citybus vehicles eventually returned to the UK, operating with Stagecoach in the south of England and becoming some of the UK's first fully air-conditioned service buses. Around seventy vehicles also went to Australia, marketed there by Scania, who were happy to do so since they did not have a midibus in their own product range.

afforded by the SLF was far superior to traditional vehicles that needed three or even four steps to board, which was not ideal for their typically aged or infirm patrons. The SLF may have been ideal for those people, but the unplanned order for the library vehicle gained so merrily by the Dennis sales team caused apoplexy among the Dennis homologation team. The reason was that Dart SLF had been type-approved solely as a passenger vehicle, while the library application classified it as a goods vehicle – meaning that many new approvals were needed to satisfy a different set of regulations.

The Dart SLF enjoyed a long production run, from 1996 through to 2006, when it was eventually replaced by the Enviro 200, which was essentially the same chassis under a new name. Component changes in that time were relatively few. The Cummins engine, of course, was steadily updated from Euro II to Euro IV, and transmissions moved from the original Allison AT545 to the later Allison 2000 series. A batch of trial vehicles was also built with a new Voith transmission, the Voith DV500. The DV500s, however, proved initially to have poor shift quality and were unreliable, with the familiar Allison units later being retrofitted following Voith's decision not to take the DV500 to production.

The Arrow Double-Decker

In 1995, a double-deck version of the Lance was offered, badged as Arrow. This was little modified from the single-decker, the changes being limited to the addition of an anti-roll bar and moving the dampers outboard. Sales were limited, at around eighty, a Dennis copycat product once again failing to make much headway against the well-established Leyland and Volvo models of the time.

DENNIS ARROW, 1995–2000

Specification as for Lance (*see* above) with the following exceptions:
Engine: Cummins C-series Euro 2
Max. power: 245PS (180kW)
Max. torque: 756lb ft (1,025Nm)
Suspension: Anti-roll bar on front axle, dampers relocated outboard
Wheelbase: 5,050mm (198.8in)
Overall length (body): 10,500m (413.3in)
Unladen weight (chassis): 5,610kg (12,368lb)
(Source: Dennis Arrow data sheet, 1996)

DENNIS SUPER POINTER DART, 1997–2001

Specification as for Dart SLF with the following exceptions:
Engine: Cummins B-series Euro 2 turbocharged and intercooled diesel
Capacity: 5900cc
Max. power: 180PS (134kW)
Max. torque: 406lb ft (550Nm)
Gearbox: Voith DIWA 823.3 3-speed fully automatic with integral retarder
or Allison B300R 4-speed fully automatic
Rear axle: Dana 09-24 single reduction hypoid
Wheelbase: 5,950mm (19ft 6.25in)
Overall length (body): 11,300m (444.9in)
Unladen weight (chassis): 4,240kg (9,348lb)
GVW: 12,960kg (28,572lb)
(Source: Dennis Dart SPD data sheets, 1999)

The Super Pointer Dart

Having observed the massive success of the longer versions of the Dart SLF, in particular in taking sales from competitors' full-size single-deckers, Dennis and Plaxton decided to stretch the Dart SLF concept yet further, to 11.3m (37ft 1in) with a project codenamed SD96, later to become the Super Pointer Dart, or SPD. At the time the Dart SLF was limited to an 11-tonne (10.8-ton) gross weight by the Allison AT545 gearbox, and also on torque capacity by the rear axle rating. A stronger Dana rear axle together with an Allison World Series transmission were therefore fitted to the SPD, while the engine power was uprated to 180bhp. This was not done without causing some apprehension to the Dennis engineers, who felt this might be a stretch too far.

The extra length of the saloon in the SPD meant that rather than having a flat saloon floor to a point just forward of the rear axle, with two steps up over the axle as on Dart SLF, the floor could be sloped gently upwards from the front axle, minimizing the step up over the rear axle. Because the SPD was very much a jointly designed project between Dennis and Plaxton, Dennis took the opportunity to integrate the floor framing into the chassis frame, simplifying and improving the bodying process for Plaxton.

The SPD first appeared at the 1997 Coach & Bus Show, with the first vehicles reaching customers in 1998. For the first two years, the model was bodied exclusively by Plaxton; subsequently, a number were bodied by East Lancs and Alexander.

The Trident Three-Axle Double-Decker

Hong Kong vehicle legislation stipulates an eighteen-year life for service buses, and in the early 1990s, many early Dragons and Condors were approaching the end of their allotted life span. Together with the territory adopting the step-free entry requirements of the UK, it was not long before it was necessary to come up with a low-floor big double-decker design. Accordingly, design work started in 1995 on a three-axle decker aimed primarily at the Hong Kong market.

As with the Dart SLF, the new model, Trident, featured a Dana (who had by then taken over Kirkstall) deep-drop beam front axle to achieve a step-free entrance and a low, wide gangway between the front wheel arches while avoiding the complexities of independent front suspension.

The Dragon had been fitted with a rear transverse engine. In developing the Trident concept, chief designer Richard Norman realized that the compact size of the Cummins M11 engine made it possible to package a lon-gitudinal engine and gearbox driving directly into the rear axle in a T-drive configuration. This would avoid the cost and complexity of the angle drive that would be necessary with a transverse engine. By angling the engine and gearbox downwards, it was also possible to get the engine under the rear seat, allowing an extra row of seats to be fitted. A bespoke portal drive axle was required, and this was developed by Dana.

The Trident 3 went on sale in 1997, quickly repeating the sales success of Dragon and Condor, despite attempts by other manufacturers, notably MAN, to break into the massive Hong Kong market.

Hong Kong is a challenging operating environment for service buses, with its combination of steep hills, heavy traffic and frequently heavy passenger loadings, and it is a testament to the design of Trident 3 that service problems were reasonably minor. Indeed, in the important measure of availability, Trident 3, and its successor Enviro 500, have consistently been among the best-performing vehicles in the territory.

DENNIS TRIDENT 3, 1997–2002

Layout and Chassis
6×2 rigid welded modular frame, rear-engined low-floor chassis

Engine
Type: 1997–2000 (approx.): Cummins Euro 2 M11-305E 6-cylinder turbocharged intercooled diesel
or c.2000–2005 Cummins Euro 3 ISMe-330 or 335 6-cylinder turbocharged intercooled diesel
or North American models: Cummins EPA-rated ISM-330 6-cylinder turbocharged intercooled diesel
Block material: Cast iron
Head material: Cast iron
Cylinders: 6 in-line
Cooling: Water
Bore and stroke: 125 × 147mm
Capacity: 10800cc
Compression ratio: Euro 2: 16:1
Max. power (DIN): Euro 2: 305PS (224kW) at 1,900rpm
Euro 3: 330 or 335PS (246 or 250kW)
EPA: 330PS (246kW)
Max. torque: Euro 2: 921lb ft (1,250Nm) at 1,200rpm

Transmission
Gearbox: Euro 2: Voith D863.3 3-speed automatic or ZF 5HP590 5-speed automatic
Drive axle: Dana portal, 13,000kg (28,660lb) capacity

Auxiliary axle: Dana T75ULF drop-centre, non-steered, 7,500kg (16,535lb) capacity

Suspension and Steering
Front: 2 airbags, multi-link location, anti-roll bar, two hydraulic dampers, rapid-kneel facility
Drive: 4 airbags, multi-link location, anti-roll bar, four hydraulic dampers
Auxiliary: 2 airbags, location by trailing taper leaf springs with panhard rod, two telescopic dampers
Steering: ZF8098 integral power
Tyres: 305/70 R 22.5 tubeless radial
Wheels: Spigot-mounted, 8.25 × 22.5

Brakes
Type: Full air, Dana S-cam drum brakes; spring brake for parking on drive and auxiliary axle
Size: 410mm (16in) diameter

Dimensions
Wheelbase: 12m body: 5,700mm (224.4in)
Overall lengths (bodied): 10,300m (405.5in)
10.6m (417.3in)
11.3m (444.9in)
12m (472.4in)
Overall width: 2,500mm (98.4in)
Unladen weight (chassis): 12m: 8,420kg (18,563lb)
GVW (max.): 24,000kg (52,910lb)
Capacity: up to 91 seats plus 37 standees
(Source: Dennis Trident 3 data sheet)

Three generations of public transport together in Hong Kong in 2005 – the tram on the left, a middle-aged Citybus Leyland Olympian in the centre and a New World First Bus Trident 3 on the right. AUTHOR

Part of the aim of the sales visit to British Columbia outlined earlier was to promote the Trident 3, and this resulted in an order for eleven, which were delivered in 1999. The Trident 3s were much more favourably received than the Dart SLFs, and further batches soon followed the initial order, BC Transit becoming a fan of the product and more than happy to act as a reference site for other North American operations, which were also beginning to develop an interest in the big double-decker.

The Trident Two-Axle Double-Decker
The success of the Dart and Dart SLF in the single-deck low-floor market made a venture into the UK low-floor double-deck arena a logical step, and in 1996 Dennis started to develop a suitable design. The proposed DD96 model used the same front module package as the three-axle Trident, with a new rear module to accommodate a single rear axle. The engineering team were initially requested to create a longitudinal T-drive package. However, they soon discovered that even using the compact Cummins C-series engine, an excessive rear overhang would result. As the front wheels of any vehicle are turned in one direction, the rearmost outer corner of the vehicle swings out in the opposite direction. This means that as the bus swings out away from the kerb at a bus stop, its back corner sweeps out, over the pavement in an extreme case. Discussions with several London operators soon confirmed the validity of the team's reservations about the long rear overhang.

The chief designer, therefore, set about looking for an alternative solution and discovered that if installed transversely, the C-series engine would fit under the rear seat, reducing the rear overhang considerably. By then, ZF in Germany had become a 'centre of excellence' in the development of low-floor bus transmission and axle components, and with increasing production volumes due to the rapid adoption of low-floor buses across Europe, prices for

Trident 2, which quickly became a common sight in both London and around the UK. ADL

these items had also reduced. This gave Dennis the potential hardware to develop a cost-effective transverse layout. Thus was born the DD97 concept, one which was quickly endorsed by the sales team. The resulting product, Trident, was launched in 1997 and was rapidly accepted by operators, particularly in London.

At almost the same time, Volvo also designed their new double-decker with a longitudinal T-drive configuration. Unlike Dennis, however, Volvo took the T-drive package right through to production. At launch it was roundly criticized for its excessive rear overhang and consequent poor manoeuvrability in city traffic, justifying the Dennis team's distrust of such a configuration. Volvo were forced into a redesign to adopt a transverse-engined layout for their B7 double-decker. This process inevitably took some time, and the resulting delay allowed the Trident to become firmly established in the marketplace.

The first two-axle Tridents entered the UK marketplace with Stagecoach in London at the start of 1999. By the summer, over 100 were in service in the city, and in less than two years, sales of the low-floor double-decker exceeded 1,000, making it the most successful double-decker in the company's history. Alexander's ALX400 bodywork was fitted to the first vehicles, with products from other bodybuilders, such as East Lancs' Lolyne and Northern Counties' President, not far behind.

Despite several updates over the years, the origins and

fundamental excellence of the Trident 2 chassis are still recognizable today in the Enviro 400 product, with over 11,000 produced by July 2019.

DENNIS EAGLE

As well as producing the Sabre cabs, the ex-Duple factory at Blackpool also made the Dennis Eagle cabs. Sharing the same basic constructional techniques, the fire and refuse vehicle cabs were nevertheless quite different in execution, being tailored very much to their intended markets.

In 1992, Dennis Eagle launched a revolutionary new refuse vehicle chassis, the Elite. For this, the cab was designed specifically for easy and rapid entry and exit, with full-height doors and one single wide step rather than the three or four steps usually needed. This was combined with a low flat floor to maximize crew space. The engine was set well back in the chassis, and the cab set well forward on the frame, allowing it to be as low as possible.

The Elite set the standard for refuse vehicle cabs, the design soon being imitated by no less than Mercedes Benz. Its low height meant that the Elite soon found customers far beyond the traditional municipal vehicle market. It became popular, for example, for airport airside applications including refuellers, where that low height assured it access into places denied to a conventional truck.

THE BEST-LAID PLANS …

In October 1997, Trinity rebranded itself as the Dennis Group, with several operating divisions including Guildford-based Dennis Specialist Vehicles, whose bus and coach market share was by then around 60 per cent, a far cry from the 10 per cent when Hestair bought Dennis in 1972.

Fire engine sales were equally buoyant in this period, thanks to the Sabre chassis, which was also highly successful. The smaller Rapier, a very agile and impressive appliance, may have achieved fewer sales due to its limited payload, but it was nevertheless a remarkable 'halo product' for the company.

So, towards the end of the 1990s, Dennis Specialist Vehicles were on a roll, dominating the UK bus market and increasingly successful overseas. By any measure – sales volume, turnover, profitability or almost any other key performance indicator – the future looked bright. The

DENNIS TRIDENT 2, 1997–2005

Layout and Chassis
4×2 rigid welded modular frame, rear-engined low-floor chassis for 9.9m–11.4m body lengths

Engine
Type: 1997–2000 (approx.): Cummins Euro 2 C-series 6-cylinder, 220PS (164kW) or 245PS (183kW)
c.2000–2005: Cummins Euro 3 ISCe 6-cylinder 225PS (168kW) or 260PS (194kW)
Block material: Cast iron
Head material: Cast iron
Cylinders: 6 in-line
Cooling: water
Bore and stroke: 134.9 × 114mm
Capacity: 8270cc
Max. power: C220-20 Euro 2: 220PS (162kW) at 2,200rpm
C245-20 Euro 2 240PS (180kW) at 2,200rpm
Max. torque: C220-20 Euro 2: 590lb ft (800Nm) at 1,400rpm
C245-20 Euro 2: 756lb ft (1,025Nm) at 1,400rpm
Fuel capacity: 275ltr (60gal)

Transmission
Gearbox: Voith D851.3 3-speed automatic with integral retarder
or ZF 4HP500 4-speed or ZF 5HP500 5-speed automatic with integral retarder
Final drive: ZF AV-132 drop centre, 13,000kg (28,660lb) capacity

Suspension and Steering
Front: 2 airbags, multi-link location, anti-roll bar, two telescopic dampers, fast-kneel facility
Rear: 4 airbags, multi-link location, anti-roll bar, four telescopic dampers
Steering: ZF8098 integral power
Tyres: 275/70R22.5 tubeless radial
Wheels: Spigot-mounted steel, 7.5 × 22.5

Brakes
Type: Air-operated, S-cam drums (early models) or Knorr 4-piston discs (later models)
Size: 410mm (16in) diameter drums

Dimensions
Wheelbases: 9.9m body: 5,250mm (206.7in)
10.45m body: 5,800mm (228.3in)
10.6m body: 5,950mm (234.25in)
Overall lengths (body): 9,900mm (389.75in)
10,450mm (411.4in)
10,600mm (417.3in)
11,400mm (448.8in)
Overall width: 2,500mm (98.4in)
Unladen weight (chassis): 6,420–6,490kg (14,154–14,308lb)
GVW (max.): 17,800kg (39,242lb)

Performance
Top speed: 48mph (77km/h) with Voith gearbox
56mph (90km/h) with ZF 5HP500 gearbox
(Source: Dennis Trident data sheet, 1999)

key to this success had come from producing products such as the Javelin, Dart SLF, Trident and Sabre that the market wanted, at a price they were willing to pay. The Dart, for example, had achieved over 1,000 sales in 1995 alone. Just one of the many attractions of Dennis chassis were their extremely competitive weights, the low weight leading directly to reduced fuel consumption – and fuel is a very significant element in the cost of bus operation.

The original step-entry Dart had a potential payload of half its gross weight, a milestone unmatched either before or since. Moreover, the low weights were achieved without any reduction in durability: structural failures on any Dennis product are rare indeed. As icing on the cake, fortune had also smiled on the company, with several external factors helping the success of the business, including the lack of market penetration of would-be competitors such as the Volvo B6 midibus and the early Volvo B7 double-decker.

Strong MoD sales of Javelin had also helped to drive sales figures to new heights.

No business can afford to stand still, however, and the Trinity management team were already considering the next steps, which they felt would once again involve manufacturing complete vehicles. The close working relationship between chassis builder Dennis and bodybuilder Plaxton has already been highlighted. It was natural therefore for Dennis and Plaxton to come together more formally, and in July 1998 a proposed deal was announced for a friendly takeover of Dennis by Plaxton's parent company, Henlys, for £190 million, a plan fully supported by the management teams of both companies. This amicable plan was soon to be derailed, however, as the next chapter reveals, by events that effectively ended Dennis's prominence as a major chassis manufacturer, relegating the company to becoming a mere supplier to a bodybuilder.

CHAPTER SEVEN

MAYFLOWER MISMANAGEMENT:
1998–2004

MAYFLOWER BUS & COACH

The plans for an amicable merger between Dennis Specialist Vehicles and Plaxton caused some consternation within the bus industry. Many people, despite assurances to the contrary, were concerned that Dennis chassis in future would no longer be available to other bodybuilders, nor would Plaxton body any chassis other than Dennis.

In particular, a rival bodybuilder, Alexander, and their parent company, Mayflower Corporation, grew concerned at the potential impact on their business, as they regularly bodied Dennis chassis. Mayflower, therefore, began their own bid for control of Dennis.

The Mayflower management team were not lacking in confidence in their ability to identify and develop previously unseen market opportunities. Moreover, they appeared to have an impressive knack of being able to extract investment funds from money markets to underpin their ambitions. Examples of this were their e3 engine venture and Mayflower Energy. The e3 engine was a new variable displacement engine promising significant improvements in fuel economy over conventional internal combustion engines, while Mayflower Energy's claim to fame was the introduction of an innovative ship designed to install wind turbines in the sea. Against a background at the time of increasing energy prices and growing concern about the environment, the enthusiasm of the Mayflower Board for these projects can perhaps be understood. Even then, however, some financial analysts were nonetheless wary of the company, justifiably as things turned out. Following the launch of the e3 engine, one was reported as saying:

The concept is very interesting. It looks to be one of those very simple concepts that is totally brilliant and could revolutionize things, but scepticism leads me to believe that things are never quite as good as Mayflower would have us think. The company tends to live on the optimistic side...

THE *MAYFLOWER RESOLUTION*

The *Mayflower Resolution* was probably the first self-elevating wind turbine installation vessel in the world. Aimed specifically at the proposed North Sea offshore wind farms, it was able to raise itself hydraulically on six legs at least 10ft (3m) above sea level to provide a stable working platform from which to hammer down a pile into the sea bed, onto which could be installed a wind turbine. Once the turbine was installed, the *Mayflower Resolution* would be lowered and could then sail to the next position to repeat the process. Up to ten turbines could be installed in this way before the ship needed to return to port.

The 14,857-tonne (14,620-ton) vessel was ordered in 2002 for build in a Chinese shipyard. Initially intended for delivery in February 2003, delays and design changes pushed the delivery back to February 2004, with a substantial rise in the cost from £20m to £53m.

The ship installed its first turbines in March 2004, in the North Hoyle wind farm off Liverpool Bay. Its second tasking, installing turbines in the Scroby Sands wind farm off Great Yarmouth was about to begin when the Mayflower Corporation collapsed into administration. Eventually bought from Mayflower's Administrators, the *Resolution* (without the Mayflower prefix) continued a successful career planting many more turbines around the coast, spawning the building of two further similar vessels.

THE E3 ENGINE

Scientist Dr Joe Erlich developed the e3 engine concept. Named for its claimed benefits to the Environment, Economy and Energy, at its launch event in October 2001 such luminaries as Sir Jack Brabham, of motorsport fame, and former UK prime minister Sir John Major were present. Mayflower's claim on the day was that their engine, although still based on traditional internal combustion engine principles, could offer at least a 50 per cent reduction in emissions combined with at least 40 per cent reduction in fuel consumption.

However, Mayflower's rationale for entering a bidding war was much more significant than merely ensuring the supply of chassis to feed Alexander's bodybuilding plant. At that time, Dennis production was at the highest-ever level, with 2,300 chassis produced at Guildford in 1999, achieving a record share of the UK bus and coach market. Seduced by this recent highly impressive performance, Mayflower were highly confident of their own ability to continue to grow and profit from the Guildford chassis business, in the process disabling a major bodybuilding competitor, Plaxton, by

cutting off their chassis supply. What they ultimately failed to understand were the temporary and limited nature of the particular market forces that had led to Dennis's current success, such as the blip of orders from the MoD for Javelins, and the ramping-down of Trident 3 sales into Hong Kong as the territory came towards the end of one of its bus-buying cycles.

After an acrimonious bidding war, and following the inevitable Monopolies and Mergers Commission investigation, Mayflower eventually took control of Dennis in October 1998. They paid £268.9 million, far above the £190 million originally agreed between Dennis and Henlys.

The resulting Dennis and Alexander consortium was given the name of Mayflower Bus & Coach. Surprisingly, given Mayflower's acquisitive tendencies, they saw no future in several of the Dennis Group product ranges, and the Carmichael fire business was soon sold off. This was followed by the sale of Dennis Eagle and Douglas Schopf.

Henlys had previously been making moves on what they saw as the lucrative US market, in 1995 taking a 49 per cent share in Prevost, a leading North American manufacturer of coaches and bus bodies, the other 51 per cent being owned by Volvo. In late 1997, a further Henlys move into the US market saw the purchase of Canada's Nova Bus Corporation, although this deal consumed much of Henlys net cash surplus.

This chart shows the number of vehicles produced by Guildford between 1986 and 2006. The steady growth in numbers up to 1999 explains why Mayflower found Dennis such an irresistible acquisition, while the decline after that date tells its own story.
RICHARD NORMAN

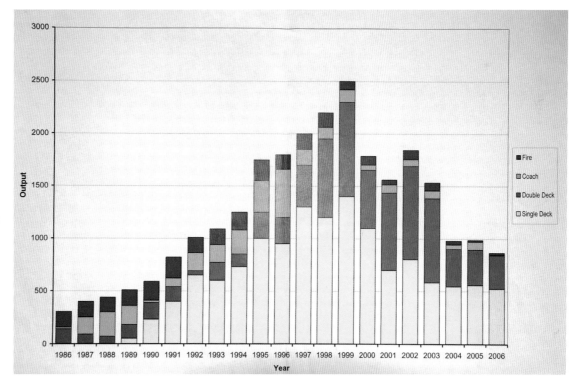

Following their failed attempt at buying Dennis, in 1999 Henlys then bought, with Volvo's backing, the US Blue Bird Corporation, which held 40 per cent of the US yellow school-bus market. Suspecting that Mayflower would refuse to provide Dart SLF chassis to them for bodying, they set up a Blue Bird subsidiary at Scarborough to develop a new midibus chassis of their own. However, by then the Henlys business was in a poor state, due to both a slow domestic market and being weakened financially by paying handsomely for Blue Bird.

FORMATION OF TRANSBUS INTERNATIONAL

In August 2000, Henlys, therefore, joined forces with Mayflower Bus & Coach, taking a minority 30 per cent share in the new enterprise, which was named TransBus International. This brought together Alexander, Plaxton and Dennis, creating a workforce of over 3,300.

Unfortunately for Dennis, however, centralized control by TransBus meant that they were no longer masters of their own destiny and free to sell chassis to the global bus market. Their only outlet for chassis was to the TransBus bodybuilders. In effect, Dennis become just another supplier to Falkirk and Scarborough, and no longer an independent chassis manufacturer. Frustratingly for the Guildford team, the policy of permitting Dennis chassis to receive only TransBus bodies was not matched by a similar exclusivity in bodybuilding, with Scania and Volvo chassis regularly being fitted with TransBus bodies.

Inevitably, this meant that as time went on, the influence of Dennis on the overall direction of TransBus waned steadily, with the Guildford operation losing much of its autonomy in critical functions such as sales, purchasing and engineering, such matters being managed, and often micro-managed, centrally.

Reality must soon have begun to set in, with Mayflower realizing that they had overpaid for Dennis. Additionally, the *Mayflower Resolution* project (*see* box) took far more of Mayflower's funds than had been anticipated, while the e3 engine absorbed the investment poured into it without any visible return, and eventually disappeared without a trace.

Cost-cutting became the order of the day, resulting in several unwelcome measures such as the sale and leaseback of the Slyfield site. Forever afterwards, this gave the company the unpleasant legacy of a massive annual rent charge.

Duple Metsec's West Midlands factory was closed in 2001, DM5000 double-deck body production being transferred to Alexander's Falkirk plant.

Plaxton's Scarborough site was also proposed for closure in the summer of 2001 with the potential loss of 700 jobs, the closure plans being blamed, unreasonably, on the fall in tourism after a foot and mouth epidemic. In preparation for the closure, Pointer body production was moved to Falkirk; however, the Scarborough plant gained a limited reprieve, with 200 staff retained after the summer break. For a time, Falkirk built both ALX200 and Pointer bodies for the Dart in parallel. However, the ALX200 soon ceased production, leaving all TransBus Dart SLFs being bodied as Pointers.

Despite the cost-cutting, it must be said that Mayflower had recognized as paramount the need to support their products in the field. As a result, during 1999 they had commissioned two major regional parts distribution centres at Wigan and Falkirk, complementing the existing Dennis parts centres in Bristol, Durham and Guildford.

In May 2002, Mayflower raised further funds from a £64 million rights issue, a share offering bought into by many small shareholders. These included many loyal employees, including the author, who believed in the future of the company and its products.

At the end of 2002, Mayflower also offloaded its short-lived Thomas Dennis joint venture bus-building operation in North America. Its 49 per cent interest in the company was sold to their partner DaimlerChrysler, whose engines were used in the joint venture products. Mayflower claimed that the reason for the sale was to free them to concentrate on double-deck production for North America rather than the single-deckers as produced by Thomas Dennis.

ADMINISTRATION – THE DARKEST HOUR

The final nail in the Mayflower coffin was probably the discovery of a £200 million black hole in Mayflower's accounts, which centred around four years of alleged financial misreporting relating to the debt factoring used by Mayflower. It was suggested that TransBus had effectively double-counted the amount of money owing to the company by its industry creditors, potentially misleading its investors. Although Britain's financial authorities investigated these allegations, no charges were ever brought against the Mayflower directors. However, by early March 2004, the stock market valuation of Mayflower, valued at £700 million in 1999, had sunk to only £22 million. Finally, with debts of £17.7 million, on 31 March 2004, Deloitte and Touche were appointed administrators to the Mayflower business.

The administrators' analysis of the assets of the business was dire. Although the company appeared to have some

£125 million in assets, the issues surrounding the company meant these were virtually non-existent. Indeed, almost the only fixed asset left in the company was the *Mayflower Resolution*. Not only that, the pension fund of the loyal workforce had been starved of investment. As a result, thousands of staff were left with only 40 per cent of their expected pensions, despite the Mayflower directors apparently having made substantial contributions into their own pension scheme shortly before administration.

Many employees, who had invested their hard-earned cash in their employer's shares via the 2002 rights issue, experienced a double blow, for their shares became worthless as a result of administration.

Fairly quickly, the administrators sold the *Resolution* to the management team of Mayflower Energy, although it only realized a knock-down £12 million rather than the £20 million at which it was valued. This was accepted, it seems, to achieve a quick sale to keep TransBus trading while a buyer was sought. The new owners of the *Resolution* set up as MPI Offshore, and after their great good fortune in acquiring their prize asset on the cheap, never looked back.

TransBus was kept trading by the administrators during this period, albeit on a very short leash, with every single item of expenditure or external correspondence needing to be signed off by the administrators' team. This led to much frustration, particularly for the engineering team, who were faced with frequently needing to explain complex technical issues in words of one syllable to the admin-istrators before being able to communicate with the outside world.

As part of the administration process, the administrators decided to make redundant around one-third of the indirect staff such as designers and clerical staff, and it was a sad day indeed when so many skills, experience and friendships were wasted. Not only that, but managers were forced into making instant decisions to select staff for redundancy, with no opportunity to consider how best to handle such a delicate situation.

Eventually, on 17 May 2004, the administrators sold the Plaxton business to its management team, led by Brian Davidson, which quickly resumed trading as Plaxton Limited.

However, despite expressions of interest from several potential buyers, including American investment firm Melrose, the Indian company Tata via its subsidiary Hispano of Spain, and, surprisingly, Wrights of Belfast, no offers were received for the rest of TransBus. The ex-management team were not able to set up a management buy-out, then a popular option in such situations, due to the substantial debts facing the company, to say nothing of the possible backlash from the alleged financial malpractice.

Days stretched to weeks with potential buyers put off by the poor financial state of the business. Small wonder that this was probably the lowest point in the history of the company, and, for a time, it looked as if closure was on the cards. However, in the nick of time a saviour appeared, as we shall see in Chapter 9.

CHAPTER EIGHT

TRANSBUS PRODUCT DEVELOPMENTS: 1998–2004

Product development under TransBus was more prolific than would perhaps have been expected, given the financial issues that increasingly afflicted the company. However, the new chassis products primarily resulted from the significant product development activity already carried out under Trinity Holdings ownership of Dennis. In particular, the plan for the replacements for the Dart SLF, Trident 2 and Trident 3, all to be branded as the Enviro family, were well advanced. This chapter describes some of the products taken to market during the TransBus era.

THE R-SERIES COACH

While the Javelin had been an undoubted sales success, its customer base was primarily of the smaller operators handling UK touring operations. In order to penetrate interurban services and European touring, it was felt that a high-specification, high-power coach was needed. In 1997, Plaxton had been looking towards an own-brand integral coach product to compete with the best European integral vehicles but recognized that they lacked chassis design and manufacturing capability. Therefore they approached Dennis to supply the running gear, the intention being that the new coach would be sold as a Plaxton product with no 'Dennis' badging.

The great virtue of working exclusively with one bodybuilder was that the underframe, which was to be built by Dennis at Guildford, could incorporate the necessary body mountings and floor framing, avoiding much of the usual extensive chassis preparation activity. Many coach chassis are supplied to the bodybuilder as ultra-short chassis, the front and rear sections of which then need to be separated by the bodybuilder, repositioned and precisely aligned to allow the bodybuilder to add their linking structure, and then all the chassis piping and wiring need to be remade. The R-series, however, linked the front and rear modules by a dedicated transit frame that

held the two modules in precise alignment until bodying was completed. All piping and wiring could, therefore, be installed at Guildford and tested on the finished chassis, needing no further disturbance or extra work by the bodybuilder. An additional benefit was that the packaging of all the chassis components could be arranged to maximize luggage space: an impressive 406cu ft (11.5cu m) was achieved.

The 1998 Mayflower takeover, however, soured the Dennis relationship with Plaxton. In fact, Plaxton almost stopped progressing the proposed high-specification coach, known internally as DC97, redeploying their engineering resources towards developing their Coach 2000 on a Volvo chassis. Mayflower, therefore, looked towards other bodybuilders for the R-series, specifically Berkhof and Caetano. However, Plaxton regained enthusiasm for the project after they came into the fold under the newly formed TransBus International in 2000. In the event, the only non-Plaxton bodied vehicles were two from Berkhof and around a dozen from Caetano.

Power for the R-series came from the well-proven Cummins M11 turbocharged diesel engine, initially at Euro 2 level, vertically mounted at the rear of the underframe. Two power output options, of 340PS and 405PS, were initially offered. Later, a de-rated R300 version was offered, which used the smaller Cummins ISCe engine like the Javelin. The initial transmission offerings were the then-novel ZF AS-Tronic ten-speed automated manual unit or a Mercedes six-speed manual unit, with either a ZF six-speed manual or the AS-Tronic transmission being offered with the 340PS engine.

The prototype underframes were built by early 1999 and were sent to Plaxton to be bodied. Recognizing the particular importance of reliability to long-distance high-speed coach operation, Dennis undertook a limited endurance test on the prototypes by shadowing National Express operations between Bristol and London for several months.

London operator Hallmark were one of the repeat customers for the R-series. ADL

This procedure successfully identified and ironed out several early-life issues.

TransBus finally launched the R-series at the October 1999 NEC Coach & Bus Show, and it was well received. The first vehicles went into service in 2001, the launch customer being Scottish operator Prentice of Hadding-ton. Subsequently, several reasonable-sized orders were received, including nineteen vehicles for Alfa Coaches of Chorley, and fourteen for Hallmark.

Some, but by no means all, of the early vehicles experienced electrical problems arising from issues with the multiplex wiring system that was fitted. While multiplex

DENNIS R-SERIES COACH, 1999–c.2005

Layout and Chassis
4×2 rigid integral premium coach underframe

Engine
Type: Cummins M11 Euro 2/ISM Euro 3 turbocharged diesel
Block material: Cast iron
Head material: Cast iron
Cylinders: 6 in-line
Cooling: Water
Bore and stroke: 125 × 147mm
Capacity: 10800cc
Valves: Overhead
Max. power (DIN): 340PS (254kW) at 1,900rpm, or 405PS (302kW)
or
Type: Cummins ISCe 6-cylinder diesel
Max. power (DIN): 300PS (224kW)

Fuel capacity: 455ltr (100gal)

Transmission
Gearbox: ZF 6-speed manual with optional Telma retarder *or* ZF AS-Tronic 10-speed automatic with ZF retarder

Suspension and Steering
Front: ZF RL85E independent using double wishbones, 2 airbags
Rear: 4 airbags and four dampers, located by C-frame
Steering: ZF 8098 integral power

Brakes
Type: Knorr Bremse disc brakes all round, with ABS and ASR

Dimensions
Overall length: 12,000mm (472.4in)
Overall width: 2,500mm (98.4in)
GVW: 18,000kg (39,682lb)
Capacity: luggage capacity 11.3cu m (400cu ft), Plaxton body
(Source: various)

systems are now universal on almost every vehicle, the R-series was probably the first PSV to be so equipped, and the unfamiliar system was viewed with much suspicion by many operators. In truth, many TransBus staff were equally apprehensive, and even needlessly scared, of working with the system. The result was that simple issues often took far too long to diagnose and resolve. The ZF AS-Tronic gearbox was another new feature that some drivers found hard to master. Both issues were, however, relatively quickly dealt with by improved training, together with attention to some build issues, and the R-series began to gain a strong following.

At one point, consideration was given to entering a joint venture with a Chinese manufacturer, and in 2002, the author was despatched to Xiamen in China to discuss the possibilities with King Long. It quickly became evident that, while King Long management were keen to progress such a joint venture, little benefit would result for Trans-Bus, so no further action was taken.

Unfortunately, just as R-series sales were growing, Mayflower, and hence TransBus International, went into administration. When the remnants eventually emerged as ADL, Plaxton were no longer part of the fold, so naturally were more interested in bodying on the well-established Volvo chassis than working with a competitor. Indeed, the fear of competition went deeper, leading Plaxton also to design and develop their own bus chassis. Dennis by then had lost their own coach sales force, limiting their ability to sell chassis for bodying elsewhere. Although a small

number of R-series chassis had been bodied by Caetano and Berkhof, the volumes were too small to justify continued production, particularly since a potential problem with engine supply was looming in that Cummins did not at that time intend to take the M11 to Euro 4, although this was subsequently rescinded with the development of the ISM engine.

THE DAGGER

In the mid-1990s, Dennis was well established as Britain's principal fire appliance maker, with Sabres or Rapiers present in the majority of brigades. Neither of these, however, catered for those brigades needing narrow, manoeuvrable appliances for rural lanes and other tight spaces. So, in 1997, the design team set out to address this by developing a narrow machine to fill the void left after models such as the F8 and D Series ceased production. The F98 (**Fire 1998**) project, later to become Dagger following Dennis's predilection for a naming policy that involved sharp pointed weapons, used almost unchanged the standard Cromweld steel cab that was so well regarded on the Sabre and Rapier, but with narrower wings to reduce the overall width to 2.3m (7ft 7in). Weight was kept to a minimum by the use of a Dart-style drivetrain using a B-series Cummins engine of 250bhp and an Allison 2000 series automatic transmission, with taper-leaf springs at the front and coil springs at the rear. The gross weight was 12.5 tonnes (12.3 tons) and, like on the Dart, the low weight permitted

Another R-series, this time of Plaxton's local operator, Acklams of Beverley. ADL

The Dagger showed promise as the smaller, low-cost alternative to the Sabre, but sadly never sold in volume.
RICHARD NORMAN

the use of 19.5in wheels, keeping the cab as low as possible to ease entry and exit. Full air-operated disc brakes were fitted all round.

Target sales included the Kent and Devon brigades, who traditionally bought narrow appliances; however, the initial sales went to Hertfordshire. These early vehicles had handling issues due to the taper-leaf springs winding up under braking. A change to conventional multi-leaf springs resolved this, but by then the narrow MAN competitor had become popular, so very few Daggers were ever sold.

THE SLF 200 THOMAS DENNIS

In 1998, a joint venture was agreed between Mayflower and Freightliner subsidiary Thomas Built Buses, to manufacture and sell an 'Americanized' version of the Dart SLF with an Alexander ALX200 body into North America. This was duly launched at the American Public Transport Association Expo 1999 exhibition. A 250,000sq ft (23,225sq m) factory in North Carolina to manufacture the bus, branded as SLF 200, was brought on stream during 1999. Some Guildford employees moved to the USA to support production and engineering activity. The prototypes and demonstrators were built in the UK, and initial US assembly took place using kits of parts and assemblies from the UK.

The vehicle was offered in several lengths, from 29ft (8.8m) to 35ft (10.7m). Early versions used the Cummins ISB EPA engine, but after pressure from Daimler Chrysler, the owners – via Freightliner – of Thomas Built Buses, 4- and 6-cylinder Mercedes Benz engines were fitted.

Sales never lived up to expectations, and TransBus withdrew from the joint venture in early 2003.

DENNIS DAGGER, 1998–

Configuration: 4×2 rigid ladder-frame forward-control fire appliance chassis
Engine: Cummins ISBe Euro 3 turbocharged and intercooled diesel
Max. power: 250PS (186kW)
Max. torque: 568lb ft (750Nm)
Gearbox: Allison 2000 series automatic
Power take-off: Chelsea type 270 suitable for 2,000ltr/min (500gal/min) pump
Rear axle: Eaton 08-24 single-reduction hypoid
Suspension: Front: Multi-leaf springs with telescopic dampers (taper-leaf on earliest vehicles)

Rear: Coil springs located by trailing taper-leaf springs with telescopic dampers and panhard rod
Brakes: Knorr Bremse 380mm (15in) discs all round, ABS
Cab: 6 crew, 42-degree tilt
Wheelbase: 3,650mm (143.7in)
   3,800mm (149.6in)
Overall width: 2,300mm (90.5in)
Overall height (over cab): 2,535mm (100in)
Unladen weight (chassis): 4,690kg (10,339lb) for 3,650mm w/b model
GVW (max.): 12,500kg (27,558lb)
Top speed: 72mph (116km/h)
(Source: Dennis Dagger specification sheet, 2003)

THE ENVIRO 300

Before Mayflower's takeover of Dennis, the decision had been made to refresh the Dart SLF, SPD, Trident 2 and Trident 3 ranges. Although this work started under the Dennis regime, it was completed by TransBus, who must have viewed it as an opportunity to stamp their mark on the new company's products. Inevitably, much of this refresh was of the bodywork, most chassis models remaining virtually untouched other than where necessary to meet legislation updates such as emissions levels.

The first vehicle to be given the Enviro treatment was the Super Pointer Dart replacement, codenamed SD99, which duly became Enviro 300. Unlike other products, SD99 was a new design rather than a makeover of the SPD. One fundamental change was that the 2.4m (7ft 10in) chassis width, which had been the same as the Dart SLF, went out to the full legal width of the day. The length also increased to 12.5m (41ft) to take advantage of legislation changes. Although the suspension was derived from the Dart SLF, the axles and frame were new, including a new front axle beam forging. The tyre width was increased to 265/70, although 19.5in rims were retained, allowing the gross weight to increase to 14.5 tonnes (14.3 tons). Rather than the Plaxton body of the SPD, an Alexander ALX300-based body was used. New styling was, however, developed by a Warwick design studio using, unusually for the bus industry, a full-sized clay mock-up of the front end.

The rationale for the Enviro 300 was that it could carry as many passengers as a competitive full-size single-decker, yet at 14.5 tonnes was considerably lighter and so more fuel-efficient. The first vehicles were registered in mid-2002 to Truronian, the Devonian operator. Sales generally were not as good as had been hoped, however, as many operators were still not too convinced by the concept of a lightweight rather than heavyweight full-size single-decker.

A subsequent, more extensive revamp in 2007 brought the Enviro 300 into line with the styling and features developed for the Dart SLF replacement, Enviro 200. By that time, sales had improved as those original reliability fears had been allayed by the excellent reputation of the earlier vehicles. Eventually, over 1,000 found homes before the model was replaced by a long-wheelbase version of the Enviro 200 MMC (Major Model Change) in 2015.

THE TS01 SMALL BUS PROPOSAL

Successive management teams both at Dennis and Trinity Holdings had long desired a small, low-cost bus to sit below the Dart and compete head-on with the Optare Solo. The engineering team's response each time they were requested to explore design solutions for a small bus was always the same – a suitable set of components at a lower cost to those on the Dart just wasn't available. Indeed, the high volumes at which Dart SLFs were selling in this period meant that the cost base of the vehicle was in any case particularly low.

This time, however, things were different. The formation of Mayflower Bus & Coach in 1998, with Plaxton initially outside the fold, had put at risk Plaxton's supply of chassis. Plaxton therefore put together a chassis design team, intending to produce their own chassis. This team, using largely Hungarian-based designers recruited following the collapse of Ikarus, the Hungarian bus-builder, quickly put together a small bus chassis design even before Plaxton joined TransBus in 2001. The design featured an extremely short rear overhang, made possible by the use of a transverse engine, with an angle drive taking the drive into the rear axle. Plaxton engineers promoted this concept, codenamed TS01, to the TransBus board, who were seduced by the highly attractive, and as it turned out, highly inaccurate costings put forward. The costings showed the build cost of the TS01 to be significantly lower than Dart SLF and conveniently underplayed the need for a completely new and expensive angle drive. Nevertheless, the project was approved, but before production could commence TransBus and its parent company collapsed into administration.

With the subsequent formation of ADL, the one-time Plaxton design team set up a new company, Enterprise Bus, touting the TD01 design to the newly formed Plaxton business that had been bought from administration by its former managers, led by Brian Davidson. Plaxton realized they needed a chassis, and agreed a deal with Enterprise Bus whereby the chassis would be made in Hungary and shipped to Scarborough for bodying. The new model, called the Plaxton Primo, started production in 2005.

In 2007, Plaxton joined ADL, bringing the Primo into the organization. By then, however, the serious and fundamental flaws in the product, such as the unacceptable driveline geometry, were becoming evident. Customers were complaining bitterly, returning vehicles and cancelling orders. This led to an embarrassing situation for ADL, who had no great need for the Primo but could not afford to ignore the customer issues. The Guildford engineers were therefore asked to come up with a fix for the Primo. Unfortunately, the problems were so fundamental that a full solution was not possible, although a package was developed to minimize the severity of the design flaws. This was then retrofitted to all the in-service vehicles starting in 2008, and the Primo model was quietly dropped from production.

THE ENVIRO 200, OR TM02: THE BUS THAT NEVER WAS

After many years of high sales of the Dennis Dart and Dart SLF, TransBus International realized, as the twenty-first century dawned, that sooner or later competitors would steal their market if their midibus product range did not develop and maintain its competitive edge.

This time around, it was recognized that the son-of-Dart would need to encompass hybrid technology, which, although in its infancy in commercial vehicles, was expected to be the drivetrain of the future. Hybrid, as well as diesel, drivetrains were therefore to be engineered from the outset. But what else could be done to set the new bus apart from the rest of the market?

Much criticism of buses in city centre operation at that time centred on the relatively long 'dwell times' at stops. These often resulted from the need for exiting passengers incarcerated in the rear section of a full bus to fight their way past standees to the centre exit door. What if, the engineers reasoned, the engine and transmission were moved across to the rear offside corner of the chassis, enabling the traditional centre door to be moved right to the back of the bus? The gangway through the bus could then become a one-way traffic flow only, boarding at the front and exiting at the rear, thus speeding passenger flow and hence reducing dwell times by more effectively utilizing the full length of the saloon.

Such a layout is common in other European countries; however, three main difficulties with this configuration seemed insurmountable. First, a midibus is, by definition, both narrower than a full-size bus and comparatively short. On a midibus of anything less than the maximum legal (at that time) 2.5m (8ft 2.5in) width, it would be impossible to engineer a gangway between the rear wheels that was wide enough to allow for both standing passengers and passengers wishing to exit the bus. Of course, even if the aisle could be made wide enough, there needed to be a step-free flat floor through to the rear, meaning that a portal, or drop-centre, rear axle would be essential.

Second, at overall lengths of anything less than around 10m (32ft 10in), there was just not enough rear overhang to accommodate a longitudinal engine, gearbox and propshaft.

Most fundamental of all, however, was the fact that left-hand-drive European vehicles were only able to achieve this configuration because of the ready availability of rear axles with an input on the left (looking from the rear of the bus). This gave the engine and gearbox, mounted of course on the left-hand side of the bus, a more or less straight entry into the rear axle. No axle with the drive offset to the right, as would be necessary for the right-hand-drive UK market, was available. With no suitable axle or gearbox being available, the concept seemed to be dead in the water.

Or was it? One of the self-imposed tasks of Richard Norman, by then the director of design, was to dig deep into the potential component supplier base to see what new hardware might be under consideration that could potentially offer unique selling points for Dennis chassis.

He uncovered an intriguing combination of opportunities that could, just possibly, provide the features for which the team were looking. They already had an extremely short engine in the Cummins ISBe 4-cylinder, but an exceptionally short transmission only 500mm long was now being considered by Voith, who had long envied the volume of sales enjoyed by their competitors Allison, the suppliers of the AT545, and subsequently S2000 transmissions, for the Dart and Dart SLF. Moreover, this new transmission, the DV500, incorporated an integral retarder, considered essential for heavier bus applications. Voith and Dennis soon agreed a joint project to develop the DV500 transmission on the basis that regardless of any new model, it would provide an alternative to the venerable Allison transmission used in the Dart.

Second, an axle manufacturer in Italy hitherto relatively unknown in the UK bus world, Graziano, were prepared to produce a right-hand-input axle suitable for a UK right-hand-drive bus. Third, Michelin, after pioneering super single tyres on articulated semitrailers, were proposing to introduce a super single tyre for buses, with a load rating suitable for a midibus.

Finally, TransBus, as part of a government-funded research project, was working with MST Technology, a spin-off business of Sheffield University, who had under development the necessary hardware to produce a hybrid bus.

A concept package thus began to take shape, featuring a very compact engine bay, which became known within the team as the 'wardrobe', tucked behind the rear right wheel. The small size of the wardrobe gave minimal space for either a radiator pack or exhaust system, so once again the engineering team came up with an innovative solution – to mount the cooling pack on the roof and fit a vertical exhaust. This took the noise, fumes and hot air away from street level, improving the environment around the bus – particularly relevant in congested London streets.

The stage was thus set for TransBus to develop their desired side-engined midibus. Initially, there was some reluctance from management to commit to the project. This was partly due to the perceived slightly unbalanced appearance of the bus, given that it would have Dart-sized 19.5in wheels at the front to minimize entrance height and retain an adequate gangway width, whereas the super singles on the rear axle would need to be 22.5in to give sufficient load capacity.

A more fundamental concern was whether the notoriously traditional target marketplace would accept such a radically different layout. A very detailed full-sized mock-up of the interior of TM02 was therefore constructed at the TransBus design office at Leyland (which was housed in the old Leyland Technical Centre). The mock-up was shown to key Transport for London personnel, who displayed great interest, to the extent of requesting a similar proposal for a double-decker! With similar positive feedback from other operators, in early 2003 the decision was made to proceed with the project.

Enviro200 is a revolutionary new midibus capable of carrying 25% more passengers. Its unique, two-door design and wide aisles will bring a new dimension to passenger transport on high-density city routes.

An amazing 77 passengers can be comfortably accommodated in a conventional 10.4m long and 2.4m wide midibus, providing total access (back and front), as well as environmental innovations that dramatically improve the street level environment, with the ultimate potential to reduce exhaust carbon emissions by a further 30%.

This is an extract from the brochure for TM02, showing its unusual door layout and the resulting passenger flow.
RICHARD NORMAN

TM02/ENVIRO 200 AND ENVIRO 200H, 2003

Configuration: 4×2 rigid, welded modular frame, rear-engined hybrid midibus
Engine: Cummins ISBe 4-cylinder diesel, side-mounted at rear
Capacity: 5900cc
Gearbox: Voith DV500 4-speed automatic with integral retarder
Hybrid package: MST
Final drive: Graziano offset drive
Suspension: Front and rear: 2 airbags, axle located by quarter-elliptic taper-leaf springs
Tyres: 19.5in front, 22.5in super-single rear
Brakes: Discs on all four wheels
Overall length: 10,400mm (409.4in)
Overall width: 2,400mm (94.5in)
Capacity: up to 77 seats
(Source: TransBus brochure)

The first of five prototypes was completed in March 2003, and the new Enviro 200 model, as it was branded at its launch at the 2003 NEC Coach & Bus Show, was received with interest. This was unsurprising, for the innovative layout gave a 25 per cent increased passenger-carrying capacity: seventy-seven in a 10.4m (34ft 1in) two-door bus. Not only that, but the 'door at each end' configuration lent itself to rapid boarding and alighting, reducing bus stop dwell times to a minimum.

No sooner were the prototypes built than fate intervened in the collapse of Mayflower and with it TransBus. This cruel stroke almost stopped the project dead in its tracks; however, the last-minute formation of Alexander Dennis Limited gave the project a reprieve.

ADL's management saw the potential of the new product, as did the London operators to whom the product was demonstrated. Indeed, the first order, for twenty-nine buses, was placed by Metroline even before the development programme had been completed.

TfL, however, and crucially for the project, were by then much less receptive, despite their initial positive reaction. One of their fears, it appeared, was that with the rear plug door open, one leaf projected beyond the rear of the bus. This was apparently considered to be a safety hazard. While this was rapidly resolved by ADL adopting an asymmetric door configuration, TfL's stance remained unchanged.

Another reason cited by TfL for rejecting the vehicle was that their drivers were trained to handle wheelchairs through the centre door, so wheelchair access through the front door was not acceptable, even though every other location in the UK operated in such a way without problems. In response to TfL's request for a double-decker design, Richard Norman had produced the ADD04 concept for a double-door, double-staircase decker. However, this also met with a lacklustre reception from TfL, even though the two-staircase principle was adopted by them with enthusiasm in the 'New Bus for London' a few years later!

The real reason behind TfL's reluctance to commit to the project probably lay in the political arena. Buses had become a significant plank of mayor Ken Livingstone's manifesto with the adoption of the much-maligned bendy buses in place of the traditional London double-decker, and nothing was to be allowed to interfere with this policy. While many within TfL privately felt that ADL's proposed side-engined midibus was ideal for London, ultimately they had to do the bidding of their political masters. Ironically, when Boris Johnson became mayor in 2008 he pledged to withdraw the bendy buses on the grounds that they were unsuitable for London; possibly the TM02 layout would then have been more favourably received, but by then it was too late.

So it was that a potentially significant new product rolled over and died. Without TfL sanction, operators could not purchase buses, and the eager initial adopter, Metroline, had to convert their order into conventional Dart SLFs. The front-end design of TM02 was, however, retained and incorporated into the more conventional layout of the Enviro 200 as we now know it.

In truth, some significant engineering issues remained unresolved in the product. The MST hybrid package, when it worked, was highly impressive. Unfortunately, however, it rarely did work for any length of time, and ADL struggled to persuade MST, who were primarily a research organization rather than a hard-nosed commercially aware manufacturing business, to address the issues or implement volume production planning within the tight timescales deemed commercially necessary. As an aside, this experience led ADL to seek alternative partners for hybrid technology, ultimately forming a relationship with BAE Systems, with the rest, as they say, being history – and very successful history at that.

Even the diesel TM02 models were not trouble-free, as the Voith DV500 transmission proved both far from smooth and very unreliable, both in the TM02 prototypes and a much bigger fleet of Dart SLFs that were built for field trials. Although Voith had solutions in sight for these issues, by then Dart sales volumes had dropped considerably, making the cost of productionizing the DV500 non-viable. The project was therefore cancelled, and the field trial Dart SLFs reworked to fit Voith D823.3 transmissions. The TM02s, however, had to retain the DV500 as both the Voith and Allison alternatives were too long to fit into the available space.

Some of the five prototypes ran for a while with a Surrey operator. However, the limited number of parts available to provide spares for the unique gearbox, axle and roof-mounted cooling system meant that their life was inevitably limited, and all bar one are now believed to have been scrapped. The remaining hybrid vehicle was bought by Andy Boulton of Dennis, who squeezed in a diesel engine and Allison T280R transmission in preparation for a possible return to the road.

This is now probably the sole surviving TM02. ANDY BOULTON

CHAPTER NINE

LAST-MINUTE SAVIOUR:
2004 ONWARDS

THE FORMATION OF
ALEXANDER DENNIS LTD

Despite much interest being shown in the assets of Trans-Bus, no firm offers were received by Deloitte. This was probably unsurprising, for the Guildford operation, in particular, was in a dire state, with little in the way of assets, many unpaid and disgruntled suppliers and a massive hole in the pension fund.

Matters had reached a point where closure was probably only days away when an offer was received from an unexpected source – a triumvirate of Scottish entrepreneurs: Angus Grossart, David Murray and Brian Souter. Alexander were a major customer of David Murray's Murray Metals business, while Brian Souter's massive Stagecoach bus operation ran thousands of TransBus vehicles. Angus Grossart, chairman of the Noble Grossart merchant bank, was the banker behind the deal.

Less charitable individuals at the time may have opined that at least two of 'the Three Musketeers' were simply protecting their own interests. Whatever the reason, it was a brave step for the Scottish team, who took on the remnants of the TransBus operation and started the slow and painful process of rebuilding not just the sales but the credibility of the business. At times they must have felt that their new venture, which they named Alexander Dennis Limited, now known to all as ADL, was a bottomless money pit. Although the new owners had, of course, bought the assets rather than the liabilities of the defunct TransBus, not only did they need to honour many TransBus debts such as suppliers' outstanding invoices, but they were also forced to reinstate warranties on many of the more recent vehicles. They may have underestimated the sheer negotiating power of their customer base, which was at that time concentrated into a handful of large bus operating companies within the UK. Those companies leaned on ADL very hard, making reinstatement of warranties a condition of further orders.

However, the new owners kept the faith, and as confidence gradually began to be regained in the marketplace, sales began to restart. The process was not without pain: almost immediately it was necessary to close the ex-Northern Counties Wigan body plant with the loss of 120 jobs, together with a further thirty positions shed at Alexander's Falkirk plant.

Significant changes were also made to the parts and service side of the business. The headquarters of this part of the company was at Anston in Yorkshire, which had been the parts and service centre of Plaxton, and its responsibilities had been subsequently widened under TransBus to cover all group products. ADL's board, though, realized that Anston was remote from the main centres of population of the customers' bus fleets, which would be better served by a new location on the other side of the country. Thus the Skelmersdale Parts and Service Centre was created, which ultimately became a 43,000sq ft (4,000sq m) global parts warehouse. This dealt with 2,500 suppliers, holding a £6.5 million inventory of over 30,000 parts lines, and shipping 1,200 parts worldwide every day. To meet the needs of the sizeable London bus park, a Guildford parts warehouse was also established in the Slyfield factory to feed the M25 area. The Slyfield operation also included a national call centre to ensure that any customer could receive assistance with just one phone call.

Some indication of the costs involved in reviving the business can be gleaned from the first set of accounts published for the new business, which covered a seventeen-month period. These show that for the first five months of restructuring, from May to September 2004, the new company made a substantial pre-tax loss of £10.6 million on a turnover of £45.4 million. However, for the subsequent full twelve-month accounting period of October 2004 to September 2005, the company achieved a pre-tax profit of £4 million on a £150.3 million turnover.

As the business became re-established, in 2007 the

opportunity was taken to repurchase the Plaxton operation, creating Britain's largest bus and coach manufacturing operation.

ADL BUS LAUNCHES

Sales were helped immeasurably by the fact that Trinity Holdings and TransBus had already started to refresh the bus product range before the business had collapsed, beginning to introduce the Enviro ranges of single- and double-deck buses that became increasingly popular under the new owners. Some of the new products and projects are reviewed below.

The Enviro 500

The Enviro 500, originally codenamed TD01, was the successor to Trident 3, the big three-axle double-decker that had found so much success in Hong Kong. In chassis terms, little changed, although the body was extensively revamped, featuring a new, crisper, family image shared with the Enviro 200, 300 and 400.

The Enviro 500 was in fact launched in 2002 in the dying days of TransBus. It was built to the latest European width limit of 2.55m (8ft 4.5in), and at that time Hong Kong leg-islation still mandated the earlier 2.5m (8ft 2.5in) width limit. Negotiation was therefore needed with the Hong Kong Transport Department before the Enviro 500 could be accepted into service. With this resolved, KMB soon became the launch customer in Hong Kong. Other Hong Kong operators were slower to order, simply because of their government-regulated age-based fleet replacement programmes.

Nevertheless, Citybus and New World First Bus, as well as the much smaller China Light and Power, all took Enviro 500s in quantity. Hong Kong operators generally split their fleets fairly equally between competitor chassis, with Volvo and Dennis each traditionally taking around 50 per cent of the market. To keep this balance, around 100 Enviro 500 bodies were mounted on Volvo B9TL chassis in 2008 for KMB and their subsidiary Long Win.

Although Trident 3 and its successor, the Enviro 500, were initially conceived for the Hong Kong market, both ADL and their predecessors had always considered the USA as a potential opportunity, notwithstanding issues of the low bridges and other infrastructure that are widely present in the USA simply because the town planners had never previously had to consider tall double-deckers. However, a sales breakthrough into North America was frustratingly slow to get off the ground, despite much sales effort and

The Enviro 500 continued the sales success of Trident 3 in Hong Kong, despite the territory being handed over to China in 1997 and the resulting reduction in British influence there. This KMB vehicle was pictured in 2005. AUTHOR

In 2005 Enviro 500s began carrying visitors along Las Vegas's Sunset Strip, and became very popular, being nicknamed 'the Deuce'. ADL

the excellent performance of the Trident 3s operating with BC Transit in Canada. Progress indeed was so slow that the ADL Board frequently agonized over their wisdom in continuing to commit considerable resource into a market showing little sign of placing orders.

There were several significant regulatory hurdles that needed to be overcome to break into the US market in any volume. First, every aspect of the vehicle had to comply with Federal standards. These are rarely aligned with the European standards adopted in the UK and elsewhere. With European standards, compliance usually needs to be demonstrated by a physical, independent test of the performance of the component or system – the 'type approval' process. In the USA, however, the process is much more one of self-certification by the supplier. The performance of a component or system only comes under scrutiny if it fails to live up to expectation, which can then involve considerable costs in the litigation-prone US environment. The second constraint on US sales was the need to demonstrate the reliability of the product by completing the Federal Bus Research and Testing Progam – the 'Altoona' trial – which is an arduous process. Third, compliance is needed with the 'Buy America' Act, which, as the name suggests, means that a significant percentage of the vehicle must be sourced in the USA. ADL was assisted in this by the fact that the Cummins

ISM engine was built in the USA, but ultimately it became necessary for ADL to build complete chassis there.

Eventually, however, all the earlier work on promoting Enviro 500 into the USA began to pay off. As the ADL Business Review for the period to 30 September 2005 was able to declare, during 2005 fifty Enviro 500s entered service with Southern Nevada Regional Transport Authority in Las Vegas, the popularity of these buses with their striking all-over advertising increasing bus ridership on the famous Strip by 50 per cent. This high-profile deal was backed up by an Enviro 500 destined for BC Transit in Vancouver undertaking a 3,000-mile (5,000km) roadshow across the USA to promote the double-decker to the US market. Another batch of twenty Enviro 500s was supplied in June 2005 to Gray Line Tours for New York sightseeing tours. Eventually, the trickle of orders turned into a veritable flood, vindicating the board's decision to keep pursuing the US market.

The Enviro 400 – First Generation
Design and planning for the Enviro 400, the replacement for the popular Trident 2 two-axle double-decker, was almost complete when TransBus International entered administration. It therefore became the first new prod-

OTTAWA

The big decker was in many respects its own best salesman, as word spread and potential customers realized its capabilities compared to the shortcomings of their existing products. As ADL's Peter Cooper, who was responsible for much of the technical sales effort into the US market later recounted:

The Ottawa authorities having been persuaded by another manufacturer to purchase a fleet of articulated buses, they were less than impressed to discover their dire performance in the snowy conditions typical of an Ottawa winter. Matters came to a head one particularly bad winter when several bendy buses jackknifed across one busy corner and brought the city to a halt. This led to an inquiry into why someone in the city had sanctioned the purchase of them without verifying their bad weather performance. Desperately keen to divest themselves of these troublesome vehicles, and hearing good things of the Enviro 500, they borrowed a Las Vegas specification Enviro 500 for extended cold weather trials. These took place in January 2007 at Transport Canada's Blainville test facility in temperatures of −35°C (−31°F), and the authorities were happy enough with the outcome to order three vehicles for evaluation. These were delivered at the end of 2008, and their success led to several hundred more being ordered by Ottawa over the next few years.

To support the North American sales effort, an Enviro 500 was cold-climate tested at the Canadian Government Test Centre in 2007. PETER COOPER

uct to be launched by ADL at the 2005 NEC Coach & Bus Show. The Enviro 400 featured a heavily reworked body: initially Falkirk-built but with the assembly subsequently shared with the Scarborough Plaxton plant. The chassis, however, was little changed from Trident 2. The quick success of Enviro 400 can be measured by the fact that over 200 orders were confirmed in the first four months of sales alone.

On Trident 2 and the early Enviro 400, the right-facing engine layout was dictated by the available hardware, which was designed for the typical left-hand-drive European low-floor single-deck bus. This put the angle drive and axle input on the left, which was not ideal for UK operation as it meant that the only space for the radiator and charge cooler pack was also on the left. In this position, it was prone to vacuuming up any debris from the gutter, with the result that cooling packs required regular cleaning to prevent the bus from overheating. This was not a popular task with operators, many of whom were reluctant to carry it out, with the result that radiators occasionally became so clogged that the vehicle failed on the road.

Not long after the launch of the Enviro 400, chief engineer Richard Norman became aware that German transmission manufacturer ZF had developed a drivetrain for the right-hand-drive Japanese market that would allow Dennis to reverse the Enviro 400 engine to face left and put the angle drive on the right. The cooling package could then be repositioned on the right where it was less likely to suck up road debris. The new installation also gave a significant reduction in cost and weight, particularly with the simultaneous adoption of the Euro 4 6-cylinder ISBe engine rather than the heavier C-series, which was then phased out.

A version of the Enviro 400 was also developed to meet a need for operations on specific routes in Hong Kong, replacing short-wheelbase Enviro 500s. A number were sold for this purpose from around 2009, although most Hong Kong double-deckers continued to be Enviro 500s. Enviro 400s also sold into other overseas markets in relatively small numbers, often as city-centre tour buses, such as those purchased by Les Tours du Vieux for Quebec in Canada in 2013 and 2014, ten bought by Honolulu in 2012 and around forty that went to various operations in New York.

One of the first Enviro 400s was this one, 'Spirit of London', built to replace the Trident destroyed by a terrorist bomb in London on 7 July 2005. It is shown here at the 2005 NEC Show launch of the Enviro 400. ADL

One highlight of Enviro 400 operations was the selection of one, heavily modified, vehicle to perform in the Beijing Olympic Games closing ceremony. Over 150 Enviro 400s were later ordered to support the 2012 London Olympics.

The Enviro 200 – Second Generation

As with other models, work had started on the replacement for the Dart SLF under TransBus. The early work on this project, TM01, was to develop a conventional layout, little changed in chassis terms from Dart SLF. As the alternative, more radical full low-floor TM02 concept gathered pace, this work was put on hold in favour of taking TM02 to production as the Enviro 200.

Following the abandonment of the TM02 version of the Enviro 200 as reported in Chapter 8, the work on the more conventional Dart SLF replacement, TM01, was reinstated, the company by then being under ADL ownership. The chassis was little changed from the Dart SLF it replaced, although the engine was necessarily uplifted to Euro 4 level. The opportunity was also taken to introduce a multiplex electrical system. The body was considerably more stylish

than either the Pointer or ALX200 offerings, with many of the styling cues shared with the other Enviro models.

The model was initially branded as the Enviro 200 Dart to differentiate it from the earlier TM02 version; however, the Dart name was soon dropped. The first vehicles entered service in mid-2006, quickly continuing the sales success of its Dart and Dart SLF predecessors. Bodybuild took place at Alexander's Falkirk factory until being transferred to Plaxton's Scarborough plant to free up space for the increasing volumes of Enviro 400s on order. Production continued until 2018, when the model, known by then as the Enviro 200 Classic, was replaced by the Enviro 200 MMC.

A significant development took place in May 2012, when Canadian bus manufacturer New Flyer started to build, under licence, a version of the Enviro 200 modified to meet the needs of the North American market. This model, known as the New Flyer MiDi, was entirely Buy America Act compliant. It was initially built at the Minnesota factory of New Flyer, and subsequently at ADL's own plant in Indiana. The specifications remained broadly similar to the UK Enviro 200 model, however, retaining the Cummins ISBe engine but with an Allison B300R transmission.

The Enviro 350H

One of ADL's forays into hybrid bus design saw them working with Hispano, under a project initially codenamed ADS09H but which later became Enviro 350H. This was a full low-floor left-hand-drive side-engined three-door 12m (39ft 4in) single-decker, unveiled at the November 2010 FIAA Show. A Cummins 4-cylinder engine was fitted in the 'wardrobe' at the rear left-hand side of the vehicle together with the generator and motor, driving to an Enviro 400 rear axle, the lithium-ion battery pack being mounted on the roof. The benefit of this configuration was, of course, that it provided lots of space for a rear door at the low floor level on a left-hand-drive vehicle.

It is believed that only forty-six were built, twelve of

This 10m (32ft 10in) 2012 Enviro 200 is operated by Reptons of Surrey. AUTHOR

ALEXANDER DENNIS
ENVIRO 200, 2006–2015

Configuration: 4×2 rigid, welded modular frame, rear-engined low-floor midibus chassis
Engine: 8.9m, 9.3m, 10.2m and 10.7m bodies: Cummins ISBe 4-cylinder Euro 4 (later Euro 5), 140PS (103kW) or 160PS (117kW)
9.1m, 9.5m, 10.4m, 10.9m and 11.3m bodies: Cummins ISBe 6-cylinder Euro 4 (later Euro 5), 205PS (131kW), 553lb ft (750Nm)
Capacity: 4500cc
Gearbox: Allison 2100 or T280R 5-speed automatic
or Voith D823.3 3-speed or D854.5 automatic with integral retarder
Retarder: (for Allison gearbox) Telma 5750 electromagntic retarder, axle-mounted

Rear axle: 8,100kg (17,857lb) capacity Dana 9-24 single-reduction hypoid
or 11,000kg (24,250lb) capacity Dana 11-26 single-reduction hypoid
Suspension: 2 airbags located by trailing taper-leaf springs and panhard rod, two telescopic dampers, fast-kneel facility on front axle
Wheelbase: 8.9m/9.1m bodies: 3,850mm (151.6in)
   9.3m/9.5m bodies: 4,230mm (166.5in)
   10.2m/10.4m bodies: 5,105mm (201in)
   10.7m/10.9m bodies: 5,675mm (223.4in)
   11.3m body: 5,980mm (235.4in)
Overall width: 2,440m (96in)
   GVW (max): up to 10.9m body: 12,580kg (27,734lb)
   11.3m body: 13,100kg (28,880lb)
(Source: ADL Enviro 200 brochure, 2008)

This CAD model of the 2011 Enviro 350H shows the side-mounted hybrid power unit. RICHARD NORMAN

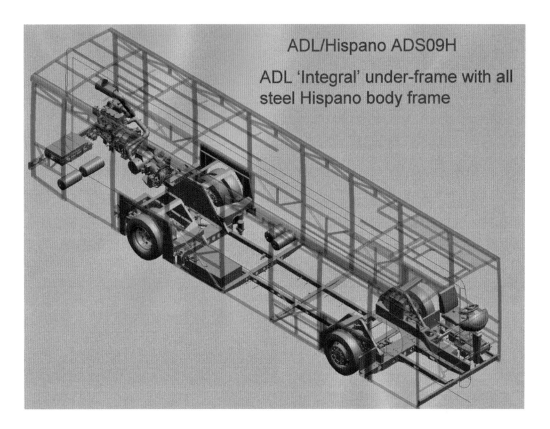

ADL/Hispano ADS09H

ADL 'Integral' under-frame with all steel Hispano body frame

which were sold to Transports Metropolitans de Barcelona, with two going to Las Palmas operators. One chassis was also bodied by Custom Coaches in Australia for evaluation by the State Transit Authority of New South Wales. The Spanish and Australian vehicles were some of the very few Guildford chassis not bodied by ADL since its inception. Although intended mainly for left-hand-drive markets, the remainder of the E350s were bodied by Alexander at Falkirk. Twenty-two found homes with Stagecoach companies Bluebird and Fife Scottish, with four being bought by First Essex.

The Enviro 500 MMC

The original version of the Enviro 500 was replaced in 2012 by the MMC or Major Model Change version. In part, this was brought about because Dana wanted to end production of their rear axles, for which ADL was the only customer. By then, the ZF AV132 drive axle was available, and this was used in the MMC package. This involved offsetting the engine to the left-hand side of the chassis, a move that also gave a better floor line. A steered tag axle option was also added in response to concerns from some customers over tyre scrub.

ADL ENVIRO 500 NORTH AMERICAN DOUBLE-DECKER

Configuration: 6×2 North American-specification low-height double-deck transit or commuter bus
Engine (current): Cummins ISL9 6-cylinder turbocharged intercooled diesel with EGR and SCR
Capacity: 8900cc
Power: 380PS (283kW) at 1,900rpm
Torque: 1,250lb ft (1,696Nm) at 1,400rpm
Gearbox: Allison B500R
or Voith D854.6
or ZF 6AP1700B
Rear axle: ZF AV-133 drop centre, 12,000kg (26,455lb) capacity
Suspension: Airbags, multi-link location, anti-roll bar and telescopic dampers
Length: 12,931mm (509.1in)
Height: 4,115mm (162in)
Width: 2,520mm (99.2in)
Gross weight: 25,700kg (56,659lb)
(Source: ADL Enviro 500 specification sheet)

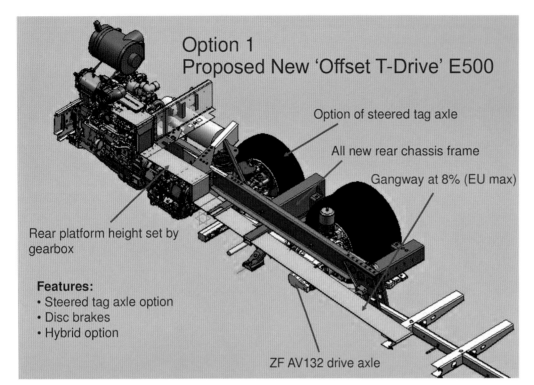

Option 1
Proposed New 'Offset T-Drive' E500

Option of steered tag axle

All new rear chassis frame

Gangway at 8% (EU max)

Rear platform height set by gearbox

Features:
• Steered tag axle option
• Disc brakes
• Hybrid option

ZF AV132 drive axle

The offset driveline of the Enviro 500 MMC model. RICHARD NORMAN

BELOW: **Operating in typical Swiss countryside is this 2018 Enviro 500 MMC Postbus, one of thirty-four.** ADL

This is the current bestselling Enviro 500 USA model. AUTHOR

Following the launch of the Enviro 500 MMC model at the 2012 NEC Show, 4,426 have been built as of July 2019, including 3,338 for Hong Kong, 266 for Singapore and 177 for New Zealand.

The Enviro 400 MMC

The Enviro 400 MMC, launched in 2014, featured a fully redesigned body based on the feedback from operator clinics together with a close analysis of every service problem reported on all Enviro 400s since 2006. In all, over 200 improvements to the previous generation were made, including a new multiplexed electrical system, a weight reduction of 880lb (400kg), increased seating capacity within the same overall length, LED lighting and a patented quick-release glass system that had the appearance of bonded glazing but allowed a pane to be replaced in minutes rather than hours.

The adoption of Euro 6 on the MMC model required a slight increase in the rear overhang to accommodate the additional emissions equipment required. One concern during the development of the Euro 6 installation was the extremely high exhaust gas temperature predicted by Cummins, which could cause problems for other road users. This led to the adoption of the unusual rectangular-shaped exhaust outlet visible under the rear bumper of MMC vehicles, which reduced the discharge speed and hence the temperature of the hot exhaust gas.

The MMC version was a stylish update of the stalwart Enviro 400 model, incorporating both styling revisions and changes requested by operator clinics. GARY AVERY

The Enviro 400 City

In 2009, ADL had become involved in the bid process for the forthcoming 'New Bus For London' project. This bid was ultimately, and disappointingly, unsuccessful, but it did highlight the potential for a new high-specification, stylish double-decker. The result was the Enviro 400 City launched in 2015, which took some themes from ADL's unsuccessful New Bus For London proposal and integrated them into an evolution of the Enviro 400 MMC. This resulted in a vehicle that gives the passenger impressive levels of comfort and a general feeling of spaciousness, aided by the unusual glazed stairwell, which also provided a unique style to the exterior of the vehicle. Moreover, this elegant vehicle was suitable for sale anywhere, not just London, and ultimately became far more successful than the London contest winner.

The Enviro 200 MMC

The Enviro 200 MMC (or Major Model Change) was launched at the 2014 Euro Bus Expo at NEC, the first vehicle entering service in 2015. A long-wheelbase version also replaced the Enviro 300 model. Some significant chassis changes were incorporated, principally the replacement of the simple suspension system with only two airbags per axle and single leaf springs for axle location. This cheap but effective system had served the Dart SLF and Enviro 200 well since the outset but was replaced by multilink location for the axles together with a four-bag C-frame rear suspension system.

A 12.8m (42ft) three-axle version, known as the Enviro200 XLB, was also released and found sales, particularly in New Zealand.

ENVIRO 400H CITY, 2015–

Layout and Chassis
4×2 welded modular frame, rear-engined vehicle

Engine
Type: Cummins ISB4.5 Euro 6 turbocharged and intercooled diesel with EGR and SCR
Cylinders: 4 in-line
Cooling: Water
Capacity: 4500cc
Max. power (DIN): 210PS (157kW) at 2,300rpm
Fuel capacity: 150ltr (33gal) aluminium tank
AdBlue capacity: 30ltr (6.6gal)

Hybrid System
Type: BAE Systems Hybridrive series system
Generator: 140kW (188hp) continuous, 195kW (260hp) peak power, water-cooled, permanent magnet
Motor power: 120kW (161hp) continuous
Motor torque: 750lb ft (1,000Nm) continuous, 1,575lb ft (2,100Nm) peak

Battery: Lithium-ion, located at rear of upper saloon
Final drive: ZF AV-132 drop centre axle, 13,000kg (28,660lb) capacity

Suspension and Steering
Front: 2 airbags, multi-link location, anti-roll bar, two telescopic dampers
Rear: 4 airbags, multi-link location, anti-roll bar, four telescopic dampers
Steering: ZF8098 integral power
Tyres: 275/70 R 22.5 tubeless
Wheels: 7.5 × 22.5 steel

Brakes
Type: Disc brakes, full air operated, electronically controlled
Size: 430mm (16.9in) diameter

Dimensions
Overall length: 10,400mm (409.4in)
    11,100m (437in)
Overall width: 2,550mm (100.4in)
(Source: ADL Enviro 400 brochure)

The City was a revamped version of the Enviro 400 MMC launched in 2015 in response to the imaginatively styled Wrights new bus for London. AUTHOR

As with Enviro 400, the **MMC** version of Enviro 200 featured both styling revisions and customer-driven updates. This unusual shot captures both front and rear aspects of two vehicles operated by First West of England. NEIL JENNINGS

It may look like a photoshopped image of an Enviro 200, but this is the 12.8m (42ft) three-axle version, the Enviro200 **XLB.** ADL

**ALEXANDER DENNIS ENVIRO
200 MMC, 2015–**

Configuration: 4×2 rigid, welded modular frame for rear-engined midibus
Engine: Cummins ISB4.5 Euro 6 4-cylinder up to 210PS, EGR and SCR
or Cummins ISB6.7 Euro 6 6-cylinder up to 250PS, EGR and SCR
Capacity: ISB4.5: 4500cc
ISB6.7: 6700cc
Gearbox: Voith or Allison
Rear axle: Dana 8,500kg (18,739lb) 09-24
or Dana 11,000kg (24,250lb) 11-26
Suspension: Full air, multi-link location, anti-roll bar, telescopic dampers

Brakes: Knorr 4-piston discs
Wheelbase: 8.9m body: 3,900mm (153.5in)
  9.7m body: 4,655mm (183.25in)
  10.5m body: 5,395mm (212.4in)
  10.8m body: 5,775mm (227.4in)
  11.5m/11.8m bodies: 6,475mm (255in)
Length: 8,900mm (350.4in)
  9,700mm (381.9in)
  10,800mm (425.2in)
  11,500mm (452.75in)
  11,800mm (464.6in)
Width: 2,470mm (97.25in)
  GVW: 12,960kg (28,572lb) with 245 tyres and 09-24 axle
  13,200kg (29,101lb) with 245 tyres and 11-26 axle
  14,400kg (31,746lb) with 265 tyres and 11-26 axle
(Source: ADL data sheet, 2018)

The Enviro 500 SuperLo

Although the Enviro 500 was by 2015 selling well into North America, the low bridges and electrical cabling infrastructure typical of most US towns and cities significantly restricted the route availability of the big deckers. A special version of the MMC model was therefore developed, the SuperLo, with an overall height of only 12ft 10in (3.91m). This represented a full 8in (200mm) height reduction over the standard US-spec Enviro 500, achieved without any reduction in the upper deck saloon headroom. It resulted from a 3in (75mm) reduction in chassis depth together with a decrease in the lower saloon headroom. Stronger solebars and additional body strengthening retained the required strength of the vehicle structure. A loss of up to seventeen seats was necessary, as the reduced headroom meant that the rear portion of the lower saloon over the rear axles could no longer be used for seating; however, it made a handy 212cu ft (6cu m) luggage area.

At the time of writing, there are 227 of these Enviro 500 SuperLo deckers in service with Go Transit in Canada. ADL

The unusual luggage compartment of the SuperLo – taking advantage of the rear saloon space where headroom is too low for passengers. ADL

The launch customer order for the SuperLo was Canada's Go Transit in 2015, with their first batch of thirty-eight vehicles being delivered in 2016. Chassis for these vehicles were built not at Guildford but in a new ADL purpose-designed facility at Vaughan, north of Toronto. Creation of this plant formed part of a deal between ADL and Ontario's Crown Transportation Agency, which resulted in orders for a total of 253 buses, of which 227 have been built at the time of writing (July 2019).

EURO 4 PROBLEMS

The Dart SLF and Trident 2 were launched with Euro 2/3 engines, in compliance with the prevailing emissions standards at that time. However, concern over diesel emissions was increasing, particularly in London, with the levels of NOx – nitrogen oxides – being considered a particular concern. The Euro 4 emissions standards, mandatory for all new vehicles from October 2005, therefore stipulated substantial reductions in NOx levels. Two methods of reducing NOx on diesel engines were available to the industry: EGR and SCR. EGR, or exhaust gas recirculation, does broadly what the name suggests – a proportion of the engine exhaust gas is routed back through the engine and reburned to reduce the NOx content. SCR, or selective catalytic reduction – is a perhaps more sophisticated process. In an SCR system, urea, a water-based ammonia solution, known by its trade name of AdBlue, is injected in precisely controlled quantities into the exhaust flow out of the engine. It then reacts with a downstream catalyst to convert the NOx to form harmless nitrogen and water vapour.

Each heavy diesel engine manufacturer had their own preferred solution to deal with the requirements of Euro 4. Most went for EGR, as it was the more straightforward solution. Indeed, Cummins adopted EGR as their design solution for their EPA-certified engines for the North American market, which was also focusing on NOx reduction. However, Cummins felt that the relatively inefficient EGR was not the right solution for the UK market, where good fuel economy was particularly important. They therefore developed their range of Euro 4 engines to use SCR. This initially proved to be a wise move, for comparative tests arranged by Transport for London between TransBus products with Cummins SCR Euro 4 engines and competitors with EGR engines demonstrated clear fuel consumption benefits from the TransBus vehicles.

However, as the Euro 4 TransBus vehicles began to accumulate service mileage, problems began to arise. During 2009, urea injection nozzles began to fail, as did the doser units that controlled the precise flow of urea into the exhaust system. Considerable investigation by both Cummins and ADL was initially unable to discover the cause of the problem. The cause was finally only uncovered by a rig-

With the introduction of Euro 6, space needed to be found for much additional equipment. This view shows the current Enviro 200 exhaust system: no longer one simple silencer! AUTHOR

orous examination of the service history of every affected vehicle. This identified that while the urea injection system worked perfectly well at normal operating temperatures, such temperatures were rarely attained in stop-start London city traffic. That meant that whenever the exhaust system cooled down, the urea that had just been injected into the system failed to mix with the exhaust gas and solidified in the exhaust pipe. This eventually blocked the pipe and injector, also causing the doser units to fail.

The solution was simple in principle but tricky to engineer, involving keeping the SCR equipment consistently hot by moving the injector and doser unit as close to the engine as possible. By the time the solution was identified and rework packages developed, continuing high sales of the Dart SLF and Trident 2 meant that in 2010 a costly but ultimately successful retrofit programme had to be carried out on many hundreds of vehicles.

HYBRID DEVELOPMENTS

Even in the TransBus era, the opportunity for hybrid buses had been identified. Buses, with their intrinsic stop-start operation, are particularly suited to hybrid application as the braking energy can be recovered to the battery to accelerate the bus subsequently. A TM02 prototype had been developed in 2003 (*see* Chapter 8) as a concept demonstrator with funding support from the Energy Saving Trust. MST supplied the motor, generator and controller, with a nickel hydride battery supplied by Varta. MST, however, were unable to satisfactorily demonstrate that they could scale their operation to provide the level of support that would be required for production volumes, so the engineering team undertook the process of looking for alternative suppliers. This proved a difficult task due to the lack of a mature market for this type of sophisticated product at that time.

However, a relationship was eventually established with BAE Systems, who had developed successful hybrid bus technology in the USA and were keen to repeat this success in the UK with their next-generation product. As the partnership progressed, in 2008 Transport for London took several hybrid versions of the Enviro 200 single-decker and Enviro 400 double-decker on trial against similar offerings from some of ADL's competitors, with the Enviro 400 hybrids, in particular, performing exceptionally well.

Further sales soon followed, both in London and then in many other UK towns and cities. In the light of the earlier successful operation of the Enviro 400 hybrids in London, it was a disappointment when a substantial contract for the New Bus for London hybrid buses was awarded to Wright-bus (who themselves went into administration in 2019) with a relatively untried hybrid package. Nevertheless, the BAE Systems/ADL hybrid vehicles have proved to be both more efficient and more reliable than their competitors'.

A hybrid system was also developed for the Enviro 500, this time using an Allison parallel system. This was fitted to vehicles for British Columbia Transit, although a development of the BAE Systems package was used on vehicles for the Hong Kong market.

THE END OF DENNIS FIRE ENGINES

While ADL senior management naturally needed to concentrate on bus production, they were not opposed to the continuation of fire engine chassis production. The two key fire products, Sabre and Dagger, thus were able to continue in production under ADL. However, over time, old ties of loyalty between Dennis Eagle and the remaining Dennis Fire staff within ADL declined, not least because many key people were lost with the massive redundancies of staff following the demise of Mayflower. Eventually, Dennis Eagle's Blackpool cab factory, which was focused on delivering the rising number of cabs needed for their own reinvigorated refuse collection vehicle market, found the continued production of fire engine cabs in unpredictable small quantities was just too much of an inconvenience. They then advised ADL that they were unable to provide cabs in batches of less than twenty-five identical units.

This put ADL in a difficult position, as fire engines were typically ordered in much smaller quantities, and each order could involve many different cab variants. ADL sales, engineering and purchasing staff fought a sterling rearguard action, first attempting to persuade Dennis Eagle to relax their stance, and when that failed, seeking to get the Dennis cab manufactured by other specialist contractors. That, however, proved prohibitively expensive. Even the feasibility of fitting cabs from other vehicle manufacturers, notably Renault, was investigated. However, this option was abandoned as it was felt that it would eliminate one of the significant benefits of the Dennis fire product – namely the uniquely purpose-designed cab.

The final measure was to attempt to amalgamate orders from the brigades to achieve the twenty-five-vehicle minimum order quantity. This foundered, however, because brigade ordering schedules were driven by their budgets and could not be readily changed.

Many firefighters regarded their Dennises as the finest fire-fighting appliances ever produced, renowned for their performance and handling, and so many brigades, including West Midlands and Tyne & Wear, were dismayed when the last Dennis Sabre chassis was quietly and unceremoniously produced in 2007.

Dennis fire appliances like this Sabre have long been popular with their crews, and are much missed. ADL

CHAPTER TEN

WHERE ARE THEY NOW?

Over the years, several companies came and went from the Dennis fold. This chapter reviews the fortunes of some of them after they were discarded.

JOHN DENNIS COACHBUILDERS

When the fire appliance bodybuilding activities of Dennis were transferred to Carmichael in 1985, John Dennis left the company founded by his grandfather and set up his own fire engine body business, John Dennis Coachbuilders. John Dennis Coachbuilders, or JDC, expanded to become a significant player in the UK fire appliance market, bodying a substantial percentage of Dennis and other competing chassis. They were based in a factory on a leased site close to the Dennis chassis plant at Slyfield in Guildford.

On the partial retirement of John Dennis, JDC was sold to new management. The new chairman was Alan McClafferty, previously managing director of Dennis Specialist Vehicles before the Mayflower takeover. At that time, JDC production numbers were around 100 bodies per year. John Dennis finally left the company bearing his name in October 2004.

JDC policy was one of diversification. One new venture was into wheelchair-accessible small bus production, using an Iveco chassis to provide seating capacity for up to twenty, or wheelchair space for up to seven passengers. However, the product faced stiff and price-sensitive competition and never became a significant success in its sector.

JDC's annual production of fire appliance bodies steadily increased to around 150, by which time they employed some 200 people. In 2010, however, the company was severely affected by a reduction in orders resulting from cuts to public sector budgets. This led to many local authorities putting new vehicle orders on hold, in turn forcing JDC to make some forty-five office and shop-floor staff redundant in November 2010, reducing the workforce by almost a third. Attempts were made at diversification, yet in 2017 the diversifications accounted for barely 10 per cent of the company's revenue and could not compensate for sliding sales in its core fire engine business.

The 2016 accounts showed that JDC's revenues, £26.5 million in 2010, had fallen to just £12.8 million. The drop was blamed on the continuing reduction in fire service budgets caused by government spending cuts. Over the same 2010–2016 period, JDC moved from a £353,000 profit to a £723,000 loss.

As a result, the company was forced to lay off yet more employees. Even with this drastic action, JDC's revenue continued to decline, and the 2017 accounts show that the company lost £1.1 million. Finally, in January 2019, the company closed its doors for the last time, leaving the final sixty or so employees jobless.

The responsibility for parts and service support for JDC products was handed over to Terberg DTS UK Ltd. Intriguingly, Terberg has swept up most of the companies that were at one time under the Dennis umbrella, including Dennis Eagle, Carmichael and the dock-spotter operations of Douglas Schopf.

CARMICHAEL INTERNATIONAL LTD

One of Mayflower's first actions after taking control of the Dennis businesses was to sell off Worcester-based fire vehicle manufacturer Carmichael International for £13.2 million.

At that time, Carmichael's 120 staff were producing about 150 appliances a year, ranging from the smallest Land Rover-based vehicles to all-wheel-drive Cobra 2 airfield crash tenders. They had a healthy £25 million order book, which included sixty military-spec 6×6 Cobra 2s and sixteen 6×6s for civil airfield crash tenders. Exports amounted to over 50 per cent of their production.

The sizeable military order was probably the high point of recent Carmichael production, for their fortunes declined afterwards, the business going into liquidation in 2004. The assets were bought by AMDAC, who themselves failed in 2016.

The assets of AMDAC Carmichael were then bought by

Carmichael Support Services, who in July 2018 also ceased trading, making all their staff redundant. As happened later with JDC, the designs, stocks and other assets were bought from the liquidator by Terberg DTS UK, who continue to provide parts and service support for Carmichael products. The airfield crash tenders they sell are however American Oshkosh products rather than those designed initially by Carmichael.

Terberg DTS UK Ltd is one of the largest specialist vehicle suppliers and support providers in the UK with an annual turnover of over £45 million per year, and is part of the 150-year-old family-owned Terberg Group with an annual turnover above €900 million (£810 million).

DENNIS MOWERS

As part of Hestair's rationalization plans when they took over Dennis in 1972, mower production was moved to Hestair's farm machinery division in Kent. In around 1976, the motor mower division was sold to one of Hestair's sub-contractors, Godstone Engineering. Production of Premier and Paragon mowers continued at Godstone, while the Guildford gang mower division was sold to Howardson Ltd (formerly Howards Engineering). Howardson, established in 1938 by Wilfred Howard, was a third-generation family engineering business looking to expand its product lines.

By 1981, the motor mower division at Godstone was struggling, with falling sales and outdated products. This allowed Howardson to buy the motor mower operations finally, and production was moved to their factory at Derby. This was an excellent fit for the mower products, as Howardson had years of experience in jig and tool manufacture. As such, they were well able to achieve the levels of precision and quality needed to produce the premium Dennis mowers.

Howardson invested heavily in developing the products, for example by improved engine installations in the Premier and Paragon ranges. As well as keeping the older products up to date, the product range was expanded by buying several other mower and allied equipment manufacturers.

In the late 1990s, the G-series mowers were developed, a range that included the Sport, G560 and G680 as well as the G760, G860 and contractor cassette machines.

Howardson won a high-profile contract in 2010 to supply mowers to South Africa for the FIFA World Cup venues. Similar agreements were received for each succeeding World Cup, culminating in the 2018 event in Russia. Here,

an impressive eighty-eight of the G860 machines, plus several Premiers, were used to prepare most of the stadiums and training grounds.

Dennis mowers are easy to recognize: to this day they share the same lozenge-shaped company logo as that used by Guildford chassis in the Trinity Holdings era.

DOUGLAS SCHOPF

Douglas Schopf was another early casualty of the Mayflower takeover of Dennis, being sold off in 1998. At some point afterwards, there was a separation of the company's product lines, with dock-spotters eventually ending up with Terberg by 2000. The aircraft tug side of the business also passed through several hands, but in 2015 was taken over by US company Textron and became part of Textron Ground Support Equipment. Both Terberg and Textron remain significant manufacturers of the same types of products as they took over from their respective parts of Douglas Schopf.

DENNIS EAGLE

Mayflower's disposal of Dennis Eagle soon after taking over Trinity Holdings was not one of their smarter moves. True, the domestic refuse vehicle market was at a low ebb at that time. On the other hand, the company had a portfolio of class-leading products, particularly the Elite chassis and Phoenix refuse vehicle body. Not only that, they operated in a market relatively unaffected by recession or world affairs, for humanity always generates waste and waste must be dealt with. Inevitably, the market returned, and following the purchase in 1999 of Dennis Eagle from Mayflower in a management buy-out, the company went from strength to strength in terms of sales.

In 2007, Dennis Eagle was bought by Ros Roca SA, a Spanish manufacturer of waste management equipment. Ros Roca then merged with Terberg Environmental in 2016, with the production of the Dennis Eagle products continuing at their Warwick and Blackpool factories.

It is an indication of just how successful Dennis Eagle became in its field that although its three-axle rigid trucks are bought primarily by the relatively small refuse-collection market sector, in 2015 Dennis Eagle nevertheless ranked second only to DAF Trucks by annual volumes in the entire three-axle, 6×2 rigid sector of the UK truck market. The Elite low-entry cab is also used by Renault Trucks on their refuse-collection trucks in continental Europe.

CHAPTER ELEVEN

ADL TODAY

CONTINUED GROWTH

ADL sales have continued to prosper, with many new markets developing around the world. Some of these have demanded local manufacture, if only to avoid punitive import duties. Several overseas build sites have therefore been established, principally in North America, Malaysia and China.

At one stage Guildford's role had declined to preparing kits of chassis parts for assembly elsewhere, overseeing the development of prototype chassis builds of new models, and carrying out low-volume or specialist chassis assembly work. However, as the company has grown, the Guildford site is again bursting at the seams with chassis production, and that situation does not look like changing any time soon.

One of the ninety Enviro 500s operated by Metrobus in Mexico City, seen here near the Angel of Independence monument. ADL

In this book, we have acknowledged that the Dennis Dart and its successor single-deck midibus models wear the crown of Britain's most successful buses, certainly by volume. However, many of the other products of ADL are equally impressive in terms of sales.

The big three-axle Enviro 500 double-decker has been an incredible success worldwide, with well over 5,000 sales. Double-deckers have always had limited sales potential, as so many countries do not have the road infrastructure to be able to use them. Other than the UK and of course Hong Kong, Berlin was one of the few places in the world where double-deck buses have traditionally been used. Thanks to ADL's efforts, all that has changed. Sales into the North American continent may have started slowly, but since the first hesitant sales into British Columbia, the big decker has made huge inroads into North America. Over 1,000 are currently in operation or on order there at the last count. These range from open-top tour buses in New York to 'Double Tall' vehicles operating at high speed on the Interstate routes around Seattle.

Not only that, but the deckers are also in service in Mexico, Switzerland, Holland, Austria, Turkey, Australia, New Zealand, Malaysia, Singapore and Spain, with more on order. Selling British-built vehicles into Germany has always been seen as virtually impossible, due to the strength of support for indigenous manufacturers. ADL, though, has achieved the impossible in signing a deal to supply up to 430 double-deckers to Berlin, replacing the entire current fleet of presently German-built deckers. Coals to Newcastle indeed!

The two-axle double-decker has also been a remarkable sales success, with almost 11,000 Trident 2s and Enviro 400s sold since their launch in 1997, many of which have been hybrids. Again, sales have been worldwide, vehicles operating as far afield as Hong Kong and Canada.

ADVANCES IN TECHNOLOGY

The days of internal-combustion engines appear to be numbered, and ADL, like most vehicle manufacturers, is forging ahead with alternative powertrain technologies, having already sold large numbers of hybrid buses into many UK cities. Over 200 ADL single-deck battery-electric buses are either in operation or on order in the UK. These chassis are made by the Chinese company BYD rather than being built in Guildford.

Seven of these electric Enviro 200s operate park and ride services around Guildford.
AUTHOR

Look – no differential! This is a prototype of an Allison ABE series electric drive axle intended for a future double-decker. AUTHOR

ADL and BYD also delivered the first batch of thirty-seven Enviro 400EV zero-emission double-deckers to London operator Metroline in mid-2019.

ADL at Guildford is, however, developing an all-electric chassis for the North American three-axle double-decker market. At the time of writing, this is still a work in progress, although significant parts of the chassis package are in place. For example, after eighteen months of development, prototypes of a new drop-centre electric drive rear axle have been produced by Allison, while the battery packaging by US partner Proterra is well advanced. Much of the battery development has been centred around reducing the height of some of the battery packs to fit under the floor, the rest being located in the space occupied on conventional vehicles by the engine and gearbox.

Perhaps the most exciting news for the future, however, is that even though the ADL hybrid buses are industry-leading, the company is not resting on its laurels. It sees hybrid drives as merely a stopgap to a carbon-free future in passenger transport and has come up with an innovative hydrogen fuel-cell bus that promises to be both extraordinarily green and cheap to run.

The key is a 30kW hydrogen fuel cell, deliberately much smaller than that used by other bus manufacturers. The fuel cell runs continuously when the bus is in operation, unlike a typical hybrid internal combustion power unit, which cuts in and out as required, creating high levels of emissions every time it starts up. This small fuel cell provides power to a battery, which can itself be much smaller than that on a conventional hybrid bus. The hydrogen to power the fuel cell is stored in four carbon-fibre tanks mounted across the rear of the bus. Between them, these will store enough hydrogen, ADL calculates, for a full eighteen-hour bus operating shift. The whole hydrogen package is much more compact than a conventional hybrid system, freeing up valuable passenger space.

Initial testing of this system has indicated a hydrogen fuel usage of around 6–7 kg/100km (0.2lb–0.25lb/mile), far less than the 12kg/100km (0.43lb/mile) of the current generation of hydrogen buses from mainland European manufacturers. At current fuel prices, that puts the operating cost of the ADL fuel cell decker similar to that of a diesel bus. The purchase price of the bus is also expected to be similar to a comparably sized hybrid bus.

Normally, the biggest concern over using hydrogen as a fuel is its availability, with the UK having only a handful of hydrogen fuelling stations, making widespread adoption of hydrogen as a fuel for passenger cars a challenge. Not so for buses, however, where the fact that a fleet of buses returns to their central depot nightly makes installation of a hydro-

ABOVE: **The prototype hydrogen-powered Enviro 400; production should begin in 2020.**
AUTHOR

The engine bay of the prototype hydrogen-fuelled Enviro 400. The blue unit on the right is the fuel cell, while above can be seen one of the four hydrogen tanks.
AUTHOR

gen fuel station in the depot feasible, particularly when a full refill takes only minutes compared to the hours needed to recharge the batteries of a fully electric bus.

The launch customer for ADL's hydrogen bus is in Liverpool – an ideal location, for the necessary hydrogen is a by-product of a nearby chemical plant, so is easily and relatively cheaply available. The first batch of these innovative vehicles should be in service by mid-2020. The fuel cells themselves will be built by Arcola at their factory in Merseyside.

ADL are also active in developing driverless vehicle technology, and in March 2019 demonstrated the UK's first full-size autonomous bus, an 11.5m (37ft 9in) Enviro 200 developed in partnership with Stagecoach and Fusion Processing Ltd. Legislation presently prevents the vehicle from being operated on public roads; therefore, trials are taking place within a Stagecoach depot in Manchester. The first public operation will be a commuter service feeding Edinburgh and running over the new Forth Road Bridge.

TAKEOVER BY THE NFI GROUP

In 2018, ADL generated a turnover of £577 million from delivering 2,533 buses globally, 49 per cent of the turnover coming from UK sales, 27 per cent from the Asia Pacific market, 12 per cent from North America and the remaining 12 per cent from aftermarket sales and developing markets. From 2010 to 2018, ADL achieved a compound annual growth rate of 10.5 per cent per annum.

In echoes of the Mayflower takeover, such levels of growth inevitably made ADL an acquisition target, and for some years there had been persistent speculation that Alexander Dennis Limited could soon come under new ownership. Possible names in the frame as new owners included BYD and New Flyer, both companies with strong links to

ADL. On 28 May 2019, this speculation was confirmed, with the news that Alexander Dennis had been sold for £320 million to NFI Group. This Canadian company is the manufacturer of New Flyer and MCI buses, with a 2018 turnover of $2,500 million (approx. £1,878 million).

The deal created a company with over 8,900 employees working from over fifty facilities worldwide, giving the apparent potential for rationalization.

At the time of writing, the implications of the NFI takeover are yet to unfold, although the new owners will doubtless want to keep the wealth of expertise of the Guildford staff. For the present, of course, while the focus has changed significantly, the vehicle building traditions started in Guildford by those two Dennis brothers 125 years ago are still very much alive and well today.

This plaque honouring the founding brothers was retrieved from the demolition of Woodbridge Works and is now on show in the Slyfield factory. AUTHOR

INDEX